Machine Annotation of Traditional Irish Dance Music

Dr Bryan Duggan Phd, MSc, BSc.
School of Computing
Dublin Institute of Technology
Kevin St. Dublin 8, Ireland.

Supervisors:
Prof. Brendan O' Shea
Dr Mikel Gainza
Prof. Pádraig Cunningham

Dublin Institute of Technology, School of Computing
June 2009

Abstract

Estimates put the canon of traditional Irish dance tunes at at least seven thousand compositions. The literature attributes this to the geographic isolation of rural communities which developed their own repertoire of tunes. Musicians playing traditional music have a personal repertoire of up to one thousand tunes. Given this diversity, a common problem faced by musicians and ethnomusicologists is identifying tunes from recordings. This is evident even in the number of commercial recordings whose title is *gan ainm* (without name).

The work presented in this PhD thesis attempts to solve this problem by developing a Content Based Music Information Retrieval (CBMIR) system adapted to the characteristics of traditional Irish music. The thesis includes a comprehensive review of the domain of traditional Irish music and presents three chapters of related work in the fields of feature extraction, melodic similarity and music information retrieval. A system is presented called MATT2 (Machine Annotation of Traditional Tunes) whose primary goal is to annotate recordings of traditional Irish dance music with useful metadata including tune names. MATT2 incorporates a number of novel algorithms for transcription of traditional music and for adapting melodic similarity measures to expressiveness in the playing of traditional music. It makes use of an onset detection function developed for the playing of traditional music on woodwind instruments such as the concert flute and tin-whistle. It uses a novel transcription algorithm based on Brendan Breathneach's observations about the transcription of traditional Irish music which provides transposition invariance for the keys and modes used to play traditional music. It incorporates a new algorithm for dealing with ornamentation notes and accommodating "the long note" in traditional music called Ornamentation Filtering. It makes use of publicly available collections of traditional music available in ABC notation. It uses a matching algorithm tolerant to errors which aligns short queries with longer strings from a corpus of known tunes, meaning that the algorithm can match entire tunes, incipits and phrases from any part of tune with equal success. The matching algorithm has also been adapted to take account of phrasing and *reversing* effects. A new algorithm is presented called TANSEY (Turn ANnotation from SEts using SimilaritY profiles) which annotates sets of tunes played *segue* as is the custom in traditional Irish dance music.

The work presented in this thesis is validated in experiments using 130 real-world field recordings of traditional music from sessions, classes, concerts and commercial recordings. Test audio includes solo and ensemble playing on a variety of instruments recorded in real-world settings such as noisy public sessions. Results are reported using standard measures from the field of information retrieval (IR) including accuracy, error, precision and recall and the system is compared to alternative approaches for CBMIR common in the literature.

Buíochas

Buíochas le mo feitheoirí, an tOllamh Brendan O'Shea, an Dochtúir Mikel Gainza ón DIT agus an tOllamh Pádraig Cunningham ó UCD as ucht an tacaíocht, treoir agus spreagadh a thug siad le ceithre bliana anuas. Ba mhaith liom buíochas speisialta a ghabháil le mo chara agus feitheoir, an tOllamh O' Shea, a raibh an radharc agus an fís aige an clár PhD a chur le chéile roinnt blianta ó shin. Buíochas freisin le hInstitiúid Teicneolaíochta Átha Cliath a thug an t-airgead le go bhféadfainn freastal ar chomhdhálacha agus a chuir an t-am ar fáil chun an obair seo a chríochnú. Buíochas le mo chomhpháirtithe i Scoil na Ríomhaireachta, an grúpa intleachta saorga, an grúpa cluichí ríomhairí agus an grúpa clostrealamh dhigiteach, go speisialta le Dr John Kelleher, Dr Brian McNamee, Dr Sarah Jane Delaney, Hugh McAtamney, Damian Gordon, Ronan Fitzpatrick and Dan Barry as ucht an t-aiseolas dearfach a chur ar fáil. Buíochas le Michael Porter agus Dave Carroll a léith an leabhar seo dom.

Buíochas leis na ceoltóirí agus na múinteoirí Maria Murphy, Rob O'Connor, Aideen Downs, Emily Sakier Donoho, Colm Ó Laoghóg, Markus Asunta, Frank Slocket, Donal Regan, Eamon Cotter, Harry Bradley, Catherine McEvoy, Dave Sheridan Treasa Harkin agus le Mick Mulvey a thug dom téip den cheoltóir Packie Duignan. Buíochas le Niall Keegan ó Oillscoil Luimnigh a thug cóip den a tráchtas dom. Buíochas freisin le Kjell Lemström ó Oillscoil Helsinki.

Buíochas le mo mhuintir agus mo cairde don cheol thar na mblianta. Ar deireadh buíochas le mo pháirtí ghrámhar Derek.

Acknowledgements

I would like to thank my supervisors Professor Brendan O' Shea and Dr Mikel Gainza of the DIT and Professor Pádraig Cunningham of UCD for their unwavering support, guidance and encouragement over the past four years. I would also like to pay tribute to my friend and supervisor, Professor O' Shea, who had the vision to initiate and develop the PhD program in the School of Computing several years ago. Thanks also to the Dublin Institute of Technology which kindly funded my attendance at various conferences and provided me with teaching relief to complete this work. Thank you to my colleagues at the DIT School of Computing, the AI Group, the Experimental Gaming Group and the Audio Research Group particularly Dr John Kelleher, Dr Brian McNamee, Dr Sarah Jane Delaney, Hugh McAtamney, Damian Gordon, Ronan Fitzpatrick and Dan Barry for their positive feedback at various stages of this work. Thank you to Michael Porter and Dave Carroll for proof reading.

Thanks to the many musicians and teachers who consented to being recorded as part of this research: Maria Murphy, Rob O'Connor, Aideen Downs, Emily Sakier Donoho, Colm Logue, Markus Asunta, Frank Slocket, Donal Regan, Eamon Cotter, Harry Bradley, Catherine McEvoy, Treasa Harkin, Dave Sheridan and to Mick Mulvey for providing archive recordings of the flute player Packie Duignan. Thanks to Niall Keegan from the University of Limerick for kindly sending me a copy of his MPhil thesis. Thanks also to Kjell Lemström from the University of Helsinki.

Thanks to my family and friends for all the music over the years. Finally thanks to my loving partner Derek.

Table of Contents

Table of Figures

Table of Tables

Associated Publications

[1]Duggan, B., O'Shea, B., Gainza, M., Cunningham, P.:"Compensating for Expressiveness in Queries to a Content Based Music Information System", 2009 International Computer Music Conference (ICMC 2009), Montreal, Canada 16–21 August 2009

Duggan, B., O'Shea, B., Gainza, M., Cunningham, P.:"The Annotation of Traditional Irish Dance Music using MATT2 and TANSEY", The 8th Annual Information Technology & Telecommunication Conference, Galway Mayo Institute of Technology, Galway, Ireland, October 2008

Duggan, B., O'Shea, B., Gainza, G and Cunningham P.: Machine Annotation of Sets of Traditional Irish Dance Tunes, Ninth International Conference on Music Information Retrieval (ISMIR), Drexel University, Philadelphia, USA, September 2008.

Duggan, B., O'Shea B., Cunningham, P.: A System for Automatically Annotating Traditional Irish Music Field Recordings, Sixth International Workshop on Content-Based Multimedia Indexing, Queen Mary University of London, UK, Jun. 2008

Zheng N., Duggan, B.: A Combinational Creativity Approach to Composing Traditional Irish Reels, 18th Irish Conference on Artificial Intelligence and Cognitive Science 29th - 31st August 2007, Dublin Institute of Technology

Duggan, B.: Enabling Access to Irish Traditional Music Archives on a PDA, Eight Annual Irish Educational Technology Users Conference, DIT Bolton St. Ireland, May 2007

Duggan, B.: Learning Traditional Irish Music using a PDA, IADIS Mobile Learning Conference, Trinity College, Dublin, Ireland, July 2006

Duggan, B., Zheng, C., Cunningham, P.: MATT - A System for Modelling Creativity in Traditional Irish Flute Playing, Third Joint Workshop on Computational Creativity, ECAI'06, Italy, August 2006

---

[1] Winner of the best presentation prize at the International Computer Music Conference (ICMC 2009), Montreal, Canada August 2009

Associated Software

These papers and all software developed as part of this PhD thesis are available for download from:

`http://www.comp.dit.ie/bduggan/music`

Source code is available via Subversion under GNU General Public License v2 from:

`http://code.google.com/p/matt2/`

Examples of tune forms, ornamentation and the test audio used in the experiments described in Chapters 7 and Chapter 8 can be downloaded from:

`http://www.comp.dit.ie/bduggan/music/`

A new, browser hosted query-by-playing search engine for traditional Irish dance tunes, with a corpus of over twelve thousand tunes based on the research reported in this PhD thesis can be accessed at:

`http://tunepal.org`

Abbreviations

ADSR – Attack Decay Sustain Release
CBID – Content Based Audio Identification
CBMIR – Content Based Music Information retrieval
DCT – Discrete Cosine Transformation
EMD - Earth Movers Distance
FAI – Frequently Accessed Index
FFT – Fast Fourier Transform
FIR - Finite Impulse Response
FMF – Fast Melody Finder
HMM – Hidden Markov Model
IR – Implication Realisation
IR – Information Retrieval
LSH – Locally Sensitive Hashing
MATT1 – Machine learning Articulation of Traditional Tunes
MATT2 – Machine Annotation of Traditional Tunes
MIDI – Musical Instrument Digital Interface
MIR – Music Information Retrieval
MM – Markov Model
MCT - Modulated Complex Transform
ODCF – Onset Detection using Comb Filters
ODF – Onset Detection Function
PCA - Principal Component Analysis
PDA – Personal Digital Assistant
PID - Principle of Intervallic Difference
PUID – Portable Unique Identifier
QBH – Query-By-Humming
STFT – Short-Time Fourier Transform
TANSEY - Turn ANnotation in SEts using SimilaritY profiles
TF × IDF - Term Frequency * Inverse Document Frequency
XML – eXtensible Markup Language
WAV –Waveform Audio Format

1 Introduction

In common with the folk music of many countries, repertoire in Irish traditional music is primarily acquired aurally. Musicians playing Irish music learn by hearing tunes played by fellow musicians in sessions, classes, workshops and from commercial recordings (Wallis & Wilson 2001). At workshops such as those held as part of the Willie Clancy Summer School (Kearns & Taylor 2003; Lynch 2008) students use electronic devices to record their classes. Increasingly students use digital audio field recorders such as the M-Audio Micro Track II, which record high quality audio directly to WAV or MP3 format (Figure 1).

Figure 1: The M-Audio Micro Track II digital audio field recorder (M-AUDIO 2008)

In this way, over the years musicians can acquire many hours of high quality field recordings in standard audio formats. Similarly, organisations such as Na Píobairí Uilleann, Comhaltas Ceoltóirí Éireann and the Irish Traditional Music Archive have been acquiring field recordings of traditional music made over the last hundred years and these organisations now possess many thousands of hours of recordings in a variety of formats and on a variety of different media (Figure 2).

Figure 2: Wax cylinder recordings of piper Patsy Touhey (courtesy of the Irish Traditional Music Archive)

In order for these archives to be useful, they must be annotated with appropriate metadata, such as tune names, time signatures, key and instruments. Additionally for musicological and ethnographic study, archives could be annotated with stylistic metadata. The main goal of this PhD thesis is to develop algorithms for automatically annotating field recordings of monophonic Irish traditional dance music. Several recent papers address the necessity of developing MIR (Music Information Retrieval) systems that are adapted to the specific requirements of ethnic music and also to the needs of musicologists studying ethnic music (Doraisamy et al. 2006; Jensen et al. 2005; Nesbit et al. 2004; Wright et al. 2008; Chordia et al. 2008). This work presents a unique attempt to develop a Content Based Music Information Retrieval (CBMIR) system adapted to the specific characteristics of Irish traditional dance music. The algorithms and systems proposed in this work take account of characteristics as slow onset times in woodwind instruments such as the concert flute and the tin-whistle, the playing of ornamentation, phrasing, reversing and the playing of tunes *segue* in sets. The work also takes advantage of ABC notation, which has been developed especially for the transcription of Western traditional music. There exist over seven thousand traditional Irish, Scots and Breton tunes freely available in ABC notation from public databases (thesession.org 2007; Norbeck 2007; Chambers 2007). ABC notation has the advantage of being based on ASCII text and so tunes in ABC can be easily processed and analysed using algorithms for textual information retrieval. Although this work focuses on traditional Irish music, it is hoped that the techniques proposed can be generalised to other genres and instruments.

1.1 Research aims

The overall aim of this research is to develop new algorithms and systems for the annotation of recordings of traditional Irish dance music. A review of the domain of traditional music is presented with details of the instruments and tune types used in traditional Irish dance music. A discussion of the keys, modes and tempos most commonly used to play Irish traditional music is included. Creativity, style and expressiveness are especially considered. This work draws extensively on authoritive sources in the domain including Breathneach's "Ceol Rince na hÉireann" series, Vallely's "Companion to Irish Traditional Music", Keegan's MPhil thesis "The Words of Traditional Flute Style" and Tansey's "The Bardic Apostles of Inisfree".

The work presented in this thesis is a Content Based Music Information Retrieval System (CBMIR) for traditional Irish dance music. These systems extract features from queries, which are digital recordings and retrieve corresponding matching musical artefacts and metadata from a corpus. A literature review of related work on the problem of feature extraction from digital audio is therefore included which includes a discussion on note onset and pitch detection in particular. A comprehensive review of melodic similarity measures employed in Music Information Retrieval (MIR) systems is included which focuses on measures that support query alignment and are tolerant to errors. A literature review in the domain of Music Information Retrieval is included which describes symbolic MIR, audio based MIR (so called audio fingerprinting) and hybrid (so called query-by-humming) systems.

The system proposed in this thesis is called MATT2 (Machine Annotation of Traditional Tunes). It addresses the problem of annotating recordings of traditional music. MATT2 incorporates a number of novel algorithms for transcription of traditional music and for adapting melodic similarity measures to expressiveness in the playing of traditional music. It makes use of an onset detection function developed for the playing of traditional music on woodwind instruments such as the concert flute and tin-whistle. It uses a novel transcription algorithm based on Brendan Breathneach's (1985) observations about the transcription of traditional Irish music which provides transposition invariance for the keys and modes used to play traditional music. It incorporates a new algorithm for dealing with ornamentation and "the long note" in traditional music called Ornamentation Filtering. The Ornamentation Filtering algorithm proposed in this thesis has no *a priori* knowledge of note durations and so is completely adaptive to tempo deviation in audio queries. It makes use of publicly available collections of traditional music available in ABC notation. It uses a matching algorithm tolerant to errors which aligns short queries with longer strings from a corpus of known tunes. The matching algorithm has also been adapted to take account of phrasing and reversing. A new algorithm is presented called TANSEY (Turn ANnotation in SEts using SimilaritY profiles) which annotates sets of tunes played *segue* as is the custom in traditional Irish dance music.

The work presented in this thesis is validated in experiments using real-world field recordings of traditional musicians from sessions, classes, concerts and commercial recordings. Test audio includes solo and ensemble playing on traditional instruments recorded in a variety of real-world settings such as noisy public sessions. Results are reported using standard measures from the field of Information Retrieval (IR) including accuracy, error, precision and recall and the system is compared against alternative approaches for CBMIR common in the literature.

Work discussed in this thesis has been presented at international conferences on Artificial Intelligence, Content Based Multimedia Indexing (CBMI), Music Information Retrieval (MIR) and Computer Music.

1.2 Use cases

This section presents several possible usage scenarios for the outputs of this research.

Maria is taking classes on the concert flute at the Willie Clancy summer school in Milltown Malbay one year. The classes take place over six days from 10am until 1pm each day. Her teacher is flute maker Eamon. Each day, Eamon spends the first half of the class teaching new tunes to the students and the second half of the class discussing technique. As the class is quite advanced, they are able to learn about two tunes per day. Maria uses a digital audio field recorder to record the classes each day. Eamon encourages the students to learn the tunes by ear and therefore doesn't give the students the notes for the tunes. Eamon has forgotten several of the titles for the tunes. In addition to the tunes he teaches the class, Eamon records additional tunes for the students to study in their own time. At the end of the week Maria feels that she has learned so many tunes that she ends up mixing them up. She has about two hours of recordings made from the classes. Mixed in with the recordings of the class, Maria has also recorded random tunes played in pub sessions she has listened to that week. At the end of the week, when she returns home, Maria transfers the MP3's of the recordings to her computer. She uses MATT2 to analyse the recordings and identify the tunes. These titles get saved in the ID3 tags of the files, so she can import the files into Windows Media Player.

Catherine is a professional flute player who is working on a new CD, with her brother John and piano player Felix. Having played music all her life, she feels she has a repertoire of at least a thousand tunes, but like many traditional musicians she has difficulty recalling the correct titles for much of her repertoire. She wishes to include tunes on the recording that she learned from local musicians when she was growing up. When arranging the sets of tunes for the recordings, she realises that several of the tunes she knows just by the name of the person who played the tunes. Several others have no name at all, even though she senses the tunes are commonly played. She plays a phrase from each of the unknown tunes and uses MATT2 to identify the tunes. Once she has the names of the tunes she looks them up in Breandán Breathnach's Ceol Rince na hÉireann series of books and uses the bibliographic notes therein to write the CD notes.

Treasa works for the Irish Traditional Music Archive. One of her jobs is to digitise analogue recordings which the archive receives. The archive is working on a project to make its collection available for streaming on the internet. The archive has just been bequeathed a set of recordings made between 1900 and 1930 by a collector in Chicago. The recordings are on wax cylinders and shellac discs and are in remarkably good condition. Treasa uses equipment in the archive to transfer the recordings to WAV format for inclusion in the public archive. When listening to the recordings Treasa is surprised to hear several unusual settings of common tunes. She uses MATT2 to annotate the WAV files with the tune titles. In one cases MATT2 returns a version of a tune from O'Neills Dance Music of

Ireland as the closest match and the same tune as transcribed in the website thesession.org as the second closest match. Treasa feels that this is an example of how the interpretation of tunes can change as a consequence of regional style and the tastes of period. She adds a bibliographic note to the recording marking it as an example of this phenomenon.

1.3 Original Contribution

The development of a novel and useful recording annotation system for traditional Irish music represents an important contribution to the traditional music community and to the study of content based music information retrieval. This work is a unique attempt to develop a content based music information retrieval system which explicitly supports traditional Irish dance music. In particular, this work improves on existing systems because it accommodates and compensates for expressive elements commonly used by players of traditional dance music. The principal specific contributions to knowledge are listed as Contribution 1 - Contribution 4 as follows:

Contribution 1. The development of a content based music information retrieval system (MATT2) which supports the input of queries played on traditional instruments. The algorithms presented were developed to support woodwind traditional instruments, but experiments reported in this thesis demonstrate that the system presented is equally effective for the fiddle, uilleann pipes, accordion, and concertina and for recordings of ensemble playing in sessions. ABC notation, the *de facto* annotation language used by traditional musicians is natively supported by MATT2. Special accommodation is included for the transposition that occurs in the tin-whistle, the most common of traditional instruments. MATT2 works equally well with short extracts, complete tunes, complete tunes played multiple times and with the use of the TANSEY algorithm given in Contribution 4 (Chapter 8), sets of tunes played segue as is the custom in Irish traditional music.

Contribution 2. The development of a new automatic transcription approach for traditional music that supports transposition invariance for the keys and modes used to play traditional music, while minimising pitch spelling errors. This transcription approach automates the approach adopted by Breandán Breathnach in the Ceol Rince na hÉireann series of tune books. Breathnach's approach was to transcribe tunes played on unusually pitched instrument as if the fundamental note of the instrument was D. Results reported in Chapter 7 demonstrate that this approach contributes to a significant improvement over transposition invariant edit distance cost functions.

Contribution 3. The development of a framework of algorithms to accommodate expressiveness in audio queries to a content based music information retrieval system. These algorithms accommodate ornamentation, the "long note", phrasing and reversing, four common techniques employed by traditional musicians. These techniques are discussed in detail in Chapter 2. In particular, a new algorithm for dealing with ornamentation is presented called Ornamentation Filtering. The Ornamentation Filtering algorithm is also tolerant of the types of tempo deviations that commonly occur in the performance of traditional Irish dance music. This thesis represents a unique attempt to specifically address the playing of ornamentation in queries to a CBMIR system. The results discussed in 7.2 and 7.3 establish that accommodating expressiveness results in a statistically significant improvement in annotation accuracy over approaches that do not accommodate expressiveness.

Contribution 4. The development of a novel algorithm based on *similarity profiles* to annotate *sets* of traditional Irish dance tunes. A set consists of multiple tunes repeated several times individually, played segue (without an interval). The playing of tunes in sets presents segmentation problems. As tunes in sets are always in the same time signature, often in the same key and can be repeated several times or not at all, there is a significant challenge in counting the repetitions of each tune and determining where each new tune begins, so that the subsequent tune can be annotated. An algorithm called TANSEY (Turn ANnotation in SEts using SimilaritY profiles) is presented that can accurately identify turns in sets played segue as is the custom in traditional music. TANSEY makes use of *similarity profiles* and it differs from existing approaches for audio segmentation that rely on recognising repetitive audio segments. Precision and recall scores are given for TANSEY on a set of thirty test recordings that establish its effectiveness.

1.4 Organisation

The remaining sections of this document are organised as follows:

Chapter 2 contains a comprehensive overview of the domain of traditional music. The main tune types are given with examples. The instruments most commonly used to play traditional music are presented and the modes and keys playable on these instruments are discussed. Initiatives to catalogue the repertoire of traditional music are described including the use of ABC notation. This chapter contains an extensive discussion on creativity and expressiveness in traditional music as these features will be referenced in later chapters. The research presented in Chapter 2 is distilled into the main challenges to implementing MIR in the domain of traditional Irish dance music.

Chapter 3 discusses work on the problem of feature extraction from digital audio focusing on the components required to build a transcription system. Onset detection approaches are presented with an emphasis on Onset Detection using Comb Filters (ODCF), an onset detection algorithm developed for the transcription of woodwind traditional instruments. An overview of relevant pitch detection approaches that work in both the time and frequency domains are also presented.

Chapter 4 describes algorithms used to measure similarity in symbolic representations of music. Simplified representation schemas common in MIR systems, such as Parsons Code and implication-realisation annotations are discussed. Geometric distances such as the Earth Movers Distance (EMD) are compared with string based measures such as the Edit (Levenstein) Distance.

Chapter 5 presents related work in the field of music information retrieval (MIR). This chapter categorises approaches as working in the symbolic domain, the signals domain (so called audio fingerprinting systems) and hybrid approaches (so called query-by-humming systems). This chapter concludes with an evaluation of the suitability of existing approaches to address the challenges presented in Chapter 2.

Chapter 6 presents a new system called MATT2. The transcription algorithms used by MATT2 are given. These are developed from the research presented in Chapter 3. A novel transcription approach is presented based on Breathneach's "fundamental note" observation in traditional music. A novel algorithm for dealing with ornamentation is presented called Ornamentation Filtering. A query and corpus normalisation approach is presented which compensates for phrasing and reversing (Chapter 2) is given.

Chapter 7 presents an evaluation of the system presented in Chapter 6 by comparing it with two alternative approaches suggested by the research presented in Chapters 4 and 5, melodic contours (Parsons Code) and a transposition invariant edit distance measure. Accuracy and error scores are given for two different categories of test audio (whole tunes and short excerpts). Statistical significance tests are presented which establish the effectiveness of the proposed algorithms when compared with the two alternative approaches.

Chapter 8 presents a novel algorithm called TANSEY (Turn ANnotation from SEts using SimilaritY profiles) which uses *similarity profiles* to annotate recordings of sets of tunes played segue as is the style in traditional Irish dance music. The TANSEY algorithm described in this chapter can identify the start and end of each repetition of a tune, can count the repetitions and can retrieve the title and associated metadata associated with each tune in a set. This enhancement to MATT2 is evaluated on a set of thirty test recordings. Measures of *precision* and *recall*, common in the domain of Information Retrieval, are given for the TANSEY algorithm for different time accuracy thresholds.

Finally, Chapter 9 concludes the thesis, summarises the main findings, restates the contributions to the body of knowledge and suggests further work which could be investigated.

2 Traditional Irish Dance Music

The main contribution of this thesis is a novel system for machine annotation of traditional Irish dance music. This chapter therefore begins this thesis by presenting the principal characteristics of traditional Irish dance music. The aim of this chapter is to establish the challenges that this form of music presents to existing CBMIR (Content Based Music Information Retrieval) approaches. New algorithms to address these challenges will be presented in later chapters.

Irish traditional music includes several musical *forms*. In the song tradition, both sean nós ("old style" singing in the Irish language) and singing in English exist. The baroque music of Turlough O'Carolan (section 2.4.5) is also considered part of the tradition (Vallely 1999). This project however, is primarily concerned with traditional dance music. The most common forms of dance tunes are: *reels, double jigs* and *hornpipes*. Other tune types include *marches, set dances, polkas, mazurkas, slip jigs, single jigs and reels, flings, highlands, scottisches, barn dances, strathspeys* and *waltzes* (Larson 2003). These forms differ in time signature, tempo and structure. For example a reel is generally played at a lively tempo and is in 4/4 time (written as eight quavers in a bar) while a waltz is generally played at slower pace and is in 3/4 time. The time signature, tempo and structure of a tune form are determined by the dance it accompanies. Most tunes consist of a common structure of two parts traditional musicians refer to as the *A* part and *B* part. Section 2.1 discusses the common tune forms in detail.

Tunes are typically arranged into *sets*. A set consists of a number of tunes (commonly two, three or four) played sequentially. Each tune in a set is usually repeated two or three times (Vallely 1999). Certain common sets were originally put together to accompany set dances (Vallely 1999), while other sets have become popular as a result of recordings made by emigrant Irish musicians in

America during the early part of the twentieth century. The origin of many sets of tunes is unknown and musicians often compile new sets "on the fly" in traditional music sessions. Chapter 8 presents a novel algorithm to annotate tunes played segue in a set.

Instruments used to play traditional dance music include the tin-whistle, fiddle (violin), uilleann (elbow) pipes, accordion, concertina, harp and the banjo (Wallis and Wilson 2001). Section 2.4 describes the main characteristics of the instruments used to play traditional Irish music, with a focus on the keys and modes these instruments typically play in.

Music is a creative art form and "individual expression" is a defining component of traditional Irish music. Creativity in traditional music takes three forms (Breathnach 1977):

1. The composition of new tunes.
2. The arrangement of tunes into sets.
3. The individual creativity of a musician in interpreting a tune.

This work focuses on developing algorithms for content based music information retrieval that specifically address points two and three above. When a traditional musician plays a tune, it is never played exactly as transcribed, though because the tune forms evolved from dances, traditional musicians never deviate from the structure of the tune. In fact an experienced musician rarely plays the same tune twice identically. Interestingly, there is no scope in traditional dance music for *rubato* (tempo flexibility). Instead, a musician will employ ornamentation and variation to interpret the tune (Larson 2003). Breathnach (1976) writes:

"Players must avoid tying themselves to a text. If they hear a turn or a twist in another setting they should make their own of it. All have equal rights in this field: they are subject only to the norms observed by players who are accepted as good performers by other bearers of the tradition."

Ornamentation plays a key role in the individual interpretation of traditional Irish music. In Irish traditional music ornamentation is played on the beat, and alters the onset of the notes (Larsen 2003). The usage of ornamentation is highly personal and large variations exist in the employment of ornamentation from region to region, instrument to instrument and from musician to musician. The playing of ornamentation presents a unique challenge to measures of musical similarity. This problem is discussed in detail in section 2.9.1 and a novel approach for dealing with ornamentation is presented in sections 6.4.1 and 6.7.

2.1 Tune types

This section presents the background and history of the most common forms of traditional Irish dance music. Table 1 summarises the main tune types[2].

[2] Audio examples of many of the tunes given in this section, played by the author on the concert flute can be listened to at: `http://www.comp.dit.ie/bduggan/music`.

Metre	Tune Types	Time Signature
Simple Duple Metre	Reel	2/2 or 4/4
	Polka	2/4
	Hornpipe	2/2 or 4/4
	March	2/2 or 4/4
	Schottische, Highland, Fling, Highland Fling,	4/4
	German, Barn Dance	4/4
	Strathspey	4/4
Compound Duple Metre	Double jig	6/8
	Single jig	6/8
	Slide	12/8 or 6/8
	March	6/8 or 12/8
Simple Triple Metre	Waltz	3/4
	Mazurka, Varsovienne	3/4
Compound Triple Metre	Slip jig	9/8

Table 1: Types of dance music (Larsen 2003)

2.1.1 Reel

A *reel* is a tune in 4/4 time usually played at a lively pace, where each bar typically contains eight quaver notes. There is an accent on the first and third beats of each bar. Most reels have an AABB form, where each "part" contains eight bars (sixty four notes). The part is repeated before the "turn"[3] (the subsequent part) is introduced and repeated. This thirty two bar melody is usually repeated two or three times before a second reel is introduced segue (Chapter 6). Although the AABB structure is the most common structure for reels other structures exist. Examples include "the Dublin Reel" (ABC) "Kiss the Maid

[3] A *turn* in traditional music is distinguished here from a turn in classical music, which is a four note ornament with a similar note sequence to a roll in traditional music (Virginia Tech 2009)

Behind the Barrel" (ABCD) and the "Banks of the Ilen" (ABB). The reel originated in France in the early sixteenth century and became played in Ireland in the eighteenth century. Many older reels originated in Scotland and it is common for variants of the same tune to appear with different titles. Reels make up the bulk of tunes played by many traditional musicians. Figure 3 shows the tune "Come west along the road" which is a tune commonly played at traditional music sessions (section 2.5) as transcribed in O'Neill's *The Dance Music of Ireland – 1001 Gems* (O'Neill 1907) (section 2.6).

Figure 3: The Reel "Come west along the road" (O'Neill 1907) (see also Figure 15 and Figure 42 and Figure 44)

2.1.2 Jig

Jigs are the second most common musical form in traditional Irish dance music. A jig is a tune in 6/8 time, usually with an AABB structure. The *double jig*, which has this structure is characterised by the rhythmic pattern of groups of three quavers. The jig tempo is usually lively when played for listening however when played to accompany for dancers in competitions, a greatly reduced tempo is often required in order to allow the dancers to execute their complicated footwork. Many traditional jigs are native in origin unlike reels which often originate in Scotland. Variations of the double jig include the *single jig*, the hop (slip) jig (a tune in 9/8 time) and the *slide,* (a tune in 12/8 time) the latter being used to accompany set (group) dances.

2.1.3 Hornpipe

A hornpipe is a complex dance tune in 4/4 time with a dotted rhythm played at a much slower tempo than a reel. Hornpipes are played in a deliberate manner to accompany a solo dance performance. Figure 4 shows the hornpipe "The Plains of Boyle"

Figure 4: The hornpipe "The Plains of Boyle"(O'Neill 1907)

2.1.4 Polka

The *polka* is a dance tune in 2/4 time. It was developed in Bohemia in the early nineteenth century, from where it spread throughout Europe due to its popularity. Polka's and slides are most commonly played in the *Sliabh Luchra* region on the border between Cork and Kerry to accompany set dances (Vallely 1999).

2.1.5 Mazurka

A *mazurka* is a tune in 3/4 time popular in the Donegal fiddle tradition. Mazurka's originated in the Mazovia province of Poland and arrived in Ireland in the middle part of the nineteenth century (Vallely 1999).

2.1.6 Slow Air

Slow airs are pieces of music in various metres, often based on the melodies to *sean nós* songs, and which are always played solo, at a slow tempo.

Taímse Im' Chodhladh

Figure 5: The slow air "Táimse Im' Chodladh" (thesession.org 2007)

The emphasis in interpretation of an air is on the expression of emotion. Slow airs are particularly suited to the uilleann pipes (section 2.4.4) and are usually part of a piper's repertoire. Often a slow air is followed by a dance tune as a way of demonstrating skill and as a method of lifting the often sombre mood which can follow the playing of an air (Vallely 1999).

2.2 Modes & tempo

Irish traditional music is modal in character. These modes, are known as: *Ionian, Dorian, Phrygian, Lydian, Myxolidian, Aeolian* and *Locrian* (Vallely 1999). Each of these modes produces a scale based on a sequence of five tones and two semitones. The Ionian and Aeolian modes are the standard major and natural minor scales in western music. Irish traditional music uses four of the seven modes: Ionian (major scale), Dorian, Aeolian (minor scale) and Myxolidian. A list of the most commonly utilised modes in Irish traditional music is given in (Larsen 2003). The same modes are repeated in Table 2, where *M** denotes that the mode *M* is less used than the rest of the modes of the list.

Mode type	**Mode tonal centre**
Ionian (major)	D, G and A*
Mixolydian	D, G and A
Dorian	E, A and B*
Aeolian (minor)	E, A and B

Table 2: Most commonly used modes by the tin-whistle, concert flute and the uilleann pipes (Gainza 2006)

The final note on which the phrases end is usually the tonal centre of the mode. If a melody is played on a tin-whistle (section 2.4.1), concert flute (section 2.4.2) or uilleann pipes (section 2.4.4) pitched in a different key, then the mode tonal centre shifts appropriately. For example, the mode of a tune in G Ionian becomes F Ionian when played on a C chanter instead of the modern standard D chanter. Breathnach (1985) writes of his transcriptions in the introduction to *Ceol Rince na hÉireann Cuid III:*

> *"In notating tunes from the playing of pipers, flutes and whistle players I have ignored the pitch of the instruments involved and proceeded on the basis that the bottom or* ***fundamental note*** *was D, the practice in use among all traditional players. Where a performer obviously adopted an unusual key in which to play a tune I notated it as played. This device is most used by fiddle players and amongst these more frequently in the United States than in Ireland."*

Section 6.6 presents a pitch spelling algorithm that exploits this "mental transposition" which is used in the transcription of traditional music. On tempo, Breathnach (1963) gives Table 3, the recommended tempo for traditional tunes to be played at, but adds:

> *"To play music at a quicker pace detracts from the melody; to play it somewhat slower can do no harm. It was customary for many of the older musicians when playing for themselves to adopt a slower pace than demanded by the dancers"*

Double Jigs	♩. = 127	Slip Jigs	♩. = 144
Single Jigs	♩. = 137	Reels	♩ = 224
Hornpipes	♩ = 180		

Table 3: Tempo for each metre of dance music (Breathnach 1963)

In (Breathnach 1976) he writes:

"A great variety is encountered in the speeds at which tunes for the sets and half sets are played."

It can therefore be concluded that a CBMIR for Irish traditional music should make no assumptions about the tempo a query recording could be played at. Section 6.4.1 presents the Ornamentation Filtering algorithm that adapts to tempo variation and deviation.

2.3 Tune titles

There is a great variety of titles for traditional dance tunes and these have no particular pattern. Carson (1997) writes:

"At any rate, the tune is not a story, but stories might lie behind the tune. For, as mnemonics, the names summon up a tangled web of circumstances; they not only help to summon the tune into being, but recall other times and other places where the tune was played, and the company there might have been. The same tune – or what is recognised by some as the same might have many names."

Titles might be classified as per Table 4.

Classification	Examples
Place (area, country, town or townland)	The Liffey Banks The Bucks of Oranmore Come West along the Road
People (the composer or person who is associated with the playing of the tune)	McFadden's Favourite Paddy Murphy's Wife Dr O'Neills
Political aspiration or event	The Home Ruler O'Connell's Trip to Parliament Repeal of the Union
Animals	The Pullet The Chicken that Made the Soup The Hare in the Corn
Aspects of nature	The Morning Dew The Rolling Wave The Green Mountain
Domestic situation or event	The Smokey House If it's Sick you are Tea you Wants
Sport related	The Foxhunters Curragh Races The Mullingar Races
Alcohol related	Dowd's Number 9 The Humours of Whiskey The Broken Pledge
Work related	The Woman of the House The Maid behind the Bar The Merry Blacksmith
Various women	Lovely Nancy The Youngest Daughter Over the Moore to Maggie
Sexual allegory and courting	Courting Them All The Night we made the Match
Unclassifiable	More Power to your Elbow Are you Willing Give us Another

Table 4: Tune titles taken from (O'Neill 1903)

2.4 Instruments

This section describes the main instruments used to play Irish traditional music currently. Music in Ireland has a history of over two thousand years (ÓhAllmhuráin 1998). In the years since the sixteenth century, Irish traditional musicians have used bag pipes, fiddles, harps, uilleann pipes, whistles, flutes and harps. Uilleann pipes from the late eighteenth century still survive in playing order as do concert flutes. Accordions and concertinas do not appear until after the mid nineteenth century. Other less popular instruments not included in this section are the mandolin, harmonica and dulcimer. The transcription algorithms described in Chapter 3, need to support the instruments given in this section.

2.4.1 Tin-whistle

The tin-whistle is a six-holed woodwind instrument which is played by blowing into a *fipple* (mouthpiece) attached on one end of the instrument. A tin-whistle player is called a tin-whistler or whistler. Most modern tin-whistle's are made from brass tubing, or nickel plated brass tubing, with a plastic fipple, though instruments can also be made entirely from plastic or from wood. Tin-whistles are a common starting instrument for musicians, since they are inexpensive, easy to play and the fingerings are identical to those on the concert flute (section 2.4.2). The tin-whistle is the most popular instrument in Irish traditional music and almost every traditional musician can play one. The oldest surviving tin-whistles date from the twelfth century, but McCullough (1987) notes:

> *"Players of the feadán are also mentioned in the description of the King of Ireland's court found in the Brehon Laws dating from the third century A.D."*

Different pitches are achieved by covering and uncovering the holes, shortening and lengthening the resonant length. With all the holes closed, the whistle generates its lowest note. In contrast to the concert flute (section 2.4.2), whose second register is achieved by narrowing the lips, the tin-whistle's second and higher register is achieved by increasing the air velocity into the fipple. The tin-whistle is a transposing instrument. It is pitched an octave higher than other instruments. For example, a D4 is sounded as a D5 on a tin-whistle. Tin-whistles are available in the keys given in Table 5. The algorithm given in section 6.6 (Chapter 6) automatically detects whether a query recording contains a transposing instrument and adapts the pitch spelling appropriately.

Key	Fundamental note (Hz)
Bb	466.16
C	523.25
D	554.37
Eb	622.25
F	698.46
G	783.99

Table 5: Tunings for tin-whistles

Table 5 is similar to Table 6 (given on page 26), with the pitches of the fundamental notes shifted up one register and the addition of the G fundamental note.

2.4.2 Flute

The "Irish flute" is also known as the *concert flute* (because it is in concert pitch), the timber flute (because it is made from wood), the simple system flute or the *fheadóg mhór* (big whistle). The flute is a woodwind instrument which is played by blowing a stream of air across the *embouchure* (hole) at the mouth end of the instrument. The stream of air is split as it hits the embouchure which sets up sound waves in the air column in the body of the instrument.

Different pitches are produced by covering and uncovering holes cut into the body of the flute. A concert flute has six holes tuned such that the lowest playable pitch; the *fundamental note*, with all holes closed is the D above middle C, and the instrument will play a D scale (D, E, F#, G, A, B, C#) as the holes are uncovered sequentially to shorten the resonant length of the bore (Figure 6). Flutes in alternative tunings are also available (Table 6).

Key	**Fundamental note (Hz)**
Bb	233.08
C	261.63
D	293.66
Eb	311.12
F	349.23

Table 6: Tunings for concert flutes

The basic flute is often augmented with the addition of up to eight keys (typically made from silver, mounted on wooden blocks) used to play pitches which are impossible to produce on the basic flute, though many traditional players do not make use of these. Many traditional tunes make use of the C natural note, which is played on a tin-whistle (section 2.4.1) by cross fingering as given in Figure 6 or by using a key on the flute if available.

●	●	●	●	●	●	○	○	○
●	●	●	●	●	○	●	○	●
●	●	●	●	○	○	●	○	●
●	●	●	○	○	○	○	○	●
●	●	○	○	○	○	○	○	●
●	○	○	○	○	○	○	○	●
D4	E4	F4	G4	A4	B4	C#5	C5	D5

Figure 6: Fingering chart for the wooden flute/tin-whistle

It is not often practical to use a key to play C natural at speed however and consequently musicians often resort to cross fingering the note or playing a C# instead, in particular when playing an ascending BCD run (Figure 16, page 50). In fact, the C and C# notes are sometimes played interchangeably and consequently the pitch spelling algorithm described in section 6.6 (Chapter 6) spells them the same.

A concert flute theoretically has a range of three octaves, though the third octave is almost never used in traditional music. The technique used to play in the second register is known as overblowing although this is generally done by narrowing the lip/embouchure rather than by blowing harder (Hamilton 1990). Playing in the third register is achieved by cross-fingering. In traditional Irish flute playing, *tonguing* as used as a note attack technique by classical flute players is rarely used. Instead a technique called *throating* is often used (the stop is produced by the throat rather than by the tongue) (Hamilton 1990). This can sometimes result in the note following the attack to be perceived as of one of the harmonics of the fundamental rather than the fundamental itself. On the flute, the timbre achieved by a musician can vary widely between a broad/breathy sound and a sharp/clear sound and naturally volume also can characterise a musician's individual style. Figure 7 depicts an unkeyed flute pitched in D and made from African black wood flute by Eamon Cotter, an unkeyed bamboo flute made by Patrick Olwell in the key of F and a six-keyed concert flute pitched in D made from African black wood by Eamon Cotter.

Figure 7: Keyed and unkeyed concert flutes

Concert flutes from the nineteenth century were originally designed to play classical music, but with the invention of the Boehm system flute in 1847, concert flutes became unpopular amongst classical musicians and thus came to be acquired by traditional musicians. Since the 1970's, there has been a renaissance in concert flute making and now many musicians play modern flutes based on the nineteenth century designs (Vallely 1999).

The flute has a strong association with the counties of Sligo, Leitrim and Roscommon (Figure 18, page 54) to which Tansey (2006) attributes to the coal mining in those areas. He argues that the flute was considered good for the development and health of the lungs of coal miners, constantly exposed to high levels of coal dust in their profession. Although the fingerings used to play the concert flute are similar to those used to play the tin-whistle (section 2.4.1), the instrument has a completely different character and timbre and is considerably more expressive in the range of tones that can be produced. Carson (1997) writes:

> *"...a flute is not a tin-whistle. Though the fingering for both is more or less identical, you can't hit the notes the same way because of the cramped posture if your hands, the added stretch, the very thickness of the flute with it's sometimes painful pressure against the inside of the palm-knuckle of the left forefinger. Then there is the question of the breath and how you take it, and how to let it out. The flute resists your breath in a very necessary way; the whistle offers no resistance, and the breathing is very different"*

2.4.3 Fiddle (Violin)

There is a long history of bowed instrument playing in Ireland, stretching back at least as far as the eleventh century (ÓhAllmhuráin 1998). The modern day fiddle was invented in Italy in 1550. It is a four stringed instrument played by drawing a bow across the strings. It is held between the chin and the chest, while the fingers on one hand press down on the strings, shortening and lengthening the resonances, thus changing the pitch. The other hand is used to draw the bow, which is made from horsehair impregnated with rosin, across the strings. The strings are tuned to the notes G3, D4, A4, and E5. Most fiddles are made from wood, but fiddles made from tin or brass were popular particular in remote areas of Donegal, where the robustness of a metal instrument was considered an advantage (Vallely 1999).

Figure 8: Fiddle player Siobhan Peoples

Most traditional musicians play in the "first position" giving the instrument a range of just over three octaves. The fiddle is a very suitable instrument for traditional music because of the relative ease by which ornamentation (section 2.9.1) can be executed (Vallely 1999). The fiddle is particular prominent in the areas of Donegal, Sligo, East Clare and Sliabh Luchra (on the Cork/Kerry border) (Figure 18, page 54), where distinctive interpretive styles have emerged. Donegal style fiddle playing is generally known for its fast pace and staccato timbre achieved with short bow strokes. The Sligo style of fiddle playing is inspired by the playing of Michael Coleman (section 2.9.3), with extensive use of ornamentation (section 2.9.1). The East Clare (Figure 18, page 54) style is known to be slower, more melodic and with a strong use of ornamentation. The Sliabh Luchra area is also particularly known for the playing of slides and polkas (section 2.1.2, 2.1.4 and Figure 18).

2.4.4 Uilleannn Pipes

The *Uilleannn Pipes* (elbow pipes) is a bellows blown bagpipe with a *chanter*, three *drones* and three *regulators* for generating sound. The uilleannn pipes is the most complex instrument of its type and Tansey (1999) describes the uilleannn pipes as the "*sacred tabernacle*" reflecting its overwhelming importance in the development of traditional Irish music.

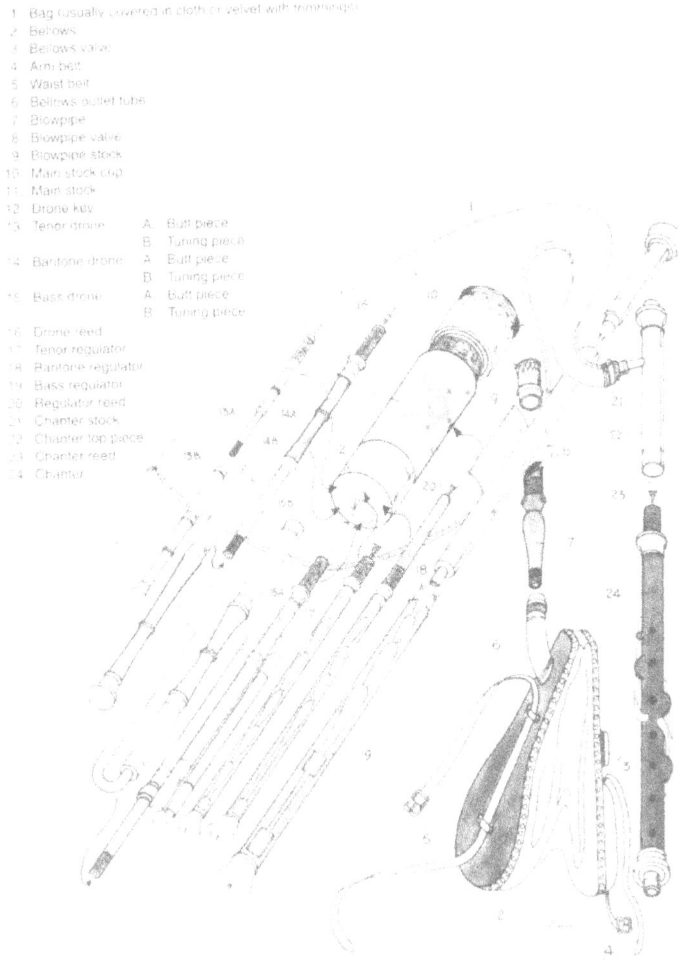

Figure 9: The main components of the uilleann pipes (Vallely 1999)

The famous piper and collector Séamus Ennis is reported to have said that it takes seven years learning, seven years practising and seven years playing to master the uilleann pipes. The player plays seated with the bag under the left arm and the bellows under the right arm. The bellows is used to blow air into the bag. The player uses pressure on the bag to maintain a constant flow of air through reads in the chanter drones and regulators to generate the sound. The chanter has a range of two octaves using the technique of overblowing, similar to overblowing on the tin-whistle (section 2.4.1) and concert flute (section 2.4.2). A fingering chart for the chanter is given in Figure 10.

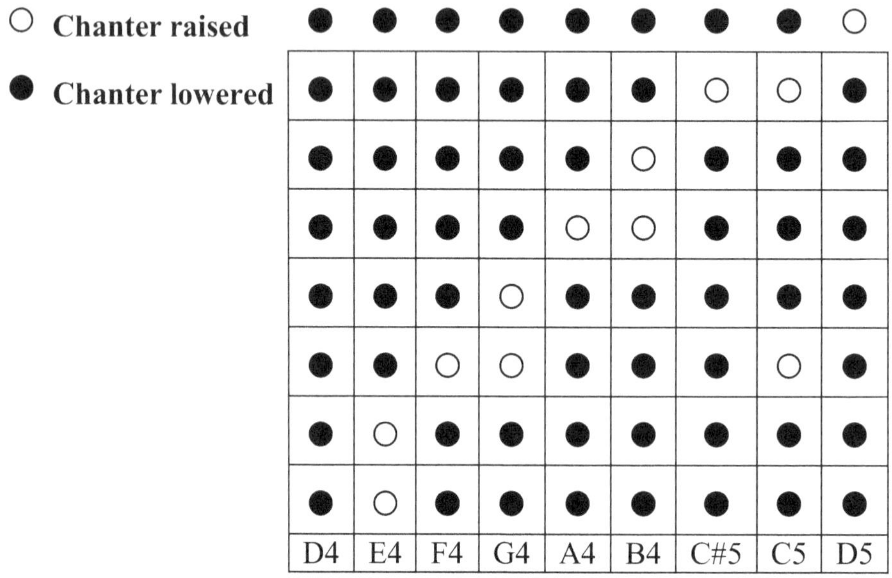

Figure 10: Fingering chart for the uilleann pipes chanter

In common with the tin-whistle and concert flute, the modern chanter is typically pitched in the key of D major, though chanters with other fundamental notes are available (Table 7).

Key	Fundamental note (Hz)
Bb	233.08
B	246.94
C	261.63
C#	277.18
D	293.66

Table 7: Tunings for uilleann pipe chanters

Sharps and flats can be achieved through the use of additional keys if available or through cross fingering. The drones are tuned to the fundamental note of the chanter, with each of the three drones pitched an octave apart.

Valves controlling the drones are typically opened for the duration of a melody providing a droning accompaniment for the melody played on the chanter. Three regulators lie on top of the drones and consist of tenor, baritone and bass. They possess keys which only sound a note when opened. They are played with the side of the hand and are used to harmonise the melody.

The uilleann pipes originated in the early eighteenth century and were originally known as the "Irish pipes" or "Union pipes". The pipes in their modern form, with three drones and regulators was introduced around 1770. The pipes idiosyncratic ornaments "yelping" and "craning" have been adapted by flute players, notably the flute player Matt Molloy, who was one of the first to introduce "craning" (section 2.9.1) to the playing of the concert flute.

2.4.5 Harp

The *harp* is the national symbol of Ireland appearing on coins and on government publications. The Brian Boru harp on display in Trinity College, is the harp from which the national symbol of Ireland is copied.

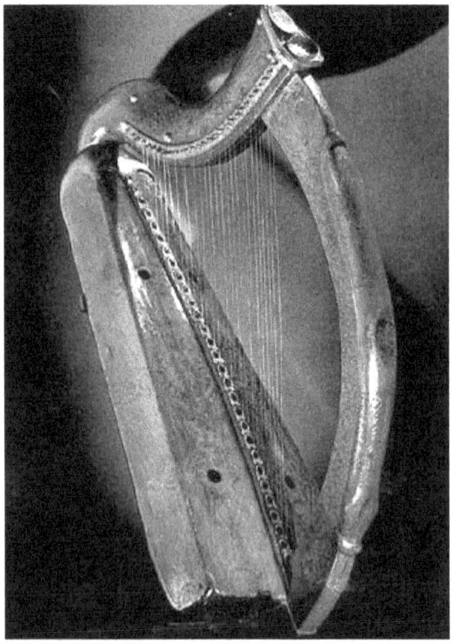

Figure 11: The Brian Boru Harp (Eagan 1998)

The earliest surviving harps from Ireland date from the 15th century. For centuries, the harp and the harpist were integral components of cultural and social life in Ireland. Turlough O'Carolan (1670-1738), the blind Irish harpist, wrote many tunes in the Baroque style - many of which are still popular amongst traditional musicians and appear in popular collections (O'Neill 1903).

The harp is a stringed instrument which has the plane of its strings positioned perpendicular to the soundboard. All harps have a neck, resonator and strings. The Irish harp went into decline in the seventeenth centaury and by the nineteenth century it had practically disappeared, until it had a renaissance since the 1950's (Vallely 1999). For further discussion on the Irish harp see (Clark 2003).

2.4.6 Free-reed instruments

Free reed instruments include the *piano accordion*, the *button accordion* and the *concertina*. In these instruments, the air stream is generated by the action of blowing a bellows using the hands, which go across a set of paired metal reeds causing them to vibrate. Each note in these instruments is produced using a different set of reeds, with a valve which is opened by pressing a key on the instrument. The piano accordion is a double draw instrument (same note on push and draw) common in *ceilí band* music. The button accordion and concertina are single draw instruments meaning that each key press can produce two notes depending on whether the player pushes or draws the bellows (Vallely 1999). The melodeon (a predecessor of the button accordion) has a set of ten keys, which produces twenty notes of the diatonic scale. A development of the melodeon is the button accordion, which includes a row of keys to produce a full chromatic scale. Since traditional music is essentially diatonic, the second row is reserved for producing ornamentations. Finally, the concertina is a small accordion with hexagonal shape, having five keys at each side (Vallely 1999).The concertina is particularly common in County Clare (Figure 18, page 54).

2.4.7 Percussion

Written and pictorial records point to Irish traditional music being melodic in nature. Where it is present percussion is usually in the form of the *bodhrán*, *bones*, *spoons*, or drums in ceilí band music. The bodhrán is a shallow, circular frame-drum with a skin of goat hide or dog skin. Before the 1960's, the bodhrán was only played on St. Stephen's day (the day after Christmas day) as part of the "wren boys" tradition (Vallely 1999), though this view seems to be contradicted by its appearance in the plays of Kerry playwright John B Keane (Keane 1986; Keane 1959). It appears to have been popularised as a result of Seán O Riada's seminal performances with radio ensemble Ceoltóirí Chualann in the 1960's. The bodhrán is played with a *beater* or *tipper*. Figure 12 illustrates the technique of holding and playing a bodhrán.

Figure 12: Bodhrán player Peter Blaney

Rib-bones from an animal and kitchen spoons, played castanet-fashion are also occasionally used to provide percussive accompaniment. Commonly heard at traditional music performances is the distinctive tapping of the feet of listeners and the musicians. Fiddle player Martin Hayes comments on this in the sleeve notes to his CD recording "The Lonesome Touch" (Hayes & Cahill 1997).

2.4.8 Lilting

Lilting, known as *port béal* in Irish, is a term used to describe a musical style known as *vocalisation*, which is found in many world cultures. It refers to the use of nonsense words, meaningless syllables or non-lexical symbols to vocalise a melody. In lilting, the placing of syllables is used to articulate rhythmic patterns and ornamentation characteristic of a musical instrument. Similar musical styles exist in Jazz, Scots, Ghanaian and Indian classical musical idioms. Lilting is very widespread and lilting might be considered as the "third instrument" of most traditional musicians, the second being the tin-whistle (section 2.4.1), which the majority of musicians can play. Vallely (1999) speculates that lilting may have developed as a response to a shortage of musical instruments. Lilting is a respected form of musical expression and Comhaltas Ceoltóirí Éireann has a separate competition for lilting in its annual *fleadhanna* (musical competitions).

Lilting is often used between musicians when they are talking about a tune or in the teaching of a tune. Although lilting is very popular, it is currently not supported as a query mechanism for any of the MIR systems discussed in Chapter 5. It is hoped to add support for lilted queries to a future version of the system presented in Chapter 6.

2.5 Solo versus ensemble playing

When traditional musicians play together, all musicians play the same melody. Breathnach (1985) criticises the trend towards the playing of accompaniment or ensemble playing in Irish traditional music and argues that it diminishes the skill of solo performance. He writes:

> *"A good performer, **playing solo – the best way of rendering this music** – will play a tune over 3, 4 or more times, introducing as he proceeds fresh forms of ornamentation, melodic and rhythmic variations."*

Nonetheless, it is common for Irish music to be played in sessions at *ceilithe* and on commercial recordings in unison. Similarly piano accompaniment has been a feature of traditional music since the availability of 78 RPM records of traditional music since the 1920's with accompaniment on piano. In the 1960s, it became popular to incorporate guitar accompaniment and in the 1970's the bouzouki was introduced. Since the 1960's it is common for traditional music to be played at *sessions* – semi-formal gatherings of musicians and occasionally dancers which often take place in pubs. Often sessions are anchored by one or two core musicians who may be paid to play, though sessions are generally open to guests of appropriate standard. The session is largely controlled by the relative status of the people playing, with the higher status musicians exercising more control over the way the session develops.

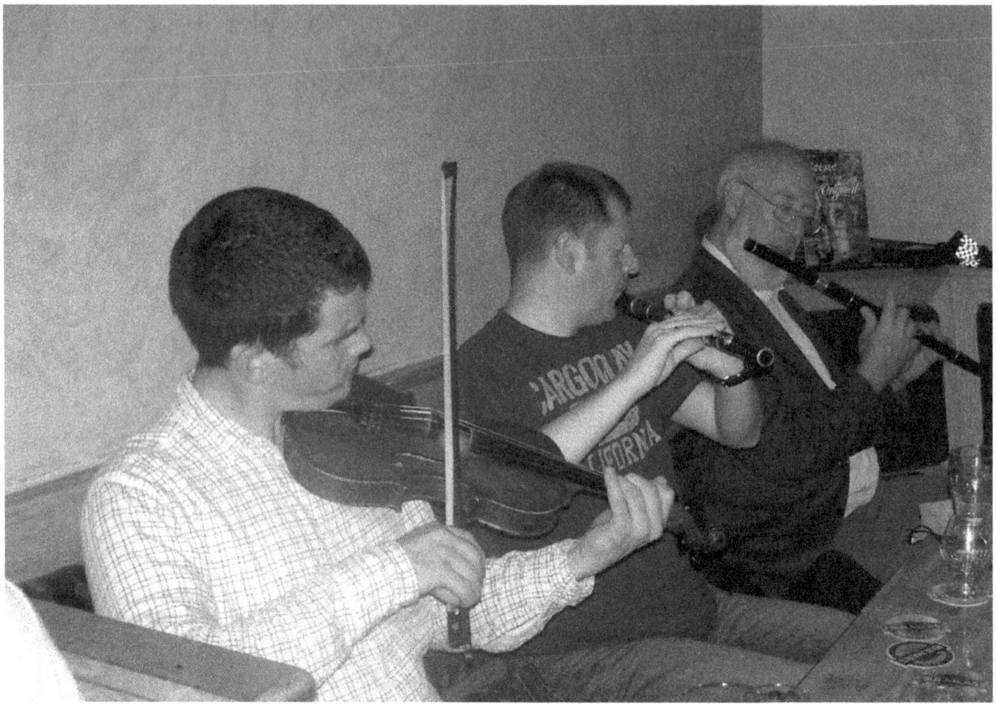

Figure 13: Fiddle player Colm Logue, the author, and flute player Patsy Hanley at an informal session at Fleadh Cheoil na hÉireann 2008

Hamilton (1990) identifies status in the session as depending on a musician's age, competence, reputation, and instrument played. Musician Charlie Lennon is quoted in (O'Shea 2006) as saying:

> *"The importance of good listeners positioned around the musicians cannot be overstated as they help to bring the best out of the musicians and make the session a success"*

Ensemble performance of Irish traditional music is a social opportunity for musicians to meet and the playing of music in sessions can be understood as a modern manifestation of the sociality of rural house dances common in Ireland before the 1930's. O'Shea (2006) writes:

> *"At two (or three) in the morning, only a handful of musicians remained and the dancers were still roaring for music. Perhaps it was the company's conviviality certainly the whiskey contributed or the fact that I was now familiar with the other musicians repertoire, but as we played together I experienced a surge of euphoria, a feeling that I was right at the centre of the music I loved, that I understood through my body the meaning of dance music, a level of exhilaration as if I were dancing myself, and to the best possible music. Other factors contributed to my sense that I was at one with the music making, for the evening was a culmination of many years of learning and playing within a cultural narrative that accorded the highest value to a house dance with older musicians such as those present. Or perhaps it was simply that, with my tapping toes at times literally under the feet of the dancers as they stamped their rhythm on the music, I was sitting in the best seat in the house..."*

2.6 Collections

There have been several notable initiatives to catalogue the canon of Irish traditional music (Petrie 1855; Bunting 1840; Joyce 1909; Shields 1998) but the majority of traditional tunes were not transcribed until the turn of the twentieth century when Francis O'Neill, the then police chief in Chicago, transcribed and documented a large body of dance tunes and airs from immigrant Irish musicians.

In 1903, he published a book of his collected tunes entitled *The Music of Ireland.* The 1,850 tunes presented in the collection were classified according to tune-type (airs and songs, Carolan compositions, double jigs, slip jigs, reels, hornpipes, long dances, marches and miscellaneous). In 1907, he published *The Dance Music of Ireland – 1001 Gems*. This collection focused entirely on the dance music repertoire and contained many tunes published in his previous collection. O'Neill's second book was considered the definitive source for traditional musicians and musicians would often refer to a tune by its reference number in the book (Wallis & Wilson 2001).

Figure 14: Police Chief Francis O' Neill and the cover of O' Neill's "The Dance Music of Ireland"

Brendan Breathnach's *Ceol Rince Na hÉireann* series in five volumes is regarded as the most significant and influential collection of traditional Irish music after O' Neill's books (Breathnach 1963; Breathnach 1976; Breathnach 1985; Breathnach 1996; Breathnach 1999). Breathnach's books contain tunes from many sources including field recordings, commercial recordings and manuscript collections of dance music held in private hands.

By identifying duplicates and variations Breathnach sought to identify the earliest occurrences of tunes and trace their history through printed manuscript collections and recordings. His books contain detailed bibliographic notes on each of the tunes included, an example of which is given in translation (Translation by Breandán Breathnach, as posted to IRTRAD-L on 15/08/98 by Terry McGee):

> *"23. Scaip an Puiteach [Scatter the Mud]: O'Neill has a setting (O'N i, 187) and Roche another, The Maids of Tramore (R i, 129). The tune [first part] which Roche has is faulty at the end, and the turn [second part] is not from this jig at all [The Eviction in Ryan's Mammoth Collection, p104, is almost identical to the Roche tune]. This jig is also called The Noonday Feast."*

2.7 Collections in electronic format

ABC is a music notation language introduced by Chris Walshaw in 1991 (Walshaw 2007) for the typesetting of traditional tunes. The format was designed primarily for folk and traditional tunes of Western European origin which can be written on one stave in standard classical notation (Walshaw 2007).

The tune given in Figure 15 is typical of the transcriptions that can be sourced in ABC from publicly available databases (see also Appendix C and Appendix E).

```
X:422
T:Come West Along the Road
R:reel
S:Session
H:See also #432, in A. This version is also played in
A.
H:1st part similar to "Over the Moor to Peggy", #710
D:Arcady: Many Happy Returns
D:Noel Hill & Tony McMahon: \'I gCnoc na Gra\'i
Z:id:hn-reel-422
M:C|
K:G
d2BG dGBG|~G2Bd efge|d2BG dGBG|1 ABcd edBc:|2 ABcd
edBd||
|:g2bg egdg|(3efg dg edBd|1 g2bg egdB|ABcd edBd:|2 gabg
efge|dega bage||
```

Figure 15: The tune "Come West Along the Road" in the ABC format (Norbeck 2007) (see also Figure 3, Figure 42 and Figure 44)

In this transcription the transcriber has helpfully included a significant amount of useful metadata with the notation for the tune such as the source of the transcription, the discography and a listing of similar tunes. ABC files are ASCII text files and so can be edited by any text editor, without the necessity for special software. Each file (known as a *tune book*) can contain multiple tunes. File sizes are typically measured in kilobytes and this facilitates easy transmission by electronic means. The small size of ABC files also makes them an ideal medium for the storage of tunes on a memory constrained mobile device (Duggan 2007b).

The header section contains amongst other fields, the title, composer, source, tempo, key, geographical origin and transcriber (Mansfield 2007). As tunes can have several titles, the title field can be repeated for a given tune. The tune body contains the notation for the tune. The body encoding supports such features as ornaments (section 2.9.1), bar divisions, sharps, flats, naturals, repeated sections, key changes, guitar chords, lyrics and variations. Appendix B gives a short tutorial on ABC notation. There is an active and vibrant community supporting ABC notation and a range of tools have been developed for a variety of platforms and purposes. Some examples include website thesession.org, a text based MIR (Music Information Retrieval) system that contains over 7,000 tunes collaboratively transcribed by the traditional music community (thesession.org 2007) (section 5.1) and TunePal an MIR system which runs on a PDA or smartphone which enables access to collections of tunes for playback in traditional music sessions (Duggan 2007a; Duggan 2007b; Duggan 2006) (section 5.1).

Between 1997 and 2000, a group of musicians under the leadership of Dan Beimborn and John Chambers, undertook a grass roots project to transcribe three of O'Neill's books to electronic format using ABC notation. As copyright had expired on O'Neill's original books, they made their work freely available on the internet (Chambers 2007). Many of the tunes from O'Neill's books are played differently by musicians today, as is normal with a living tradition. Around the same period (the late 1990's) Henrik Norbeck collected nearly two thousand tunes in ABC notation from various sessions and recordings. Again this collection was made freely available on the internet. This collection contains many modern settings of tunes from O'Neill's books (Norbeck 2007). The experiments presented in Chapter 7 and Chapter 8 use Norbeck's reel and jig corpus to identify recordings of tunes.

2.8 Musical creativity

Götz (1981) relates creativity to "making" and defines creativity as "the process or activity of deliberately concretising insight". Boden (1996) distinguishes two types of creativity. Psychological creativity (P-creativity) occurs when an individual has an idea which is novel to that individual, regardless of how many other individuals have had the same idea. Historical creativity (H-creativity) defines ideas that are novel not only to an individual, but also novel in the history of human endeavour. P-creativity is therefore judged by an individual. H-creativity is judged by society at large. The concept of two levels of creativity is also proposed by (Gardner 1993), who distinguishes between "little c" and "big C" creativity.

There are examples in traditional music of both P-creativity and H-creativity as defined in (Boden 1996). Individual expression (P-creativity) is in fact a defining component of traditional Irish music. In the introduction to the revised edition of O' Neill's Music of Ireland, Krassen (1975) describes a typical scenario:

> *"It seems that on this particular occasion Touhey wanted to learn a tune from McFadden. He had McFadden play it for him several times and then tried his own hand at it. Of course McFadden had to play it again, pointing out several "errors." This happened a number of times until Touhey finally gave up, for McFadden was playing the tune a little differently each time through!"*

A traditional musician will usually employ variations, ornamentation, timbre and phrasing to interpret a tune (Larson 2003). How these elements are accommodated in this work is described in Chapter 6.

H-creativity by definition, more rarely occurs in traditional music. Some examples might include the introduction of the concert flute in the nineteenth century, the development of the ceilí band form in the 1920's and 1930's, the renaissance of traditional music led by Sean O' Riada and Ceoltóirí Chualann in the 1960's and the introduction of the Bouzuki in the 1970's (Wallis and Wilson 2001).

The cognition of individual creativity implies that an individual musician demonstrates a style which can be recognised. Meyer (1989) defines musical style as:

"a replication of patterning...that results from a series of choices made within some set of constraints".

Keegan (1992) again associates the concept of style with creativity and claims that the technique of an individual and their musical style are one and the same thing.

2.9 Style & expressiveness in traditional Irish dance music

Until the 1940's there existed distinct *regional* styles of playing Irish traditional music attributed mainly to the isolation of rural communities prior to the advent of mass communication (Keegan 1992). This section concentrates on flute and tin-whistle styles, though the techniques explored in this section are also used in other traditional instruments to varying extents and each instrument adds its own idiosyncrasies.

There are a number of authoritative sources which describe characteristics that can define an individual musician's style. For the concert flute, these include Valley's, "Timber: The Flute Tutor", and his PhD thesis, "Flute Routes to 21st Century Ireland" (Vallely 2004), Larson's "The Essential Guide to Irish Flute and Tin Whistle", McCormack's, "Fliúit: Irish Flute Tutorial", Keegan's (1992) MPhil thesis "Words of Traditional Flute Style". In addition there is Casey's "Traditional Irish Flute Music from East Galway A Regional study and Documentary Field Collection". Additionally Tansey's (1999) "The Bardic Apostles of Inishfree", a profile of Sligo musicians makes reference to ornaments (section 2.9.1) not described in any of the other literature, (*bark*, *backstitch, run* and *pop*). In personal interviews he has elaborated on the meaning of these terms (Tansey 2006). Breathnach's (1963) *Ceol Rince na hÉireann Cuid I* and *Cuid III* contain detailed tables indicating how ornamentation should be performed on the pipes, whistle, fiddle and the accordion.

Although there are some disagreements in definitions of certain features, the literature generally agrees that interpretative style can be characterised by features that include use of ornamentation, phrasing (where a musician takes a breath), use of variation, staccato or legato playing (with throating/ tonguing attacks), the timbre a musician achieves with an instrument, bowing style on the fiddle, tempo, choice of tune, choice of tune type and the arrangement of tunes into sets. Certain instruments are also more popular in some regions of Ireland than others, such as the flute in counties Sligo, Leitrim and Roscommon (sections 2.4.2 and 2.9.3) the fiddle in Donegal (section 2.4.3) and the button accordion in Sliabh Luchra.

2.9.1 Ornamentation

Larsen (2003) defines ornamentation as:

> "*...ways of altering or embellishing small pieces or cells of a melody that are between 1 and 3 8-note beats long. These alterations and embellishments are created mainly through the use of special fingered articulations.*"

The playing of ornamentation is a defining characteristic of traditional Irish music. The sound of most ornaments is very brief. Although generated by inserting additional notes, Larsen (2003) argues that the notes are played at such speed that they are not perceived as having a discernible pitch or duration.

Breathneach's (1963) descriptions of ornaments however seems to contradict this view as he distinguishes different fingerings for ornaments played on different instruments. Keegan (1992) similarly suggests that the use of different fingerings is a characteristic of musical style and ability.

Further, there are differing opinions as to the origins of ornamentation in traditional Irish music. Larsen (2003) suggests that ornamentation is derived from the playing of the *píob mór*, a mouth blown bagpipe which predated the development of the modern uilleann pipes. The píob mór had no capacity for momentary interruptions to the flow of air and thus melodies were played as unbroken streams of sound. In order to generate a stop between two notes of the same pitch, a musician would play a third note momentarily between the two notes.

Tansey (1999) however argues that ornamentation developed as an attempt to mimic the sounds of nature. He compares for example the sound of a *cran* to that of a sheep's "baa" and postulates that the ornament was developed by shepherd's who played wooden flutes while tending sheep:

> *"I put it to you therefore that it had to come from the throats of birds, the wild animals, the ancient chants of our forefathers, the hum of the bees and the mighty rhythms of the galloping hooves of wild horses all moulded together..."*

The main types of ornamentation are now identified[4].

A *cut* is defined as an articulation used to separate two notes. A cut is articulated by playing a middle note momentarily at a higher pitch than the second

[4] Audio examples of each of the ornaments described in this section can be listened to at: `http://www.comp.dit.ie/bduggan/music`

note. The overall length of the two notes does not change when cutting and so the length of the second note must be shortened very slightly to accommodate the cut.

A *tap* (referred to in some sources as a *strike* or a *bounce*) is an articulation also used to separate two notes. A tap is articulated by playing a middle note momentarily at a lower pitch than the second note.

A *long roll* is an ornament used to separate three notes. The second note in the sequence is cut and the third note is tapped. Again, the overall length of the three notes does not change. A *short roll* is similar to a long roll, but the first note in the sequence of three is dropped. Jackie Small in the introduction to (Breathnach 1996) describes a roll as similar to a *gruppetto* in classical music, but with a different emphasis. He writes:

> *"The use of the roll is best learned by traditional musicians: notation cannot adequately express the secret of this little rhythmic 'knot' which is such a characteristic of Irish traditional dance music. Where a roll or triplet is indicated...one could play the roll appropriate to one's instrument, or a triplet or other ornamental device; or indeed no ornament at all and instead opt for 'the long note'"*

Rolls therefore can be played or not according to preference and so melodic similarity metrics (Chapter 4) should consider a phrase played with or without ornamentation to have a distance of zero. This requires that the measure will be a non metric (Chapter 4).

Uilleann pipes' chanters (section 2.4.4), concert flutes (section 2.4.2) and tin-whistles are usually pitched in D. As there is no note lower than a low D on these instruments, a tap on the low D is not possible. Instead, to execute a "roll" type ornament on a low D, a musician will play a *cran*. In order to play a cran, the musician replaces the tap with a second cut. The second cut uses a different note, usually higher than that of the first cut. This creates a "bubbling" sound characteristic of the playing of flute player Matt Molloy. In cases where the instrument is pitched differently (Table 5, Table 6, Table 7) the pitches generated by craning are adjusted as appropriate. Not all musicians use crans, for example, the flute player Catherine McEvoy rarely plays crans. Although Larsen (2003) suggests that crans can be done on any note, most other sources suggest that crans are only played on the low and middle D and E (Vallely 1999; Vallely 1986). They can be played long or short as with rolls. An example of the several ways in which the musical phrase GGG (3 quaver length G4's) in ABC notation may be interpreted is given in Table 8 (see also Appendix B).

Example (in ABC format)	**Meaning**
GGG	3 quaver notes
ggg	3 quaver notes transposed 1 octave
~G3	A G roll, 5 notes
~g3	A G roll, 5 notes, transposed 1 octave
G~G2	A G followed by a 4 note roll
g~g2	A G followed by a 4 note roll, transposed 1 octave
G3	A dotted crochet (The long note)
g3	A dotted crochet (The long note), transposed one octave
G2z	A crochet G followed by a breath
g2z	A crochet G followed by a breath, transposed one octave
G{B}G{D}	A 5 note G roll, ornamented with an unusual fingering. Many variations are possible.

Table 8: Variations on the notes GGG in ABC notation

With the above articulations, the actual pitch of the "extra" notes may vary depending on which finger the musician feels most comfortable lifting at speed (Keegan 1992). Using different fingers to perform the ornamentation also gives the ornament a specific character which can be part of a musician's unique sound. Breathnach (1963) writes:

"The single grace note is shown as being the next highest note to that being ornamented although in fact this may not have been so; this form also varies from instrument to instrument"

This contrasts with Larson's (2003) more limited explanations of ornamentation.

A *trill* is defined as a rapid alteration of the principal note and the note above it. A trill may begin on either the principal note or on the higher ornamental note. Trills are usually played for short durations in traditional music, with longer duration trills being considered too much of an allusion to classical music.

A *tight triplet* also called a *treble* in (Tansey 1999) is a stepwise rising or falling sequence of 3 notes played in quick succession in the rhythm of two notes. A specific type of tight triplet mentioned in (Tansey 1999) is a *back stich* which he describes as a treble using the notes BCD.

A *run* as described by Tansey (2006) is a descending sequence of two tight triplets as illustrated in Figure 16. In the note sequence, the first four notes are played without the use of a run while the second sequence of six notes are two tight triplets, in other words a *run* on the four note sequence.

```
K:D
M:Reel
=cABG (3=cBA (3BAG
```

Figure 16: An example of a *run* in ABC notation (see also Appendix B and `http://www.comp.dit.ie/bduggan/music`)

Figure 17 gives examples of the ornamentation discussed in this section in piano-roll format. As can be seen from the diagram the inserted notes take duration from the subsequent note. This characteristic is exploited in the Ornamentation Filtering algorithm presented in section 6.4.1.

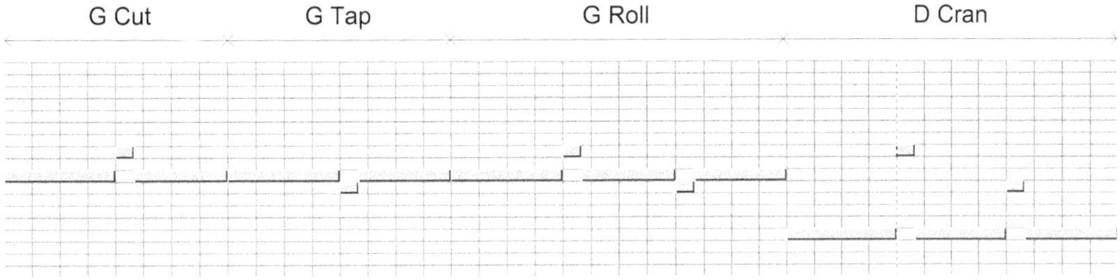

Figure 17: Examples of ornamentation in piano roll format (see also `http://www.comp.dit.ie/bduggan/music` for example audio recordings)

Switching between octaves on a wooden flute or tin-whistle is achieved using *overblowing* (Hamilton 1990). Overblowing is also used as a technique in the sounding of a *hard D* on a concert flute. A hard D is achieved on a wooden flute by overblowing the D in the lower register to the extent that the note is perceived as a group of harmonics of D which can be impossible to distinguish (Keegan 1992). The hard D is also played on the pipes.

Reversing is a technique common in the Donegal fiddle tradition which is also popular amongst certain flute players. Reversing describes where a musician transposes a melody by one octave in order to add a "baser" sound. This commonly occurs in the B part of a tune which is usually played in the high register of an instrument. In ensemble playing, this has a similar effect to the technique of *doubling* (playing the melody in two octaves simultaneously) on the concertina and it can be used to create a simple polyphony. Reversing can be done whereby a phrase or entire part of a tune is transposed (Robinson 1999). Many examples of this phenomenon can be heard on the CD recording "O Bhéal go Béal" by Marcas O'Murchu (O'Murchu 1997). This is also a characteristic technique of the flute player Seamus Tansey which Carson (1997) describes as a "*Tansey stock-in-trade, blowing the high notes low and visa-versa, jumping octaves all the time*". This seemingly random transposition by octave will affect measures of melodic similarity described in Chapter 4 and so this is compensated for in section 6.7.

2.9.2 Phrasing

Phrasing in concert flute and tin-whistle music is easily identified as the timings in a performance of a tune where a musician takes a breath.

Ornamentation	Single-note	Cut
		Tap
	Multi-note	Roll
		Cran
		Triplet
		Run
Breathing	Phrasing	
	Throating (attacks)	
	Overblowing	
	Timbre	
Variation		
Repertoire	Reels	
	Jigs	
	Hornpipes	
	Polkas	
	Slides	
Sets		
Tempo	Fast	
	Slow	
	Tempo deviation	

Table 9: Features which characterise creativity in traditional Irish flute playing

Traditional music scores are not annotated with breath marks and it is up to an individual musician to decide where a breath should be taken. Taking a breath usually means leaving out a note or several notes from the score in a performance. Phrasing is therefore more obvious in music played on the flute and tin-whistle than on any other traditional instruments. Keegan (1992) in his interviews establishes that phrasing (and in particular the length of phrases) is a strong indicator of a particular regional and individual style. Table 9 (previous page) summarises the features elaborated upon in this section.

2.9.3 Regional Styles

Canainn (1978) describes regional style as the common features which distinguish the majority of performances by musicians from a particular area. Keegan (1992) attempts to understand the cognition of regional styles of Irish flute music by conducting a series of interviews with prominent musicians. He reports that four regional flute styles were identified by his subjects, though his work suggests that the characteristics which distinguished these styles varied somewhat. The regional styles identified in his work are: The West Clare style, the Ballinakill/East Galway style, the Fermanagh/Northern style and the Sligo/Roscommon style. Figure 18 shows a map of Ireland with the locations of the four regions identified by Keegan.

The West Clare and Ballinakill/East Galway styles he describes as demonstrating much use of ornamentation and accidentals, with the melody played at a relatively slow pace. These styles differ in repertoire and use of breath articulation, with The West Clare style being characterised by the use of throating to emphasise rhythm. The Ballinakill/East Galway style developed from the playing of the musicians in one of the first ceili bands, The Ballinakill Traditional Players. Keegan suggests that the Ballinakill/East Galway sound is more legato, with an emphasis on melody rather than rhythm. This is evident in the repertoire played by musicians in that style, which contains tunes with several parts. He suggests that in the past a substantial group of East Galway musicians have adopted the Boehm system flute or other fully keyed instruments, which are more suitable for the repertoire which involve tunes in unusual keys and with accidentals.

Figure 18: Geographic origin of regional style (Source: Author based on (Keegan 1992))

The Fermanagh/Northern style he describes as being sparsely-ornamented, but with heavy stress on breath articulation techniques. Keegan (1992) states that there exist two styles of phrasing. In some examples, there is an emphasis on natural-phrasing (regular two-bar phrases), while other musicians demonstrate short irregular phrasing, characteristic of the music of North Leitrim (and hence similar to the Sligo-Roscommon style).

There is a strong concentration of flute players in the Leitrim/Sligo/Roscommon area which Tansey (2006) attributes to the prevalence of coal mining in the region. He argues that the flute was considered good for the development and health of the lungs of coal miners, constantly exposed to high levels of coal dust in their profession. Vallely (1999) suggests that the Sligo style was inspired by the playing of emigrant fiddlers of the 1920's such as Michael Coleman, whose 78 RPM records were very popular at the time. Although Keegan's (1992) subjects reported contradictory opinions on many aspects of the Sligo/Roscommon style, they agreed that the style is very rhythmical because of the use of breath articulation and emphasis. They also suggest that the overuse of ornamentation is not characteristic of many musicians of the Sligo/Roscommon style (though he points out several notable exceptions). Vallely (1999) seems to disagree with this assessment and suggests that phrases and variations are ornate in the Sligo style, with an emphatic puff from the diaphragm accenting each new phrase. This is evident in the playing of modern archetypal Sligo flute players Seamus Tansey, Catherine McEvoy and Matt Molloy.

Vallely (1999) distinguishes a distinctive Leitrim style of flute playing inspired by the flute player John McKenna of Arigna, near Drumshambo who recorded extensively in the early part of the twentieth Century (Figure 19).

Figure 19: John McKenna (flute) and Michael Gaffney (banjo)

He proposes that the Leitrim style pre-dates the Sligo/Roscommon style and is reminiscent of an older flute playing style, likely at one time to be common to both Sligo and Leitrum. McKenna's style was driving, breathy and comparatively sparing in the use of ornamentation, with short melodic phrasing.

2.9.4 Expressive examples

To better illustrate the variation that occurs in the employment of the expressive elements outlined in this chapter, Appendix H presents note for note transcriptions of the tune "Ambrose Moloney's" played by two expert flute players, Catherine McEvoy and Eamon Cotter. Catherine McEvoy plays in the Sligo/Roscommon style and in fact has a released a CD recording entitled "Traditional Flute Music in the Sligo-Roscommon Style" (McEvoy 1998). Eamon Cotter combines elements of the East Galway flute style and elements of the East Clare fiddle tradition in his flute playing (Hurley 2005). These transcriptions show marked differences in how each musician has chosen to interpret the tune. The first difference is that McEvoy has chosen to play the reel three times, while Cotter plays the tune just twice. There are many examples of variation in the employment of both ornamentation and phrasing. Consider the phrase from the B part of the tune the first time around:

```
dgbg a2fa|gedB GABd|
eaag agef|g2bg age2|
```

Which McEvoy interprets as:

```
dzb a{c'}ag{g}ea|{c'}g{g}edB ~g3d|
{f}a4{c'}a {b}g{b}ed|gzbg abge|
```

McEvoy has taken a breath in the first and last bars, employed cuts at the onset of many of the notes in the second register, played a `g` roll in the second register instead of the phrase `GAB` (in the lower register) and replaced the phrase `eaag` with "the long note" `a4` with a corresponding cut at the onset, amongst other melodic and ornamental transformations. In contrast, Cotter plays the same phrase as:

```
dgbg ~a2f{ag}a|gedB GDBD|
ea{b}a^g a{gf}=gef|gzbg{b}a{gf}gez|
```

He takes two breaths, but in the last bar and in different places to McEvoy. He replaces the phrase `a2` with a short roll on the note `a` and again cuts at the onset of many of the notes in the second register. Cotter however also plays trills instead of cuts at the onsets of the notes `a` and `g`. Interesting Cotter makes use of the accidental g# (transcribed as `^g` in ABC notation), the use of accidentals being a characteristic of the East Galway flute style (Hurley 2005).

2.10 Conclusions

From this introduction to the domain of traditional Irish dance music, it can be concluded that an MIR system for traditional dance music must deal with many challenges which would present difficulties for the MIR systems presented in Chapter 5. These challenges are distilled into P1-P10 in Table 10.

P1	Support for traditional instruments
P2	Commonly used keys & modes
P3	Reversing
P4	C, C# similarity
P5	Phrasing
P6	Transposition in tin-whistles
P7	Ornamentation
P8	The long note
P9	Tempo deviation
P10	The playing of tunes in sets

Table 10: Summary of the main challenges in performing CBMIR on traditional music sources

Firstly and most obviously, the system should support the input and annotation of queries played in traditional instruments such as the flute, tin-whistle, fiddle and uilleann pipes or alternatively lilted queries (P1, P6). Irish traditional music is usually played legato and so any transcription system needs to support legato note onsets (section 3.1). Interestingly, although some of the Query by Humming MIR systems described in Chapter 4 contain traditional Irish dance tunes in their corpora, they do not generate positive results when queries are played on the tin-whistle or wooden flute (as tested by the author).

Stylistic variation (P3, P5, P8, P9) is very common even within the same performance of a tune and therefore any system developed needs to be robust to melodic variations. The use of ornamentation (P7) means that transcribed melodies are always augmented when performed. From Breathneach's comments, it can be understood that the playing of ornamentation is optional and according to Keegan, is an indication of personal and regional style. Ornamentation can be played or not or replaced by "the long note" according to preference and so melodic similarity measures (Chapter 4) should consider a phrase played with or without ornamentation to have a distance of zero. The MATT2 system proposed in Chapter 6 filters ornamentation notes "intelligently" and also deals with the long note in traditional music.

Where a musician makes use of reversing (P3), this should be considered the same as a melody played without reversing. As a simple example, the musical phrase GGG in ABC notation may be interpreted in many ways as indicated in Table 8. This will affect melodic similarity measures (Chapter 4) that depend on exact matches.

The collection of tunes into sets played in a *segue* creates segmentation problems (P10). An input query to a CBMIR system for traditional music may consist of a phrase from any part of a melody, an entire melody, an entire melody played multiple times or multiple melodies played multiple times without an interval, in the same time signature and often in the same key. The challenge therefore is in segmenting a query appropriately so that each individual tune in a set can be annotated correctly. This challenge is address in Chapter 8 with the introduction of a new algorithm called TANSEY (Turn ANnotation from SEts using SimilaritY profiles).

Given the dominance of concert pitch instruments used to play traditional dance music, transposition invariance is only required for the keys and modes playable on the concert pitch instruments given in Table 5, Table 6 and Table 7 (P2). This can be achieved by modifying the pitch spelling algorithm as described in section 6.6 to suit the fundamental note (section 2.2) of the instrument playing the query, rather than by using a transposition invariant similarity measure (section 4.4) which doubly weights replacements, insertions and deletions. Polyphony also does not need to be considered as, when Irish traditional music is played in unison the same melody is simultaneously played by all the performers. Where accompaniment is present, Gainza's (2006) work on the separation of melody from accompaniment in recordings of traditional music can be used to extract the melody component of the signal.

Chapter 3 considers the problem of how to build a transcription system that can extract note onset time and pitch information from query recordings and reviews a number of the main approaches to these problems.

3 Features of Music

CBMIR (Content Based Music Information Retrieval) involves the extraction, and analysis of information from audio signals. The aim of this thesis to develop an approach whereby a digital recording of traditional music can be annotated by comparing it against a representation of a melody in a symbolic format. In order to achieve this, it is necessary to extract a representation of the melody contained in the digital recording by performing a transcription.

Audio signal features can be categorised into *low-level* and *high-level* features. Examples of the former are frequency spectrums, spectral centroid or Mel-frequency cepstral coefficients (MFCC's). High-level features describe properties like rhythm, tempo, melody and structure. In general, low-level features are closely related to the audio signal, whereas high-level features represent more abstract properties of music (Schedl 2008). Developing even a monophonic transcription system that performs as well as a human is an open research question as Dixon (2004) writes:

> *"The main problem in music signal analysis is the development of algorithms to extract sufficiently high level content from audio signals. The low level signal processing algorithms are well understood, but they produce inaccurate or ambiguous results, which can be corrected given sufficient musical knowledge, such as that possessed by a musically literate human listener. This type of musical intelligence is difficult to encapsulate in rules or algorithms that can be incorporated into computer programs."*

This chapter presents the main features of music and discusses techniques to extract these features from digital signals. In particular, this chapter focuses on note onset time and pitch extraction techniques as these will form the basis for the transcription components of the CBMIR system presented in Chapter 6.

3.1 Onset-detection

A note onset describes the start time of a note. A note offset gives the end time of the note. In music played legato, the offset of a note is concurrent with the onset of the subsequent note. Timbre (section 3.3) is related to note onset, as listeners use the attack of a note in distinguishing notes played on different instruments. For example, note attack in percussive instruments such as the piano (Figure 21, page 64) sound different to note attack in a concert flute (Figure 20).

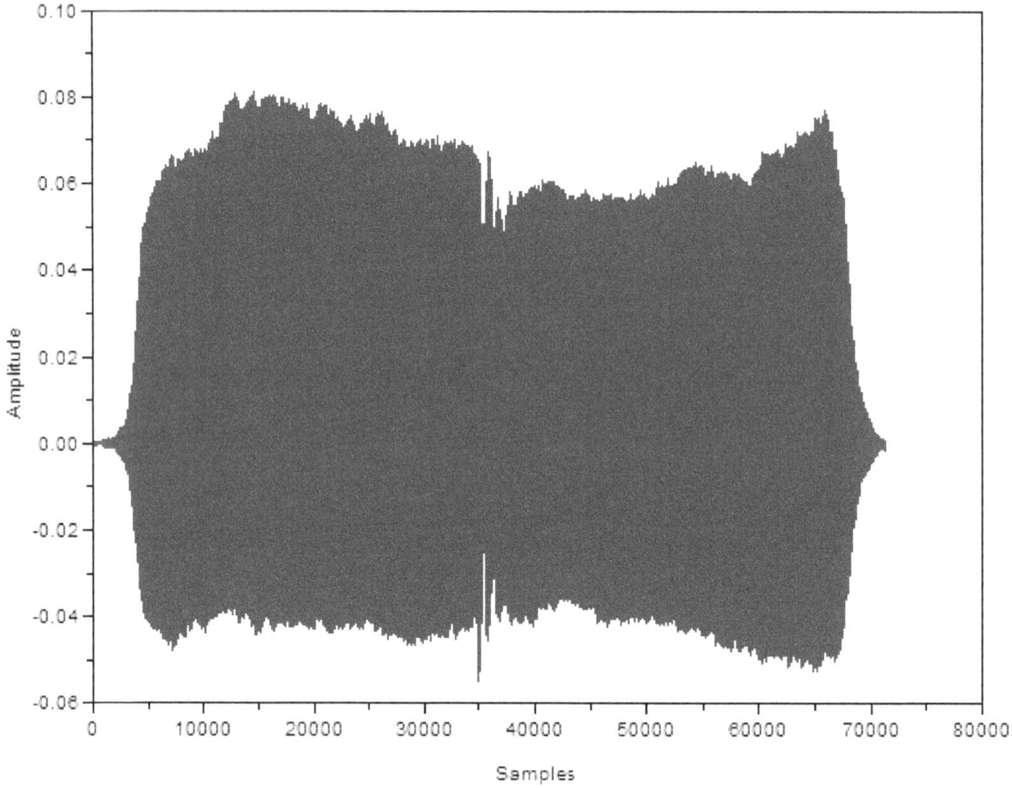

Figure 20: Waveform plot of a concert flute playing the notes A to G legato

Figure 20 and Figure 21 compare waveform plots of a concert flute playing the notes A to G legato with waveform plots of the same notes being played on a piano. As can be seen from these figures, there is a significant energy change in the plot from the piano between the offset of the first note and the onset of the second note, whereas with notes played legato on the wooden flute there is a no significant energy change from one note to the next. Also significant in these plots is the contrast in onsets between the two plots. In Figure 20, the onset to the first note is gradual as the energy builds up, in contrast to the second plot, where the signal reaches maximum energy very quickly.

Vos & Rasch (1981) distinguish between actual and perceived onset times of musical notes, and showed that the perceived onset occurs when the tone reaches a level of approximately 6 – 15dB below its maximum value. Dixon (2006) identifies factors such as masking, temporal order thresholds and "*just noticeable differences*" that make the definition of onset for real-world audio data a challenge. For example, in polyphonic music, the onsets of nominally simultaneous notes (chords) might be spread over tens of milliseconds.

Algorithms that identify note onsets typically try to identify transient regions in the signal. Transient regions can include a sudden change in energy, or a change in the profile of the frequency spectrum of a signal, for example. Onset detection algorithms derive a function called an Onset Detection Function (ODF) from the audio signal at a lower sampling rate than the original signal and apply a peak-picking algorithm to locate the onsets (Bello et al. 2005; Dixon 2006). The peak picking algorithm is normally limited to identifying local maxima above a defined threshold. Thresholds can be fixed or adaptive. A fixed threshold can be employed on signals with little dynamics, however as music can have has significant amplitude changes over the course of a performance, a fixed threshold will tend to generate false negatives in quiet passages and false positives in noisy ones. For this reason, adaptation of the threshold to the characteristics of the signal is usually employed (Bello et al. 2005). Note-onset detection is an important subproblem in the domains of automatic transcription, instrument identification and rhythm estimation (Gainza 2006).

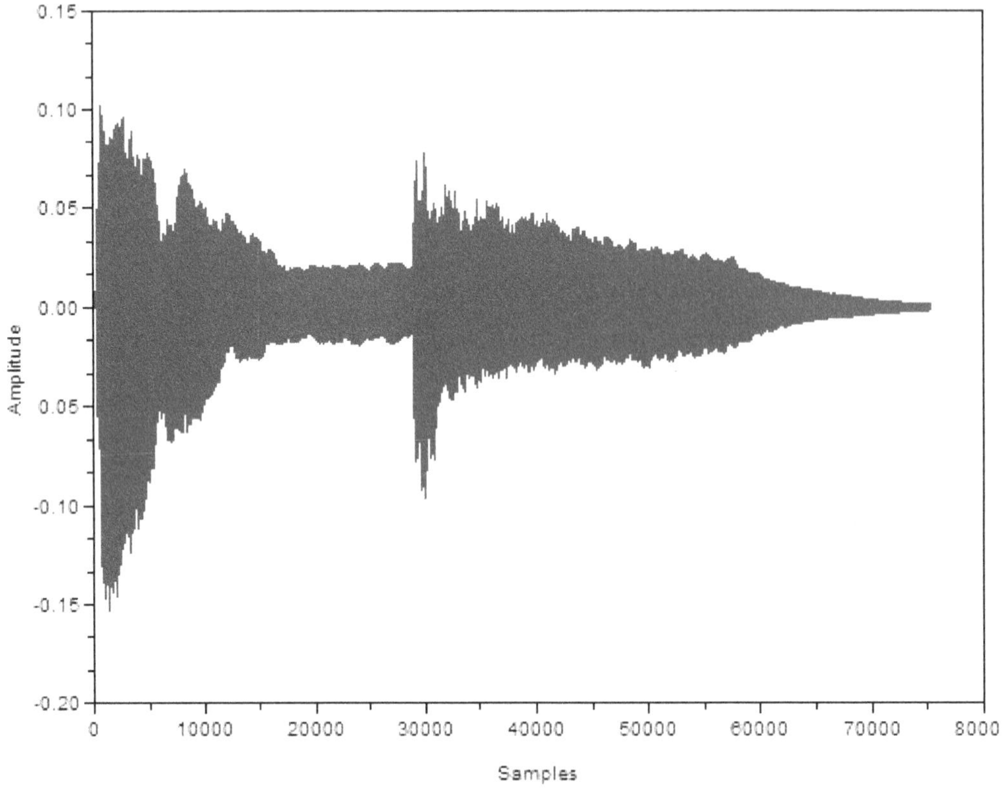

Figure 21: Waveform plot of a piano playing the notes A to G

Onsets can be classified as either *sharp* or *slow*. A sharp onset has a short duration and is characterised by a sharp change in the energy profile of the signal. Instruments with a sharp attack include the piano and the plucking of a string on a guitar. Woodwind instruments such as the concert flute and tin-whistle in contrast have a slow onset meaning that the signal takes much longer to reach maximum amplitude.

Early methods of onset detection were derived from the observation that the onset of a note is often accompanied by an increase in the signal's amplitude (section 3.4). An envelope following onset detector can be derived by low pass filtering the signal and applying a peak picking algorithm to the subsequent signal (W. Schloss 1985). Chafe & Jaffe (1986) analyse the amplitude envelope of the entire input signal however their approach only works for signals with prominent onsets. Dixon (2004) uses a simple energy based onset detection function in the time domain that looks at the energy changes in successive frames. The author claims that this approach worked well for percussive instruments such as the piano, but admits that the algorithm often detected false onsets and also failed to detect onsets for simultaneously sounding notes.

Several onset detection studies separate the signal into frequency bands in order to more accurately analyse the salient components. Masri (1996) proposes using *spectral flux* (section 3.3) restricted to positive changes and summed across all frequency bins to detect onsets. He also proposes a *high frequency content* (HFC) function which looks at changes between frames, in the high frequency component of a signal. The HFC function is reported to produce peaks in the note attack phase and is notably successful when faced with percussive onsets, where transients consist of bursts of white noise. Scheirer's (1998) approach is inspired by psychoacoustics. He separates the signal into six frequency bands, covering an octave each. He then extracts the amplitude envelope for each band which is smoothed using a half Hanning window (section 3.2) (Figure 25). These are fed into comb-filter resonators in order to estimate the tempo of the signal. Klapuri (1998) develops the *relative difference function* by dividing Scheirer's (1998) first order difference by the amplitude envelope to give an onset detection function that works better for slower onsets. Klapuri (1999) employs a filter bank which divides the signal into eight non-overlapping bands. In each band, onset times and intensities are detected and finally combined. The eight filter-bank model is used as an approximation of the mechanics of the human cochlea.

When a new note is played, it is likely that the new note will be out of phase with the previous note, and so irregularities in the phase of various frequency components can also indicate the presence of an onset (Dixon 2006). A *phase vocoder* is an algorithm which modifies the Short-Time Fourier transform STFT (section 3.2) of an input signal, before re-synthesising the sound. Phase vocoders can be used to achieve high quality time scale and pitch modifications of a signal (Dolson 1986). A phase based onset detection approach based on phase vocoder theory is proposed in (Settel & Lippe 1994). This approach looks at phase differences in the frequency bins between consecutive frames in an STFT of the signal (section 3.2). These differences are used to separate steady and transient bin components of the STFT. The work of (Settel & Lippe 1994) is developed by (Duxbury et al. 2001) who suggest combining the transient separation with energy based onset detection methods into a complex domain method. Their approach however requires the user to manually input a threshold to be used in the calculation of note onsets. Methods which analyse the distribution of phase deviations across the frequency domain are proposed in (Duxbury et al. 2003; Bello & M Sandler 2003). In the steady-state part of a signal, phase deviations approach zero, thus a histogram of the distributions of phase deviations will have a peak in the zero bin. During attack transients, values increase, widening and flattening the distribution. To measure the spread of the distribution per frame, they compute the Inter Quartile Range (IQR); that is the difference between the 75th and the 25th percentiles of the data being analysed.

Duxbury *et al.* (2002) present a complex domain method which splits the signal into four frequency bands. The two lowest frequency bands use a function based on spectral difference. The highest two bands use energy based methods. A statistical analysis is carried out on the onset detection function to set the threshold above which onsets are identified.

Lacoste & Eck (2005) use an artificial neural network (ANN) to classify frames of audio in a signal as either onset or non-onset. They propose two algorithms which they call *single-net* and *many-net*. The single-net algorithm computes the spectrogram of the signal, uses a neural network to find an onset trace and then makes use of a peak picking algorithm to identify candidate onset times. The many-net algorithm repeats the single-net algorithm n times with different hyperparameters and then combines the classifications using another neural network. Tempo information is used to filter spurious onsets. Their many-net algorithm scored highest in the MIREX 2005 onset detection competition, but they comment on the poor performance of the algorithms due to the inefficiency of neural networks.

Gainza *et al.* (2005) propose an onset detection method based on comb filters which specifically addresses the problem of how to detect slow onsets in woodwind traditional instruments such as the concert flute and the tin whistle. Onset Detection using Comb Filters (ODCF) discovers harmonic characteristics of the input signal and is therefore more tolerant to energy changes in an input signal and is also better at detecting onsets in legato playing, where there is no significant change in energy at the onset of a new note. To generate the Onset Detection Function (ODF) using ODCF, the input signal is first sampled at 44100Khz. The input signal is then segmented into overlapping frames of 2048 samples (approximately 46 milliseconds). Each frame overlaps with the previous frame by 75%. Each frame is then passed through a bank of twelve FIR (Finite Impulse Response) comb filters.

A FIR comb filter works by summing the time domain input signal with a delayed version of the same input signal (section 3.2). The delay of the filter is calculated as being the length in time of a single period of a waveform at the frequency. This has the effect of amplifying the frequency or a harmonic in the input signal which matches the frequency being filtered. Thus, the energy of the input signal is doubled only if the peaks of the signal coincide with the peaks of the FIR comb filter. This will only occur for a given delay and its integer multiples (Smith 1997). Equation 1 which gives the output power of each of twelve filters *E*(*m*, *D*) with different delays corresponding to the twelve semitones in the key of D3, where *m* is the frame, *D* is the delay in samples, *x* is the signal being filtered and *N* is the length of the frame being filtered (Gainza & Coyle 2007). Figure 37 (Chapter 6) gives an extract from the author's implementation of Equation 1 in Java.

$$E(m, D) = \frac{\sum_{n=D+1}^{N}[x(n) + x(n-D)]^2}{4 * x^2(n)}$$

Equation 1

For each frame of audio examined, the outputs of the frame for each of the twelve filters are calculated. A value for the ODF is then calculated as being the sum of the difference between the outputs of each of the twelve filters in successive frames squared, as given by Equation 2 (Gainza & Coyle 2007).

$$ODF(m) = \sum_{i=1}^{12}[E(m, D_i) - E(m-1, D_i)]^2$$

Equation 2

A dynamic threshold is then calculated above which peaks in the ODF are recognised as being candidate note onsets. The dynamic threshold is calculated as the mean of the amplitude of the entire signal plus the standard deviation for the frame being considered (Gainza et al. 2005).

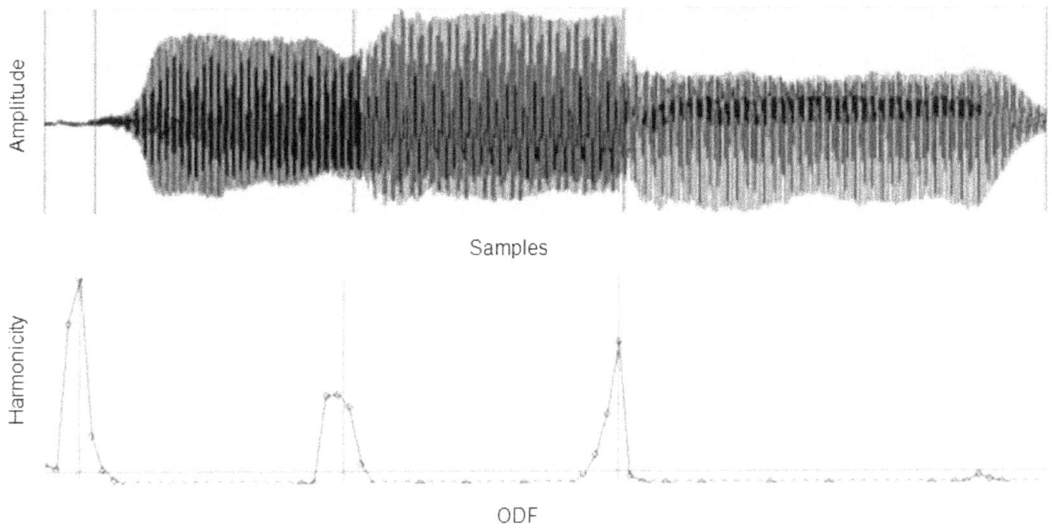

Figure 22: Onset Detection Function (ODF) for a musical phrase calculated using ODCF implemented by the author in Java (Chapter 6)

Figure 22 shows the ODF calculated in this way (using the authors implementation in Java described in Chapter 6) with an input signal of a wooden flute playing the notes D, E and F# legato. As illustrated, the onsets detected correspond to the onsets of each new note.

Collins (2005) thesis is that stable pitch queues can be used to segment a signal into note onsets. He uses a pitch tracker based on cross correlating a harmonic template with a constant Q spectrum, with the signal to extract the best fitting F0 estimation (section 3.2). He uses 4096 point FFT with a step size of 512 samples. He post processes the output of the pitch tracker to remove momentary octave errors and rogue outliers. Further, he employs both a vibrato suppression algorithm and silence detection algorithm to filter spurious onsets, and generates an ODF by tracking pitch changes between successive frames. To extract peaks from the onset detection function, an adaptive threshold is used similar to those described in (Bello et al. 2005; Gainza 2006; Gainza et al. 2005). Reported results show that Collins (2005) ODF gives better performance than Bello et al.'s (2005) phase deviation algorithm. Collins (2005) attributes this improvement to the incorporation of vibrato suppression which establishes the importance of modelling higher level musical features into music analysis systems.

Dixon (2006) improves on phase analysis approaches discussed by (Bello et al. 2005) by proposing *weighted phase deviation* (WPD) and *normalised weighted phase deviation* (NWPD). Using WPD, frequency bins are weighted by their magnitude and using NWPD the sum of the weights is factored out. In their reported experiments on test audio from various instruments, WPD and NWPD perform significantly better than phase deviation alone and are comparable with spectral flux (Masri 1996), and complex domain methods (Bello et al. 2004). Further, Dixon (2006) proposes *rectified complex domain* (RCD) as an improvement on the complex domain methods proposed by (Duxbury et al. 2002) and (Bello et al. 2004) which adapts Masri's (1996) usage of positive changes in spectral flux.

3.2 Pitch

Pitch represents the perception of the fundamental frequency of a sound. The fundamental frequency (F0) is given as the number of oscillations per second. In Western music pitch information is considered to be more discriminative than rhythm, since there are more possibilities for a sequence of *n* pitches than for a sequence of *n* durations (Lemstrom & Perttu 2000). Sounds generated by real instruments and by the human voice usually contain *overtones*, also known as *partials*. When these partials occur at integer multiples of the fundamental frequency, they are known as *harmonics*. Algorithms to detect pitch can work in either the time domain or the frequency domain. Figure 23 shows a plot of a wooden flute playing the note D4, with the normalised absolute values of the

Discrete Fourier Transform (DFT) of this signal given in Figure 24. Harmonics of the fundamental frequency are clearly visible as periodic peaks in the plot.

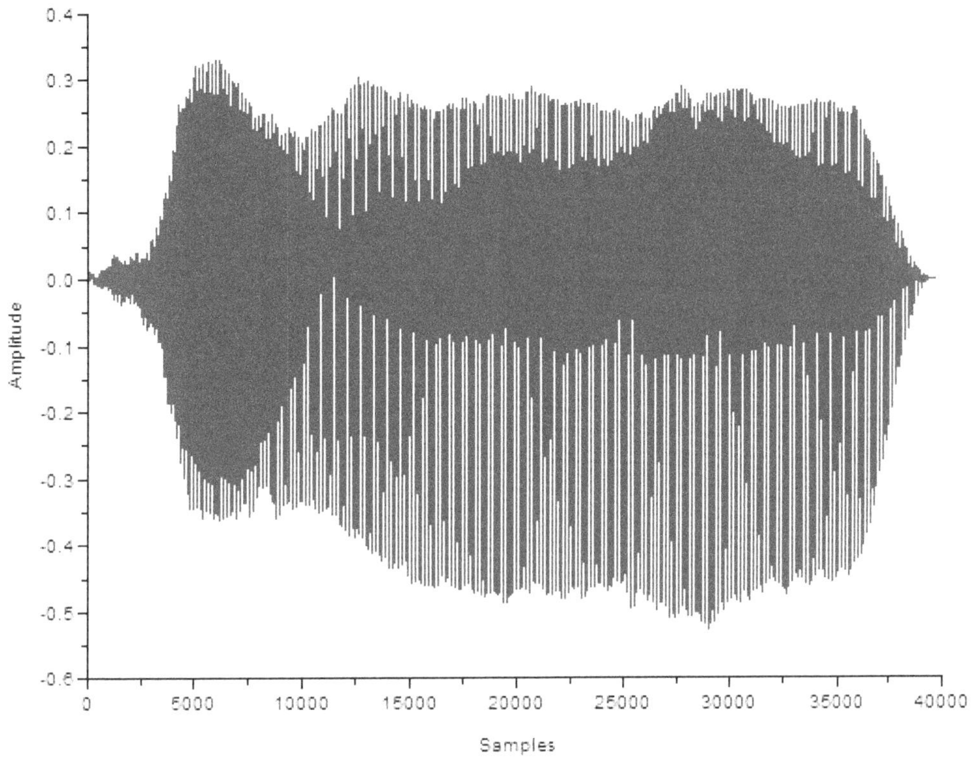

Figure 23: A concert flute playing the note D4

In the time domain, Rabiner *et al.* (1976) suggest that are peak and valley measurements, zero-crossing measurements, and autocorrelation measurements may be used to estimate pitch, but that these measurements are sensitive to noise. Pitch estimation based on maximum likelihood is proposed in (Wise et al. 1976). Maximum likelihood pitch estimation analyses the periodicity of the autocorrelation function in the time domain.

Finite Impulse Response (FIR) comb filters are used in the work of (Moorer 1975; Miwa et al. 2000; Tadokoro et al. 2003; Cheveigne 1991). Comb filters are so named because the peaks and troughs in their magnitude frequency response resemble the teeth of a comb. A FIR comb filter works by summing the input signal with a delayed version of the same input signal. The delay of the filter is calculated as being 1 / frequency being filtered (the length in time of a single period of a waveform at the frequency). This has the effect of amplifying the frequency (or a harmonic thereof) in the input signal which matches the frequency being filtered. For example, given a sample rate sr=44100 and a frequency of 293Hz, the delay is 151 samples. The output of a comb filter can be calculated in the time domain as given in Equation 1 (see also section 6.2).

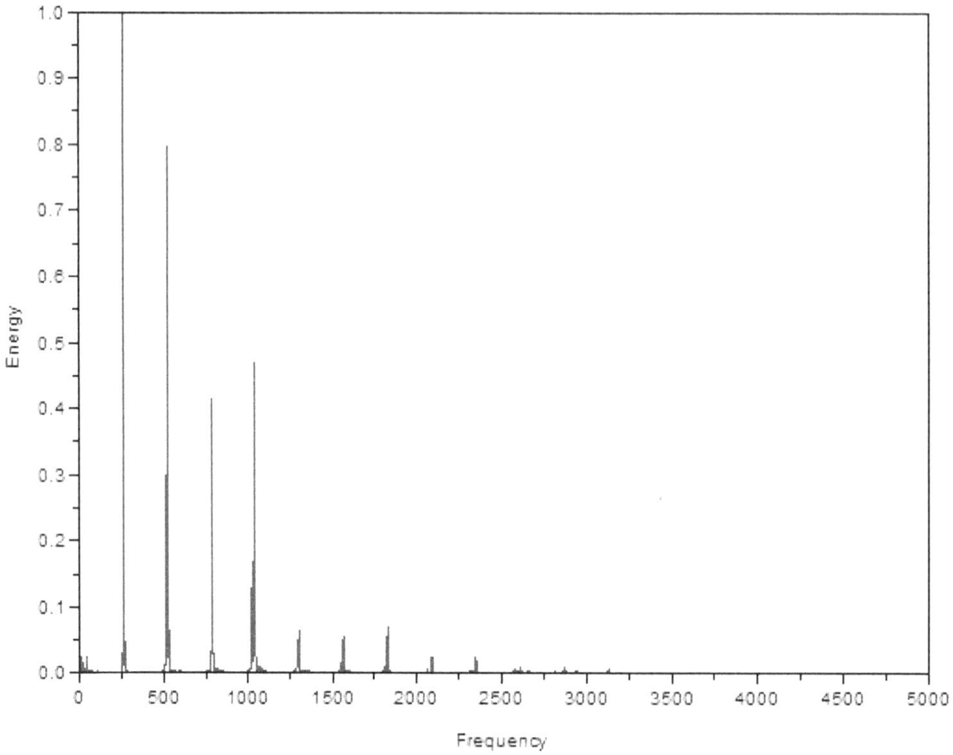

Figure 24: The normalised absolute FFT values of the signal from Figure 23

Autocorrelation as a means of estimating pitch, is suggested in (Brown 1993). Autocorrelation is the correlation of a signal with itself in the attempt to discover repeating patterns in the signal such as the presence of a periodic signal.

The autocorrelation algorithm exploits the fact that a periodic signal will be similar from one period to the next. The autocorrelation function is defined as the sum of the absolute difference between the two signals over some interval. The resulting function will have peaks at integer multiples of the signal period in a similar manner to a comb filter. The frame of audio being analysed should have a length N at least twice as long as the longest period being searched for. Ghias et al (1995) use autocorrelation to estimate pitches in their QBH (Query By Humming) system (section 5.3), but report that autocorrelation is subject to aliasing (picking an integer multiple of the actual pitch) and is computationally complex.

To convert a time domain signal to a frequency domain signal, the Discrete Fourier Transform (DFT) is computed. The DFT takes a signal and decomposes it into a sum of sines and cosines of different frequencies. In Equation 3, x is the signal in the time domain, and a_n and b_n are unknown coefficients of the series. The integer n has units of Hertz(Hz) and corresponds to the frequency of the wave (Storey 2002).

$$f(x) = a_0 + \sum_{n=1}^{\infty} (a_n \sin(2\pi nt) + b_n \cos(2\pi nt))$$

Equation 3

Figure 24 (page 72) shows the absolute values of the FFT of a wooden flute playing the note D4. The short-time Fourier transform (STFT) is used to convert local sections of a signal from the time domain to the frequency domain. An STFT is usually calculated on a frame of audio windowed using a Hanning function (Figure 25) so that out of phase signal components from the start and end of the frame have minimal impact on the energies computed. This is also known as *spectral leakage* (Smith 1997).

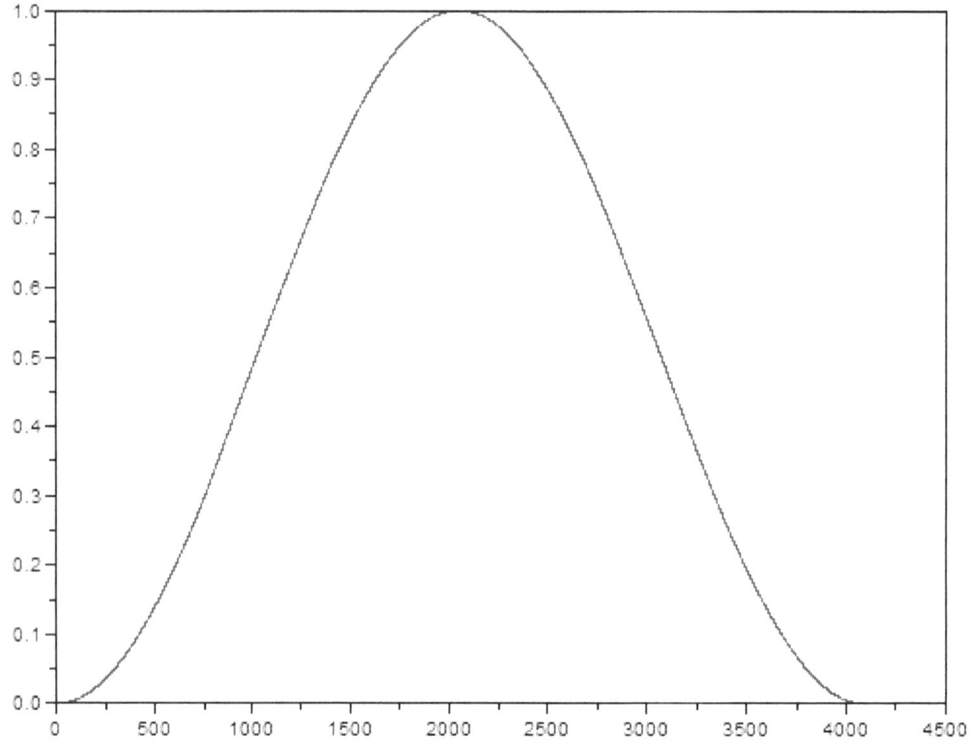

Figure 25: Hanning function

Figure 26 shows the effect of windowing using a Hanning function on a frame of audio from the sample given in Figure 23 (page 71).

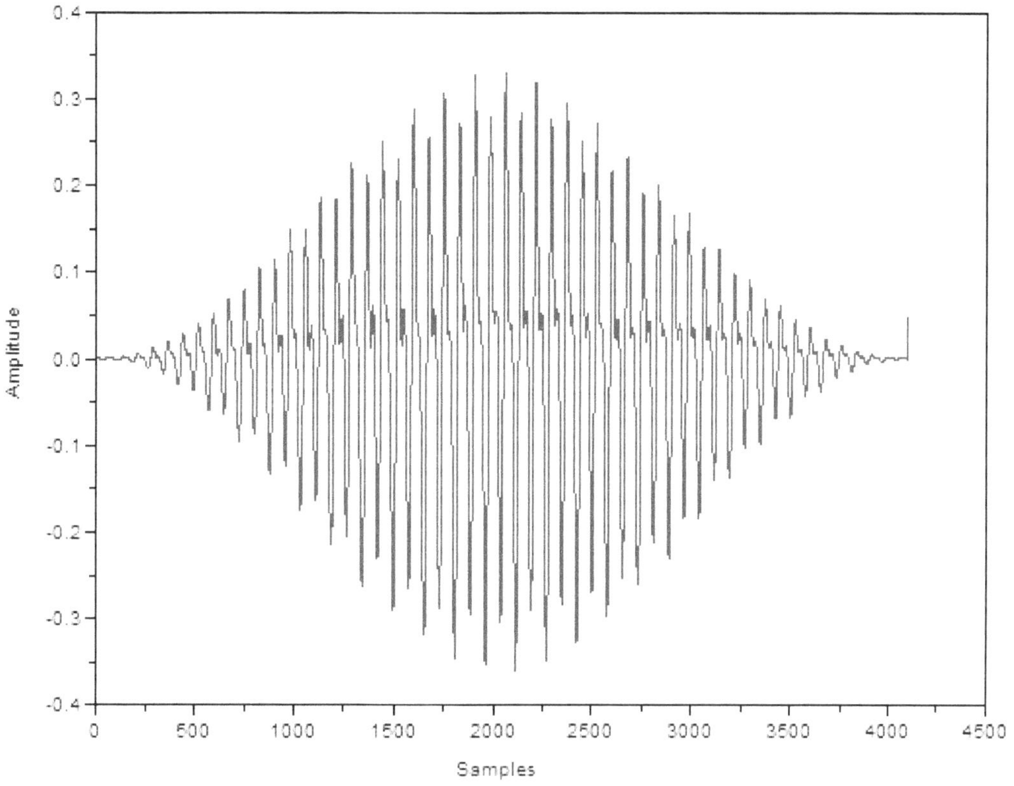

Figure 26: A frame of audio from Figure 23 windowed by the Hanning function from Figure 25

The STFT is given by Equation 4 where *w(m)* is the window which selects an L length block from the input signal $x(m)$, n is the frame number and H is the hop length in samples (Gainza et al. 2005).

$$X(n,k) = \sum_{m=0}^{L-1} x(m+nH)w(m)e^{-j\left(\frac{2\pi}{N}\right)km}$$

Equation 4

Evaluating these sums directly would take $O(N^2)$ arithmetical operations and so this is usually achieved using the Fast Fourier Transform algorithm (FFT).

An FFT is an algorithm to compute the same result in O(N log N) operations. In the straightforward case, the fundamental frequency (F0) will be the frequency bin with the highest energy, though this is not always the case. Sometimes a harmonic of the fundamental frequency will contain the highest energy in the spectrum and peak picking algorithms have been widely employed to retrieve the FFT bin which corresponds with the perceived pitch (Kasi & Zahorian 2002; Dogan & Mendel 1992; Atal 1973; Klapuri 1998; Klapuri 2003).

In the frequency domain, autocorrelation can again be used (Kunieda et al. 1996), though harmonics of the fundamental frequency will also correlate using this method. Brown (1992) cross-correlates the spectrum with spectral representations of different harmonics, where the frequency components are logarithmically separated. In this representation, harmonic frequency components are equally spaced in the frequency domain regardless of the fundamental frequency. A pattern is built for all pitch candidates and cross-correlated with the spectrum to give a maximum in the position of the fundamental frequency. Klapuri's (2003) approach is similar. He splits the signal into 17 overlapping logarithmically distributed frequency bands. A weighted vector is then calculated for each candidate fundamental frequency to obtain the fundamental frequency that best explains the energy band.

Frequency domain periodicity methods such as those described are susceptible to both high and low octave pitch detection errors (Gainza 2006). A comprehensive review of pitch detection algorithms and their applicability to transcription in traditional Irish music is given in (Gainza 2006).

3.3 Timbre

Timbre is the quality of a sound which distinguishes different types of sound production, such as a note played on a concert flute compared to the same note played on an accordion. The physical characteristics of sound which affect the perception of timbre include the harmonic series generated by the instrument and the ADSR (Attack, Decay, Sustain, Release) amplitude envelope of a note played on the instrument. *Brightness* is a measure of the energy in higher-frequency bands of the signal. The *spectral-centroid* is an indication of the "center of mass" of the frequency spectrum. It is calculated as the weighted mean of the frequencies present in the signal, with their magnitudes as the weights as per Equation 5.

$$Centroid = \frac{\sum_{n=0}^{N-1} f(n)x(n)}{\sum_{n=0}^{N-1} x(n)}$$

Equation 5

Bandwidth can be computed as the magnitude-weighted average of the differences between the spectral components and the spectral-centroid of the frequency spectrum (Smith 1997). It is zero for a single sinewave, while ideal white noise has an infinite band-width (Typke et al. 2005). *Spectral flux* measures the change in magnitude in each frequency bin of an STFT of a signal (Dixon 2006).

3.4 Loudness

Loudness is the perceived amplitude of a sound. The perception of loudness varies from person to person and is affected by parameters other than sound pressure, including frequency and duration. Loudness is commonly measured on a logarithmic scale, called *decibel SPL* (Sound Power Level). On this scale, 0 dB SPL is a sound wave power of 10^{-16} watts/cm^2, the weakest sound detectable by the human ear. Normal speech is at about 60 dB SPL, while painful damage to the ear occurs at about 140 dB SPL (Smith 1997).

3.5 Rhythm

Rhythm is the term which denotes the organisation of sound in time; the temporal quality of sound. Rhythm is related to the concepts of *grouping*, *metre* and *structural accents*. Music is organised to equal sized bars, where each bar contains the same number of beats. *Metre* gives the number of beats in a bar, while *accent* gives the measure of which beats receive emphasis (Lerdahl & Jackendoff 1983). An onset detection function is often used to estimate rhythm. For example Scheirer (1998) uses an onset detection function (section 3.1) to extract beat and tempo information from digital audio. The *BeatRoot* system is given in (Dixon 2004). BeatRoot models the perception of beats in a piece of music. BeatRoot first analyses the input signal to extract note onsets. Dixon's first attempt to extract note onsets used a time domain algorithm which looked at the energy changes in successive frames. The authors claim that this approach worked well for percussive instruments such as the piano, but admit that the algorithm often detected false onsets and also failed to detect onsets for simultaneously sounding notes. Their second attempt improves accuracy by separating the signal into frequency bands and looking for onsets in each band. The system then uses an array of agents initialised with a tempo hypothesis. The agent then predicts further beats and is evaluated according to how well the predicted and actual beat times correspond. The system was evaluated against a corpus of Mozart sonatas and popular music and the authors claim a success rate of 90%.

3.6 Structure

Tonal music is usually organised into higher level groupings of musical segments aligned with the rhythm. In pop music for example, these segments might be labelled as intro, verse, chorus and refrain with segments such as verse and chorus being repeated at intervals in the music (Peiszer et al. 2008). In classical music, a *fugue* opens with a main subject, which is transformed and repeated in the parts (voices) of the fugue. These transformed subjects are known as *countersubjects* and must be *contrapuntal* (sound different from each other, but harmonious when played together). These contrapuntal variations may imitate the main subject, be transformed in pitch or rhythm be augmented or diminished or the melody may be inverted (Hofstadter 1979).

In Irish traditional dance music, tunes are usually structured in repeated monophonic sections known as the A part and the B part of a tune. Occasionally there can also be a C and D part. An AABB reel for example contains a 64 note sequence repeated and then followed by second 64 note sequence repeated after which the entire tune is repeated. An ABC jig contains a 48 note sequence followed by a second 48 note sequence followed by a third 48 note sequence, after which the entire tune is usually repeated.

The automatic inference of structure from digital audio recordings of music is known as Automatic Audio Segmentation. Foote (2000) uses a self similarity matrix of pitch based features vectors extracted from each frame of audio using an STFT (section 3.2). The similarity of frames on the horizontal axis to frames on the vertical axis is plotted in a matrix. Using this approach, musical structure can be inferred from patterns in the matrix. A measure of novelty is extracted from the matrix by calculating the correlation of the matrix with a "checkerboard kernel", with peaks in the novelty profile used to extract segment boundaries. The size of the kernel is varied to detect novelty over different time scales.

Maddage *et al.* (2004) use high level metadata such as rhythm extracted from the signal in combination with low level features to improve segmentation accuracy. Firstly, the rhythm structure of the audio is inferred using an Onset Detection Function (section 3.1). The audio is then segmented into beat length frames. A statistical learning method based on Hidden Markov Models (section

4.5) is then used to identify chord sequences in the frames and to detect vocal/instrumental boundaries. Finally repeated chord patterns and vocal content analysis is used to define the structure of the song.

Peiszer (2007) expands Foote's (2000) work by developing a two phase approach to segmentation. First, various features are extracted from each frame of audio such as the spectrogram, Mel Frequency Cepstrum Coefficients, rhythm-based features and harmony related features. Then, the self-similarity matrix between these feature vectors is calculated and a novelty profile generated. The novelty profile is then smoothed using a low pass filter and peaks are extracted as candidate segment boundaries. In phase two, the extracted segments are clustered. Segments that cluster together are labelled identically.

3.7 Conclusions

The aim of this thesis is to develop an approach whereby a digital recording of traditional music can be annotated by comparing it against representations of melodies in a symbolic format. In order to achieve this, it is necessary to extract a representation of the melody contained in the digital recording by performing a transcription. Transcription systems can be built by combining onset and pitch detection. This chapter contained a review of several of the main algorithms used in pitch and onset detection. Energy based onset detection approaches can achieve a high degree of accuracy when the input audio signal contains significant energy transitions around the onset of new notes. This is the case in instruments such as the piano for example. However, in the case of traditional Irish dance music played on woodwind instruments in particular, legato playing is the norm. Typically these instruments do not generate transients and will have slow onsets difficult to detect using energy based methods. Also the playing of ornamentation (section 2.9.1) will be difficult to isolate using the energy based approaches described.

Phase based methods are sensitive to noise which increase the number of spurious onsets. In order to address the unique problems of transcription in traditional Irish dance music, Onset Detection using Comb Filters is proposed in (Gainza et al. 2005; Gainza 2006). These papers report extensive testing using this approach on recordings of various traditional instruments. This is therefore the approach taken in developing MATT2 described in Chapter 6.

Various approaches for performing pitch detection are given in section 3.2. FIR comb filters, autocorrelation functions and maximum likelihood are approaches used in the time domain as monophonic pitch detectors. To convert a time domain signal to frequency domain representation a Fast Fourier Transform is performed. Both time and frequency domain pitch estimation approaches report octave pitch estimation errors. For monophonic music, peak picking from the frequency spectrum can be employed. In implementing MATT2, described in Chapter 6, a variation of Klapuri's (2003) peak picking approach for multi-pitch estimation is employed.

The output of the transcription system will be a representation in a symbolic format. Chapter 4 continues by describing approaches used to compare symbolic representations of music.

4 Melodic Similarity

The output of the transcription subsystem described in sections 6.2 and 6.3 will be a time indexed vector of pitches and durations extracted from a query recording. It will then be necessary to compare these extracted features against a corpus so that an annotation can be made. This chapter therefore describes several of the main methods for gauging similarity between melodies. These measures may be more accurately described as *dissimilarity metrics* as each of the methods presented calculates the distance between melodies. A higher distance implies that the melodies are less similar. A *metric* is a function on a set $S, d : S \times S \rightarrow \mathbb{R}^{+} \cup \{0\}$ with the following properties (Typke 2007):

i. Self-identity: For all $x \in S$, $d(x,x) = 0$
ii. Positivity: For all $x \neq y$ in S, $d(x,y) > 0$
iii. Symmetry: For all $x, y \in S$, $d(x,y) = d(y, x)$
iv. Triangle inequality: For $x, y, z \in S$, $d(x,z) \leq d(x, y) + d(y, z)$

For measuring melodic dissimilarity in a way which agrees with human perception, a measure should possess the self identity property. This implies that two identical melodies should have a distance of zero. Typke (2007) states that positivity is usually, but not always desired. This implies that it is usually desirable for different melodies to have a positive distance. This fact has been explored in sections 2.8 and 2.9, where it is suggested that a melody can be interpreted differently by different musicians, but perceived as the same (having a distance of zero) by a human listener. This is the premise behind the expressiveness accommodation algorithms developed in section 6.4. Typke (2007) further states that symmetry, while useful may not correlate with how humans perceive melodic dissimilarity. Included in this chapter also are alternative representation schemas whose aim is to present a simplified representation of a melody so that comparisons can be more easily made.

4.1 Melodic contour (Parsons code)

Parsons' thesis is that a simplified encoding which ignores most of the information in the melody can provide sufficient discriminatory power to distinguish between significant numbers of tunes. Parsons Code includes only the directions of melodies and ignores pitch, duration and rhythm. Each pair of consecutive notes is coded as "U" ("up") if the second note is higher than the first note, "S" ("same") if the pitches are equal, and "D" ("down") otherwise. Figure 27 shows the first two bars from the tune "Banish Misfortune" in ABC notation and in stave music notation, with the corresponding Parsons Code.

```
=fed cAG|AGd cAG
```

```
DDDDDDUDUDDD
```

Figure 27: The first 2 bars from the tune "Banish Misfortune" in ABC format and in music notation, with the corresponding Parsons Code

The opening note of any melody is used only as a reference point and does not show up explicitly in the Parsons Code representation. An enhancement of this idea is presented in (Downie 1999) where monophonic melodies are represented as string of note intervals (*n*-grams). His corpus contains 9354 folksongs. He uses three different encoding schemes to represent the interval set.

Each encoding scheme is based on a different representation of the intervals. Set C3 represents all melodies as "a" (no interval) "b" (negative interval) or "c" (positive interval) Set C7 represents negative 1,2,3 as "b", "c", "d"; positive 1,2, 3 as "B", "C", "D"; all negatives <=-4 as "d"; all positives >= +4 as "D". Set C15 represents negative 1to 6 as "b" to "g"; positive 1 to 6 as "B" to "G"; all negatives <=-7 as "h"; all positives >= +7 as "H". Section 5.1 discusses Downie's MIR system based on this representation.

4.2 Implication-realisation

Grachten *et al.* (2005) present a similarity measure based on Narmour's Implication/Realisation (IR) model (Narmour 1992). Narmour's theory applies gestalt principals to music. According to Narmour, certain melodic structures imply subsequent structures in order to be "closed". The Principle of Registral Direction (PRD) states that small intervals imply an interval in the same registral direction. A small upward interval implies another upward interval and a small downward interval implies another downward interval. Large intervals imply a change in *registral direction.* A large upward interval implies a downward interval and a large downward interval implies an upward interval. The Principle of Intervallic Difference (PID) states that a five semitone or fewer intervals implies a similarly-sized interval and a seven semitones or more interval implies a smaller interval. Based on these two principles, melodic patterns are identified which either satisfy or violate the implication as predicted by the principles. Such patterns are called *structures* and labelled to denote characteristics in terms of registral direction and intervallic difference.

To use this model as a similar measure, Grachten *et al.* (2005) have developed an annotation system which annotates monophonic melodies in MIDI format with the appropriate IR tags. Since the annotations are sequential, they propose using edit distances (section 4.4) with parameterised editing costs to compare melodic strings. They suggest that concrete melody representations better discriminate on the short range of melodic similarity and that a more abstract melody representation such as IR representation provides more discriminatory power on the long range of similarity. They present the results of an evaluation of 11 queries against 558 incipits, where they received a favourable ranking compared to other similarity measures (including those discussed in section 4.3), but note that the test corpus had had grace notes removed to make the task easier.

4.3 Transportation distance

The usage of transportation distances to measure melodic dissimilarity is proposed in (Typke 2007; Typke et al. 2003). First melodies are converted into *weighted point sets* in 2-dimensional Euclidian space. The dimensions are the onset time (horizontal) and pitch (vertical) of each note, while the weight is the duration of the note. The Earth Movers Distance (EMD) between two weighted point sets measures the minimum amount of work required to transform one into the other by moving weight (Rubner et al. 2000). Flow is measured as weight unit multiplied by ground distance. If $A = \{a_1, a_2..a_m\}$ is a weighted point set such that $a_i = \{(x_i, w_i), 1 \leq i \leq m$, where $x_i \in \mathbb{R}$ and $w_i \in \mathbb{R}^+ \cup \{0\}$, $W = \sum_{i=1}^{m} w_i$ is the total weight of set A. EMD can be formulated as a linear programming problem (Hitchcock 1941).

Given two weighted point sets A and B, $f_{i,j}$ is the flow of weight from a_i to b_i over the distance $d_{i,j}$. If W and U are the total weights of A and B, the set of all possible flows of $f_{i,j}$ is defined as by the constraints set out in Equation 6.

1. $f_{i,j} \geq 0, 1 \leq i \leq m, 1 \leq j \leq n$
2. $\sum_{j=1}^{n} f_{i,j} \leq w_i, 1 \leq i \leq m$
3. $\sum_{j=1}^{n} f_{i,j} \leq w_i, 1 \leq j \leq m$
4. $\sum_{i=1}^{m} \sum_{j=1}^{n} f_{i,j} = \min(W, U)$

Equation 6

Constraint one allows moving weight from *A* to *B* and not vice versa. Constraints two and three limit the amount of weight which can be sent by the elements in *A* to their weights, and the elements in *B* to receive no more weight than the weight they can hold. Constraint four means that the total transported weight is the minimum of the total weights of the two sets. The total cost for transforming *A* to *B* is the sum of the weights $f_{i,j}$ multiplied by the distance $d_{i,j}$, normalised by the weight of the lighter set as per Equation 7.

$$EMD(A, B) = \frac{\min(\sum_{i=1}^{m} \sum_{j=1}^{n} f_{i,j}\, d_{ij})}{\min(W, U)}$$

Equation 7

EMD is a metric as described in the introduction to this chapter, if the ground distance is a metric and if EMD is applied to two sets with equal weights. In the case of unequal total weights, the EMD does not obey the triangle inequality. The Euclidian distance is used as the ground distance as per Equation 8 (Typke 2007).

$$d = \sqrt{(x_2 - x_1)^2 + (w_2 - w_1)^2}$$

Equation 8

In order to recognise augmented or diminished versions of a melody as similar, Typke (2007) proposes stretching the melody with the smaller maximum time coordinate, but leaving the durations (represented as point weights) of the notes unchanged. Typke (2007) proposes two methods of making the measure transposition invariant. First, he proposes moving one or other of the melodies up or down until a minimum distance is reached, with a corresponding repeated application of the dissimilarity measure and increase in computational complexity. The second method he proposes is to transform one of the melodies so that the weighted average pitch is equal. This second method works to the extent that transposed versions of the same melody appear closer than other melodies from his test corpus of melodies. Time and pitch are also normalised so that transportations in time and pitch are equally expensive (Typke 2007).

This method was evaluated in a number of ways. For example the EMD was used to identify 80,000 incipits from anonymous composers by comparing the incipits against the RISM/A/II (Répertoire International des Sources Musicales International Inventory of Musical Sources) corpus in Plaine & Easie (Howard 1997) format. Using this method 3.9% of previously unidentified incipits could be now be identified. This compares favourably with (Schlichte 1990). A segmentation algorithm is also reported in (Typke 2007), where incipits from the corpus and queries are split into segments of between five and sixteen notes. This is used to match incipits and queries in the case where different length musical sequences are to be matched. The author reports that this technique provided good results at the MIREX 2006 (Music Information Retrieval Evaluation eXchange) competition. The author attributes this to the fact that the distance measure is continuous (in that small changes to either of the melodies result in small changes to the distance) and works well with non-quantised data such as hummed queries. Transportation distance is used in Musipidia (Prechelt & Typke 2001) (section 5.3).

4.4 Edit (Levenshtein) distance

Edit distance, also known as Levenshtein distance or evolutionary distance is a concept from information retrieval and it describes the number of edits (insertions, deletions and substitutions) that have to be made in order to change one string to another. It is the most common measure to expose the dissimilarity between two strings (Levenshtein 1966; Navarro & Raffinot 2002).

The edit distance *ed(x, y)* between strings $x=x_1 \ldots x_m$ and $y=y_1 \ldots y_n$, where $x, y \in \Sigma*$ is the minimum cost of a sequence of editing steps required to convert x into y. The alphabet Σ of possible characters *ch* gives $\Sigma*$, the set of all possible sequences of $ch \in \Sigma$. Edit distance can be calculated using dynamic programming (Navarro & Raffinot 2002). Dynamic programming is a method of solving a large problem by regarding the problem as the sum of the solution to its recursively solved subproblems. Dynamic programming is different to recursion however. In order to avoid recalculating the solutions to subproblems, dynamic programming makes use of a technique called *memoisation*, whereby the solutions to subproblems are stored once calculated, to save recalculation.

To compute the edit distance *ed(x,y)* between strings x and y, a matrix $M_{1 \ldots m+1, 1 \ldots n+1}$ is constructed where $M_{i,j}$ is the minimum number of edit operations needed to match $x_{1 \ldots i}$ to $y_{1 \ldots j}$. Each matrix element $M_{i,j}$ is calculated as per Equation 9, where $\delta(a, b) = 0$ if $a = b$ and 1 otherwise. The matrix element $M_{1,1}$ is the edit distance between two empty strings.

$$M_{1,1} \leftarrow 0$$

$$M_{i,j} \leftarrow \min \begin{cases} M_{i-1,j} + 1 \\ M_{i,j-1} + 1 \\ M_{i-1,j-1} + \delta(x_i, y_j) \end{cases}$$

Equation 9

The algorithm considers the last characters, x_i and y_j. If they are equal, then $x_{1..i}$ can be converted into $y_{1..j}$ at a cost of $M_{i-1,j-1}$. If they are not equal, x_i can be converted to y_j by substitution at a cost of $M_{i-1,j-1} + 1$, or x_i can be deleted at a cost of $M_{i-1,j} + 1$ or y_j can be appended to x at a cost of $M_{i,j-1} + 1$. The minimum edit distance between x and y is given by the matrix entry at position $M_{m+1,n+1}$.

Table 11 is an example of the matrix produced to calculate the edit distance between the strings "DFGDGBDEGGAB" and "DGGGDGBDEFGAB". The edit distance between these strings given as $M_{m+1,n+1}$ is 3.

		D	**G**	**G**	**G**	**D**	**G**	**B**	**D**	**E**	**F**	**G**	**A**	**B**
	0	1	2	3	4	5	6	7	8	9	10	11	12	13
D	1	0	1	2	3	4	5	6	7	8	9	10	11	12
F	2	1	1	2	3	4	5	6	7	8	8	9	10	11
G	3	2	1	1	2	3	4	5	6	7	8	8	9	10
D	4	3	2	2	2	2	3	4	5	6	7	8	9	10
G	5	4	3	2	2	3	2	3	4	5	6	7	8	9
B	6	5	4	3	3	3	3	2	3	4	5	6	7	8
D	7	6	5	4	4	3	4	3	2	3	4	5	6	7
E	8	7	6	5	5	4	4	4	3	2	3	4	5	6
G	9	8	7	6	5	5	4	5	4	3	3	3	4	5
G	10	9	8	7	6	6	5	5	5	4	4	3	4	5
A	11	10	9	8	7	7	6	6	6	5	5	4	3	4
B	12	11	10	9	8	8	7	6	7	6	6	5	4	3

Table 11: Edit distance matrix for the strings "DFGDGBDEGGAB" and "DGGGDGBDEFGAB" with the minimum edit distance position highlighted

An alternative expression of the edit distance equation which gives identical results is given in Equation 10, which is equivalent to Equation 9 because neighbouring cells in M differ by at most 1.

$$M_{i,1} \leftarrow i-1, M_{1,j} \leftarrow j-1$$

$$M_{i,j} \leftarrow \begin{cases} M_{i-1,j-1} & \text{if } x_i = y_i \\ 1 + \min(M_{i-1,j-1}, M_{i-1,j}, M_{i,j-1}) & \text{else} \end{cases}$$

Equation 10

The algorithm can be adapted to find the lowest edit distances for x in substrings of y. This is achieved by setting $M_{1,j} = 0$ for all $j \in 1 \ldots n+1$. In contrast to the edit distance algorithm described above, the last row $M_{m+i,j}$ is then used to give a *sliding window* edit distance for x in substrings of y as per Equation 11 (Navarro & Raffinot 2002).

$$eds(x, y) = \min_{1 \geq j \geq n+1} (M_{m+1,j})$$

Equation 11

An example of this variation on the edit distance applied to search for the pattern "BDEE" in "DGGGDGBDEFGAB" is given in Table 12. The minimum edit distance positions are highlighted. Variations on the edit distance algorithm have been applied in domains such as DNA analysis and automated spell checking and are commonly used in MIR systems (Birmingham et al. 2001; Lemstrom & Perttu 2000; Rho & Hwang 2004; McPherson & Bainbridge 2001; Prechelt & Typke 2001).

Instead of using dynamic programming, bit-parallelism can be employed to compare strings with at most n errors. Bit-parallel algorithms simulate classical string matching algorithms, but use bit-masks to store the number of errors allowed. In this way, the algorithms are limited by the word size of the masks used (Navarro & Raffinot 2002). Bit-parallel algorithms have the advantage of having faster execution times, but the disadvantage of limiting of the maximum number of allowable errors to the word size of the bit-masks used (Lemstrom & Perttu 2000; Navarro & Raffinot 2002).

		D	**G**	**G**	**G**	**D**	**G**	**B**	**D**	**E**	**F**	**G**	**A**	**B**
	0	0	0	0	0	0	0	0	0	0	0	0	0	0
B	1	1	1	1	1	1	1	0	1	1	1	1	1	0
D	2	1	2	2	2	1	2	1	0	1	2	2	2	1
E	3	2	2	3	3	2	2	2	1	0	1	2	3	2
E	4	3	3	3	4	3	3	3	2	1	1	2	3	3

Table 12: Edit distance for the string "BDEE" in "DGGGDGBDEFGAB". This string represents the first 13 notes from the tune "Jim Coleman's" in ABC notation

It is understood from experiments with human listeners that humans perceive transposed melodies to be similar. Interestingly studies in animals have demonstrated that this ability is unique to humans (Kenneally 2008). Hence there have been several attempts to adapt the edit distance algorithm for melodic dissimilarity to provide *transposition invariant* melodic dissimilarity. Mongeau & Sankoff (1990) for example use intervals between successive pitches to represent a melody for a dissimilarity comparison instead of the absolute values of pitches. Their algorithms can be understood by first considering the note alphabet Σ to be $= \mathbb{Z}$ or $\mathbb{R}$, the integer or real alphabet. The string x' represents the transposed copy of x, transposed by t, if $x' = (x_1 + t)\ (x_2 + t)...(x_m + t)$. For example if a melody was represented by the string $x = \{3, 7, 5, 5, 8, 7, 7,5 ,3\}$ it could be relatively encoded as $x' = \{4, -2, 0, 3, -1, 0, -2, -2\}$. Using this scheme, there is naturally one less element in interval representation of the melody then in the original melody. The crucial property of this representation is that it is transposition invariant. In other words, if x and y are transpositions of each other, then $x' = y'$. The limitation of this approach becomes apparent if the case of an insertion or a deletion is considered. Consider the two strings $x = \{1, 2, 3, 4, 5\}$ and $y = \{1, 3, 4, 5\}$. The edit distance between these strings $ed(x, y) = 1$. When converted to an interval representation these strings become $x'=\{1, 1, 1, 1\}$ and $y' = \{2,1, 1\}$. The edit distance between these strings $ed(x', y') = 2$. Hence each insertion and deletion has a double weighting on the calculation of the transposition invariant edit distance of two melodic strings. Lemstrom & Ukkonen (2000) state that using interval encodings; when intervals are calculated on the fly from absolute sequences, a deletion or insertion transposes the rest of the melody and so as an alternative, they propose instead adapting a cost function for local transformations (insert, delete, replace) which is transposition invariant. A "standard" edit distance cost function considers the insertion, deletion and replacement of each pair of elements in x and y. In Lemstrom & Ukkonen's (2000) proposed transposition invariant edit distance calculation, the cost function is adapted to consider in addition, the previous and current characters in x and y. Equation 12 provides a transposition invariant method of calculating edit distance which is equivalent to Equation 9 for calculating transposition invariant edit distances.

$$M_{1,1} \leftarrow 0$$

$$M_{i,j} \leftarrow \min \begin{cases} M_{i-1,j} + 1 \\ M_{i,j-1} + 1 \\ M_{i-1,j-1} + \left(If\ x_i - x_{i-1} = y_j - y_{j-1}\ then\ 0\ else\ 1 \right) \end{cases}$$

Equation 12

Algorithms for calculating transposition invariant distances (Hamming distance, longest common subsequence, edit distance) between strings are also given in (Makinen et al. 2003). Their transposition invariant minimum edit distance *edt* between x' and y, where x and y are melodic strings and x' is x transposed by t, is given in Equation 13.

$$edt(x', y) = \min_{t \in T}(ed(x + t, y))$$

Equation 13

$T = \{x_i - y_j \mid 1 \leq i \leq m,\ 1 \leq j \leq n\}$, in other words, the set of all possible values for t which would result in an alignment between x and y. In order to calculate $edt(x',y)$, they propose using a brute force approach by calculating $ed(x + t,y)$ for all T. This is similar to the approach described in section 4.3. This obviously increases the computational complexity of the algorithm over a straightforward edit distance calculation between the two strings. In order to speed up the calculation, they propose using sparse dynamic programming. Sparse dynamic programming was introduced in (Eppstein et al. 1992a; Eppstein et al. 1992b). The main idea behind these techniques is that only elements in a string associated with a match are visited. In order to achieve this, the authors propose calculating an ordered set of matching elements in x' and y for every value of t such that $M_t = \{(i, j) \mid x_i + t = y_j\}$. Using sparse dynamic programming, the computational complexity of the transposition invariant edit distance algorithm is $O(mn \log n)$ compared to $O(mn)$ for standard edit distance. They also present a measure called "Longest Common Hidden Melody", which is a transposition invariant version of the longest common subsequence measure.

Edit distances are calculated in the SEMEX MIR system (Lemstrom & Perttu 2000) described in section 5.1, in Musipidia (Prechelt & Typke 2001) (section 5.3), in Lu *et al.*'s (2001) QBH MIR system (section 5.3), in Fast Melody Finder (Rho & Hwang 2004) described in section 5.3, in (Grachten et al. 2005) and (Duggan et al. 2006) amongst others (section 5.3).

4.5 Hidden Markov Models

A Markov Model (MM) is a *probabilistic model* of a system which transitions through a sequence of states $S = S_1, S_2...S_N$. The Markov property of the model states that the probability of the current state S_i is based only on the previous state S_{i-1}. This is described as a first order Markov process.

Hidden Markov Models (HMM) extend the concept to include the case where an observation O is a probabilistic function of the state. Rabiner (1989) describes a HMM as:

> *"a doubly embedded stochastic process with an underlying stochastic process that is not observable (it is hidden), but can only be observed through another set of stochastic processes that produce the sequence of observations".*

In other words, given an observation, what is the probability of a particular state? A HMM is formally defined as a triple $\lambda = (A,B,\pi)$, where A is the state transition matrix, B is the confusion matrix and π is a vector of the initial state probabilities. The state transition matrix A is a matrix which gives the probability of every state following every other state. If there are N states, this matrix will be of size $N \times N$. In the case where a state cannot follow another state, the probability is given as 0. The confusion matrix gives the probability of each state given each observation O. If there are M observations, then the confusion matrix will be of size $M \times N$.

There are three basic problems that HMM's can be used to solve. Firstly to calculate $P(O|\lambda)$, the probability of an observation sequence $O=O_1,O_2...O_M$ given a model λ. This can be calculated efficiently using the *forward* algorithm with a complexity of $O(N^2M)$ (Rabiner 1989). If multiple models exist, then this algorithm can be used to decide which model most likely gave rise to the set of observations.

Secondly, a HMM can be used to calculate the sequence of states $S = S_1, S_2 \ldots S_N$ most likely to have generated the set of observations $O=O_1,O_2 \ldots O_M$. To solve this, the Viterbi dynamic programming algorithm can be used (Viterbi 1967; Forney Jr 1973). The third problem that can be addressed by a HMM is to adjust the model parameters (A,B,π) to maximise the probability of the observation sequence given the model. This can be computed using the forward-backward algorithm (Rabiner 1989).

The probability distribution of a HMM allows modelling of uncertainties such as a singer's inability to accurately sing the exact pitch or rhythm of a query to a CBMIR system. Features of melodies such as pitch, interval or rhythm sequences, can be used to calculate Markov chains. A Markov chain is a state graph, where nodes represent states and weighted directed edges represent the probabilities of state transitions. States can correspond with features such as pitch levels, intervals, or note durations. Transition probabilities are calculated as the counts of subsequent states. Similarity between a query and a candidate piece in the corpus can be determined by calculating the product of the transition probabilities, based on the transition matrix of the candidate piece, for each pair of consecutive states in the query (Birmingham et al. 2003). HMM's are used in Guido/MIR (Hoos 2001) (section 5.1) and in Birmingham et al.'s (2001) Musart QBH system (section 5.3).

4.6 Conclusions

The output of a transcription system based on the algorithms described in Chapter 3 can be considered to be a set N, whose elements N_j consist of vectors of the features $\{os, of, f\}$ possibly containing transcription errors, where os and of are the onset and offset respectively and f is the extracted frequency. From Chapter 2, it is clear that a query will contain ornamentation and phrasing resulting from the creative interpretation of music by the musician; however matching polyphonic queries to polyphonic transcriptions is not required due to the essentially monophonic nature of traditional music. The algorithms discussed in this chapter describe methods of calculating distances between representations of melodic sequences. Methods based on transportation distance, edit distance and Hidden Markov Models are given, which work on representations including Implication/Realisation annotations, MIDI sequences, MIDI intervals and melodic contours. The task being considered in this work is to retrieve the human annotated musical sequence from a corpus which is the closest match for the transcription vector N. Any distance measure therefore needs to support the following characteristics:

1. Alignment should be possible so that short queries can be matched against segments of longer musical strings from the corpus. Short queries should not be penalised.
2. An unknown number of possible transformations may have occurred in the query as a result of creative interpretation and transcription errors, but the nature and scope of many of these transformations is understood. It will be possible to accommodate interpretative elements such as those described in Chapter 2. How this is achieved is discussed in Chapter 6, however distance measures still need to be tolerant of errors (Chapter 3).
3. Transposition invariance is required to the extent that the keys and modes discussed in section 2.2 are supported. Similarly the transpositions that occur from the playing of instruments with the fundamental notes given in Table 5, Table 6 and Table 7 should be supported.

Although melodic contours are widely used in query-by-humming systems (section 5.3) as a means of compensating for singer error, the literature suggests that this representation schema results in too many false positives (Lu et al. 2001; Schlichte 1990; Adams et al. 2003; Downie 1999) and so a more discriminate representation should be used. Similarly, ornamentation involves inserting additional notes at higher and lower pitches which means that strings can be transformed in a way which makes the original string difficult to recognise (section 4.1).

Typke's (2007) implementation of Earth Movers Distance has the advantage of being a linear measure, in that small modifications to a query result in corresponding small changes in the distances calculated. He also proposes two methods for calculating transposition invariant distances. However aligning short queries with longer corpus strings is only possible by expanding the query so that its length is the same as the corpus string. This is not true alignment however and short phrases will not match with substrings of long corpus strings using this method. A further limitation with this measure is that there is no obvious method for calculating appropriate weights when queries are played at different tempos to melodies from the corpus (section 2.2).

Hidden Markov Models can be developed which make use of the forward-backward algorithm to maximise the probability of the observation sequence given the model. Models can be built from pitches, intervals and rhythm sequences with example queries. The disadvantage of HMM's is that they require a large number of ground truth example queries with errors, in order to be error tolerant (Birmingham et al. 2003).

Edit distance is difficult to use for polyphonic music, but widely used for monophonic comparisons as in the case in traditional Irish music. This is therefore the approach used to measure melodic similarity in the MATT2 system described in Chapter 6. Lemstrom & Ukkonen (2000) point out that when comparing music, the transposition invariant version of the edit distance is generally more useful except when it is known *a priori* that strings x and y being compared are in the same key. Using the transposition invariant edit distance requires that pitches are quantised to the nearest semitone. This method also doubly weights insertions and deletions. If it is known that the melodies being compared are in a particular key, then it is better to quantise pitches to the playable notes on the instrument so that transcription errors are avoided. Also as highlighted in (Typke 2007; Schlichte 1990), the transposition invariant edit distance algorithm suffers from another problem: classifying melodies with similar intervals as similar, when the melodies are in fact different.

Section 6.6 proposes a pitch spelling algorithm to transcribe melodies to playable notes on an instrument rather than the nearest semitone, and so the standard edit distance can be used. Similarly, edit distance supports alignment based on (Navarro & Raffinot 2002). This method is exploited particularly in the TANSEY set segmentation algorithm given in Chapter 8. Edit distances are tolerant of insert, update and delete substitutions but cannot explicitly accommodate ornamentation. Section 6.4.1 proposes a method of effectively filtering ornamentation notes in melodies so that they can be compared using edit distances. Moreover, the expressiveness accommodation algorithms proposed in section 6.4 are actually independent of the metric used and any of the metrics discussed in this chapter would be improved with their employment.

Chapter 5 shows how the techniques explored in this and the previous chapter have been combined to produce experimental systems for content based music information retrieval.

5 Content Based Music Information Retrieval

This chapter describes a number of related systems and approaches to the CBMIR system proposed in this thesis. Music Information Retrieval can be defined as:

> *"the task of extracting from a large quantity of musical data, the portions of that data with respect to which some musicological statement is true"*
>
> \- (Kassler 1966)

The origins of this field of research are in paper collections of *incipits*, short melodic fragments drawn from the opening phrases of pieces of music. These collections were manually compiled by researchers or librarians, and usually covered one narrow field of music (Lemstrom & Perttu 2000). The term Music Information Retrieval is first mentioned in the context of computer science literature in (Kassler 1966). In this work the author presents MIR, an assembly like language for formulating musical queries and navigating scores. He suggests that MIR could form part of a "library of the future" although he recognises the limitations of the language proposed.

More recently it is suggested that there are three main classifications of MIR systems: those for searching symbolic representations of music, those for searching audio data and those systems that combine both approaches by first converting audio data to a symbolic representation and then searching for a match in a corpus of symbolically notated music (Typke et al. 2005; Typke 2007). Downie (2003) proposes analytic/production systems and locating MIR systems, a classification analogous to the first two classifications. This section presents related work in each of the three classifications of MIR system given in (Typke et al. 2005; Typke 2007) and concludes with an analysis of the suitability of the existing approaches explored to perform MIR for traditional Irish music.

5.1 Searching symbolic representations

Symbolic MIR has its origins in dictionaries of musical themes such as (Barlow & Morgenstern 1948). Monophonic music can be represented as a one-dimensional string of characters, where each character represents a musical note. Strings can be made up of characters representing pitches, pitch intervals or melody contours. In systems which use this format, standard string matching algorithms such as Knuth-Morris-Pratt, Boyer-Moore, Levenstein (Edit) Distance (section 4.4), longest common sub-sequence or regular expression searching have been applied (Navarro & Raffinot 2002).

Themefinder is a symbolic MIR system that provides a web-based interface to the Humdrum *thema* command (Kornstadt 1998). The *Humdrum Toolkit* is a set of software tools for music researchers which manipulate ASCII data conforming to the Humdrum syntax (Humdrum 2008) . The *thema* command allows searching of corpora of musical themes or incipits. There are almost ten thousand themes in the Themefinder collection encoded in the kern music data format (a markup language for musical scores). Queries can match the incipit or any part of a theme in the corpus, but the system requires knowledge of the *Humdrum Syntax*. Figure 28 is a screenshot of the interface to Themefinder which illustrates some of the query possibilities.

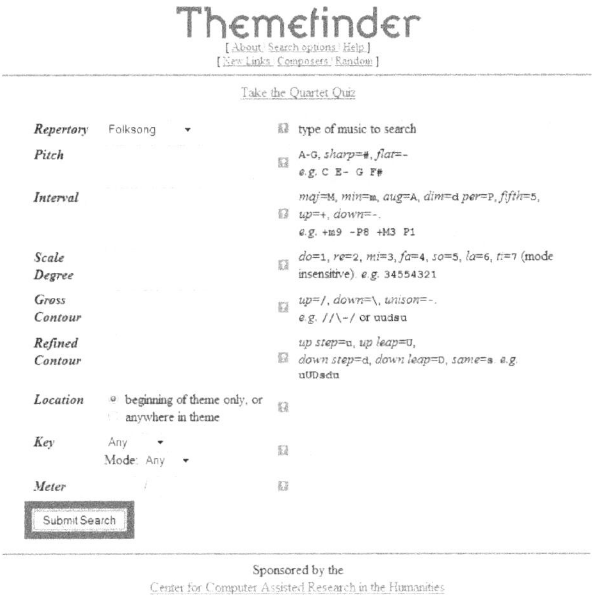

Figure 28: The Themefinder user interface

The encoding scheme for melodies discussed in section 4.1 is used to build a symbolic MIR system using the SMART Information Retrieval System in (Downie 1999). The SMART system has the advantage of being an *off the shelf* textual information retrieval system. Downie (1999) builds *n*-grams of note interval sequences where n = 4, 5, and 6, by treating melodies as long strings of intervals and taking all substrings of a fixed length. His hypothesis is that there is an equivalency between interval only melodic *n*-grams (i.e. "musical words") and "real words"; intervals and letters. To retrieve matching melodies, he uses the TF × IDF (Term Frequency * Inverse Document Frequency) ranking method from information retrieval and text mining. TF × IDF is a statistical measure used to evaluate how important a word is to a document in a corpus. The importance increases proportionally to the number of times a word appears in the document but is offset by the frequency of the word in the corpus. Variations of the TF × IDF weighting scheme are used by search engines as a tool in scoring and ranking a document's relevance given a user query. Downie uses melodic strings, extracted from melodies in the corpus as queries to evaluate the system. He artificially creates expansion, compression, repetition and omission errors in the queries to simulate potential error types that might be introduced by human subjects (see also section 5.3).

SEMEX (Search Engine for Melodic Excerpts) has a corpus where strings are represented as integer pitch levels of the notes (Lemstrom & Perttu 2000). Rhythm is not considered. Queries are similarly represented, but are usually considered to be shorter than strings from the corpus and so edit distances with alignment are calculated to find a match. SEMEX makes use of the transposition invariant cost function given in (Lemstrom & Ukkonen 2000) (section 4.4) in the calculation of edit distances, using bit-parallelism instead of dynamic programming to allow queries to match strings from the corpus with at most n errors, with low computational complexity. Bit-parallel algorithms simulate classical string matching algorithms, but use bit masking to store the number of errors allowed. In this way, the algorithms are limited by the word size of the bit masks used (Navarro & Raffinot 2002). Monophonic queries can be matched against polyphonic music from the corpus by either reducing the corpus to a monophonic representation or by using an algorithm known as MonoPoly, which makes it possible to locate occurrences that are distributed among several voices. SEMEX is implemented in C++ and has a command line interface.

GuidoMIR is a symbolic MIR system which has a native corpus of melodies in the Guido/XML music notation language (Hoos 2001). The authors claim that using a symbolic musical score language such as Guido/XML has a number of advantages over MIDI, a format designed for playback. They cite the ability to store metadata with the melody as the main advantage, but list several others. They also do not use any form of database engine and instead their system is built entirely in Perl and uses a database of flat files. Although their corpus is text based, the authors use a probabilistic matching algorithm based on first order Markov chains to match queries to corpus strings (section 4.5). Their system supports queries based on both pitch and rhythm.

C-Brahms uses nine different algorithms which support monophonic, polyphonic, rhythm invariant, transposition invariant, partial or exact matches for queries against a corpus of polyphonic music in a database of symbolically encoded music, drawn from MIDI files (Makinen et al. 2003; Ukkonen et al. 2003; Wiggins et al. 2002; Lemstrom et al. 2003). The algorithms use a number of different techniques, including dynamic programming, bit-parallelism and a two-dimensional geometric representation of music. In the latter algorithms, music is represented as horizontal line segments in Euclidean two-dimensional space. The horizontal axis represents time and the vertical axis, the pitch values. Some of these algorithms are discussed in section 4.4. C-Brahms has a public user interface available on the web so that the different algorithms can be evaluated.

In (Widmer et al. 2005) the authors describe a system which uses web mining to classify music by genre. Their system called GenreCrawler applies Term Frequency × Inverse Document Frequency (TF × IDF) (Salton and Buckley 1988) to extract meta data about a term (for example an artist name) from the results of Google queries. They hierarchically cluster the results using a Self Organising Map (Kohonen 2001). They do not present any results for this system, but suggest that it is only useful for well known (and hence well documented) artists.

TunePal is an MIR system whose main advantage is that it runs on a mobile device such as PDA or smartphone and so can be used in traditional music sessions and workshops (Duggan 2007b; Duggan 2006). Figure 29 shows musicians comparing tunes using TunePal at a traditional music session. TunePal has a corpus of approximately five thousand traditional Irish dance melodies in ABC notation (section 2.7 and Appendix B & C) drawn from transcriptions of

O'Neill (O'Neill 1903; Krassen 1975; Chambers 2007) and Henrik Norbeck (Norbeck 2007).

Figure 29: Musicians in a session compare tunes using TunePal

The system supports text queries on melodies or any of the metadata such as tune name, type or composer. For melodic queries, the system requires knowledge of ABC notation. It has an elementary query normalisation algorithm which normalises text queries into the same register and removes ornamentation from corpus strings, but otherwise it requires exact matches with strings from the corpus.

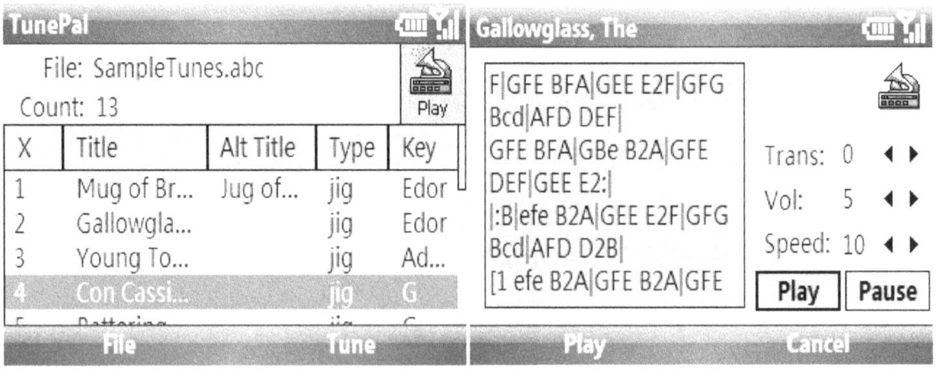

Figure 30: Screenshots of TunePal running on a Windows Mobile Smartphone

TunePal's main purpose is as an *aid memoir* for a musician who wants to play a tune, but can remember the name the tune and not the melody. Hence matching melodies can be easily converted to MIDI and played back at an adjustable tempo. Figure 30 shows screenshots of TunePal running on a Windows Mobile smartphone.

Website thesession.org (thesession.org 2007) is not discussed in the literature, but is important because it contains a collection of over seven thousand traditional Irish dance tunes in ABC notation (section 2.6) entered by the traditional music community that can be searched using text queries by any of the metadata associated with a tune or by melodic queries in ABC notation. The website is significant, because unlike much of the work discussed in this chapter that has grown out of academic research projects, thesession.org is supported by an active community of thousands of musicians who regularly contribute tunes, report on traditional music sessions (section 2.5) and engage in lively discussions. Figure 31 shows an example of the search results generated for the query "broom". Appendix E gives an extract from a discussion on the tune "Down the Broom" which is returned when this search is entered.

Figure 31: thesession.org user interface. (See also Appendix E)

5.2 Searching audio data

Systems that match digital recordings of audio to digests or hashes of known recordings are known as Audio fingerprinting or Content-Based Audio Identification (CBID) systems (Cano et al. 2005). Using fingerprints and matching algorithms, these systems have several requirements:

1. They must be robust to compression and noise in the transmission channel.
2. They must be able to identify whole titles from excerpts a few seconds long.
3. They should be computationally efficient.

In order to index audio, it must be reduced in dimensionality. This is known as fingerprint extraction. Fingerprint extraction derives a concise set of relevant features of a recording. Extracted fingerprints must support discrimination over large numbers of other fingerprints, be invariant to distortions, compact and efficient to compute. Audio is sometimes preprocessed to simulate the channel. For a telephone task, the audio could be band pass filtered to emulate the frequency bandwidth of telephone audio. Audio is then segmented into overlapping tapered frames (section 3.2) and transformed. Some common transformations include Fast Fourier Transform (FFT) (section 3.2), the Discrete Cosine Transform (DCT), the Haar Transformor the Walsh-Hadamard Transform (Subramanya et al. 1997), and the Modulated Complex Transform (MCLT) (Mihgak & Venkatesan 2001). Additional transformations are then applied in order to generate the final feature vectors for each frame. Mel-Frequency Cepstrum Coefficients are proposed in (Blum et al. 1999). Spectral Flatness Measure (SFM) is used in (Allamanche et al. 2001). Band representative vectors; an ordered list of indexes of bands with prominent tones are used by

(Papaodysseus et al. 2001), while (Burges et al. 2002) use principal component analysis (PCA) to find to find the optimal representative features.

A set of features is usually extracted for each frame of audio examined and a fingerprint derived by summarising the multidimensional vector sequences of an entire piece of audio in a single vector. Some systems include high-level musically meaningful attributes, like rhythm (section 2.2 and 3.5) or prominent pitch (section 3.2) (Relatable 2008; Blum et al. 1999).

Matching algorithms usually employ indexing as sequential scanning will be too slow. Indexing algorithms build sets of equivalence classes, discard some classes and search the rest exhaustively (Chávez et al. 2001). Algorithms should have a low False Rejection Rate (FRR), be memory efficient and should allow insert, delete and update operations (Cano et al. 2005). Euclidian distances are used in (Blum et al. 1999). Allamanche et al. (2001) use Hidden Markov Models (section 4.5). (Mihgak & Venkatesan 2001) reports on the use of a measure called "Exponential Pseudo Norm".

Finally thresholding is used to determine if a correct identification has been made. In the process of comparing fingerprints extracted from queries against the corpus of known fingerprints, scores (resulting from distances) are calculated. If a score is less than a certain threshold, then this indicates that a system has confidence in its classification. Several factors influence the identification of a threshold including the fingerprint model employed, the discriminative information of the query, the similarity of the fingerprints in the corpus, and the corpus size. Larger databases increase the probability of false positives.

Commercial examples of audio fingerprinting systems include Shazam and MusicBrainz (Shazam 2008; MusicBrainz 2008). Shazam is a subscription based service, aimed at mobile phone users. To use the service, users dial a special phone number and play a segment of the audio to software listening on the other end. Shazam includes an application for the Apple iPhone, which identifies audio and then allows a user to purchase the identified track from the iTunes music store (Apple 2008).

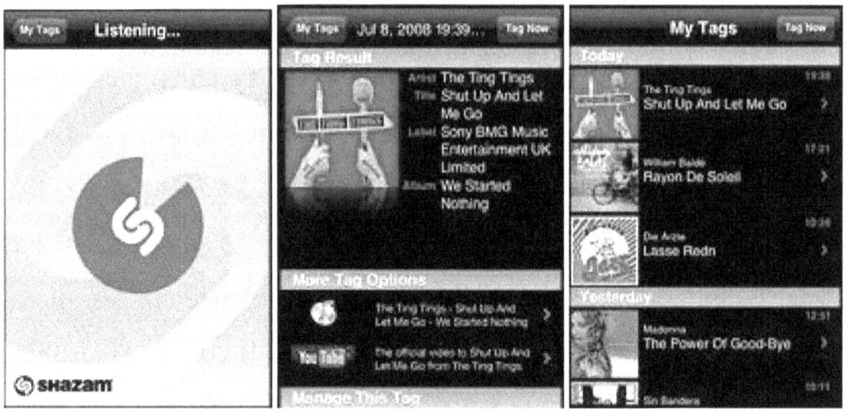

Figure 32: Shazam audio fingerprinting running on an iPhone (Shazam 2008)

MusicBrainz is an "*open source community music metadatabase*", with clients for a number of operating systems including Windows, Mac OS X and Linux (MusicBrainz 2008). MusicBrainz clients generate a fingerprint known as a PUID (Portable Unique Identifier). To annotate a file with metadata, the PUID is sent to a server, which compares it with the PUID's of known audio. If a match is found, the server returns the set of metadata for the audio file which includes artist name, album, track name and track number. The MusicBrainz corpus is maintained by a community of users.

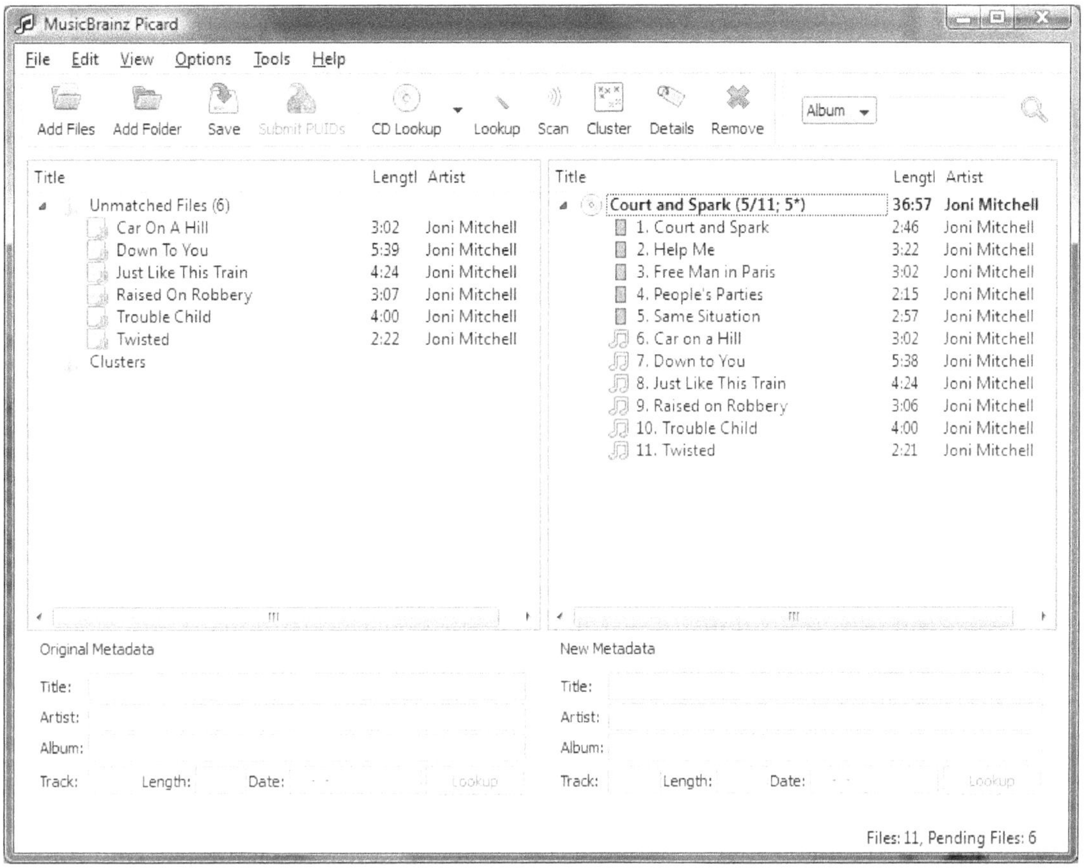

Figure 33: The "Picard" MusicBrainz client

For a more detailed profile of algorithms used in audio fingerprinting, refer to (Cano et al. 2005)

5.3 Hybrid approaches

Most research into hybrid MIR systems has focused on developing Query-By-Humming (QBH) interfaces to corpora of symbolically annotated melodies. QBH describes music information retrieval systems where audio clips of singing, humming or whistling act as queries. The premise is that if user wants to retrieve a melody from a large collection of music, a natural option is to sing, hum, or whistle a part of the melody into a microphone and let the system retrieve the matching melodies. The QBH task can be divided into two sub problems (Ryynanen & Klapuri 2008):

1. Converting a query into a format which enables searching. This problem is explored in detail in Chapter 3.
2. Matching the query with melodies in the corpus. This problem is explored in detail in Chapter 4.

The former problem is one of automatically transcribing a query into a sequence of note events (Chapter 3), whereas the latter is the problem of measuring melodic dissimilarity between the query string (which may contain errors) and strings from the corpus (Chapter 4).

Cornell's Query-By-Humming is one of the earliest examples available of a query-by-humming system (Ghias et al. 1995). It has a corpus of 183 pieces of music in MIDI format stored in a flat file database. Pitch tracking is performed using Matlab, chosen for it's built in audio processing facilities. The system transcribes hummed queries into Parsons' Code (Section 4.1) using a modified autocorrelation algorithm (section 3.2) (Dubnowski et al. 1976). The corpus is then similarly converted to Parsons' Code and matched against a query using Baeza-Yates & Perleberg's (1996) approximate string matching algorithm. This algorithm matches strings with a configurable maximum of *n* errors. The authors report a success rate of 90% using their techniques for queries of between ten and twelve characters.

The MELDEX system has a pitch tracking interface which allows users to sing queries (McNab et al. 1997; McNab et al. 1996; McPherson & Bainbridge 2001). The system depends on the user separating each note by singing "da" or "ta". The articulation of the consonant is used to detect the onset of each note. As queries are generated by humans, they naturally contain errors. The classification of the errors into four types: expansion, compression, repetition, and omission (see also section 5.1) is reported in (Downie 1999). MELDEX has a database of approximately ten thousand folk songs, compiled from the Essen collection. The system uses the approximate string matching methodology of (Mongeau & Sankoff 1990) (section 4.4). This methodology was designed explicitly for the musicological analysis of melodic strings. Melody contour searches use Parsons (1975) interval direction method (section 4.1). Matching melodies are ranked based on the degree of similarity between query and the items returned. Initially, MELDEX supported queries based on incipit's (McNab et al. 1996), however subsequent improvements facilitated the matching of queries where the match occurs not only in the incipit, but also anywhere within a melody (McNab et al. 1997).

Figure 34: MELDEX Interface. A user can play a part of melody or record a query for transcription

Early reported performance of the system is quite poor, with simple, exact match searches, taking an average of five hundred milliseconds to perform and twenty note approximate search pattern, requiring approximately twenty one seconds. Nevertheless, Downie (2003) describes MELDEX as a "gold standard" in monophonic, symbol-based, locating retrieval systems. Figure 34 (previous page) shows a screen shot of the interface to a typical MELDEX screen.

Musipedia (previously known as Tuneserver) is a web-based MIR system which supports queries entered by whistling, playing on a virtual piano keyboard, tapping the rhythm on the computer keyboard, or entering the melodic contour (Prechelt & Typke 2001). For whistled input, the audio is first sampled and a Fast Fourier Transform, frequency domain algorithm is used to estimate pitch (section 3.2). Note onsets (section 3.1) are noted using a combination of silence windows and pitch changes between consecutive frames of audio. The audio is then converted to Parsons Code (section 4.1) and a melodic contour search calculates the weighted edit distances (section 4.4) between the query and strings from the corpus. Results are ranked in order of ascending distance from the query. The authors report a success rate of approximately 80% for queries with an average of sixteen notes, where the correct melody was within the top forty matches. The correct melody was returned as the closest match in just 44% of queries. The authors ascribe mistakes to transcription errors and queries which were too short to discriminate similar representations of different melodies. The front end to Musipedia is also known as Melodyhound. Interestingly, although Musipedia contains traditional Irish dance tunes as part of its corpus, it does not generate positive results when queries are played on the tin-whistle or wooden flute (as tested by the author). A later implementation of Musipedia supports pitch and onset time-based searches by representing the query as a weighted point set and calculating the Earth Mover's Distance (section 4.3) for each query point set and pre-computed point sets representing segments of melodies from the database.

The "query by tapping" method which only takes the rhythm into account uses the same algorithm as the pitch and onset time method, but assumes all pitches to be the same. The system accelerates searches using an indexing technique based on vantage objects (Typke et al. 2004; Typke et al. 2003).

Lu *et al.* (2001) describe a QBH MIR system which represents queries as a triplet consisting of pitch contour, pitch interval, and duration, where pitch contour is U, or D, pitch interval is the difference between the frequencies of two consecutive notes and duration represents how long a note is played or hummed. The authors convert their MIDI corpus to this format using a heuristic to extract the melody line from a polyphonic MIDI representation of the audio. To convert audio to a query, they use an energy based onset detection function to determine the onsets of new notes in query audio (section 3.1). The authors point out the flaw in this method given that humans usually hum melodies *legato* and hence their algorithm misses onsets. Their corpus consists of approximately one thousand melodies in MIDI format. To match a query to a melody, their system first calculates the edit distance between the query and strings from the corpus. Strings whose edit distances are above a threshold are discarded. Strings for further consideration have interval and duration similarity calculated. They describe this as a "hierarchical matching algorithm". The final measure of similarity is the weighted sum of the three similarities. They observe that people hum the pitch variations more correctly than rhythm and conclude that errors are more likely to involve rhythm than pitch interval. Hence they assign a larger weight to the duration similarity. In 74% of queries, the correct song was listed among the first three matches and that 59% of queries, the corresponding correct song was retrieved as the first match.

Fast melody Finder (FMF) is a web based music information retrieval prototype whose key feature is that it indexes the corpus according to a scheme known as FAI (Frequently Accessed Index) (Rho & Hwang 2004). The principal behind FAI is that a piece of music is often identifiable from a few specific melody segments of the overall melody. In FAI, segments are automatically induced from previous user queries. Each entry in the FAI structure has four variables: access count, age, repetition and size. The authors propose an index maintenance system which supports merging of similar indexes.

Their prototype system has a corpus of twelve thousand MIDI files that they pre-process to extract meta data in XML format such as time signature and key. Melodies are represented as pitch (U, D, S) and time contours (L, S, S) (section 4.1). Queries can be input by humming or by drawing the melody on a graphical representation of a five line stave. The system presumably incorporates a transcription subsystem, but this is not discussed in the work. Matching is achieved using the Boyer Moore algorithm (Navarro & Raffinot 2002) initially to search for an exact match and if an exact match is not found the system falls back to calculating the edit distance using dynamic programming (section 4.4). Index entries are searched in order of access count. The authors present results which indicate that queries using both pitch and time contours are more accurate than pitch contours alone and also that their indexing scheme increased the performance of the system.

Ryynanen & Klapuri (2008) describe a QBH system which uses Locality Sensitive Hashing (LSH) to speed up retrieval of matching melodies. They use a corpus of 6030 melodies in MIDI format. They use a transcription algorithm described in detail in (Ryynanen & Klapuri 2006). This algorithm uses a frame based pitch salience estimator to measure the strength of different fundamental frequencies in successive frames. The algorithm also applies a musicological model to filter note transitions. As an output, the algorithm produces a sequence of notes in the format $\{p_i, b_i, e_i\}$ where p_i is MIDI note number (Table 22, page 150), b_i is the onset time and e_i is the offset time of the note in seconds. Their system then generates sub-sequences of the transcribed melody the authors refer to as pitch vectors, with different durations. This process is carried out not only on the transcribed melody, but also on each melody from the corpus. The similarity of melodic fragments is measured using the Euclidean distance between pitch vectors. To obtain a sub-linear time complexity, the authors employ LSH (Andoni & Indyk 2006). LSH is an algorithm for searching approximately nearest neighbours in high dimension spaces. The principal behind LSH is that points whose distances are within the threshold r will be hashed to the same bucket. Each query pitch vector is matched against melodic fragments in the database using LSH. The LSH returns the nearest neighbours and their distances to the query as matches. To obtain the final list of retrieved melodies, the candidate melodies are ranked according to their distance to the entire query note sequence. They report a top-three hit rate of 90% for 427 queries and a performance increase of between four and twenty times compared to exact nearest neighbour search.

The QBH system TuneBot which develops singer profiles by learning from user provided feedback on the search results is presented in (Little et al. 2007). This happens automatically, letting the performance of the system improve while deployed. Figure 35 illustrates the TuneBot user interface.

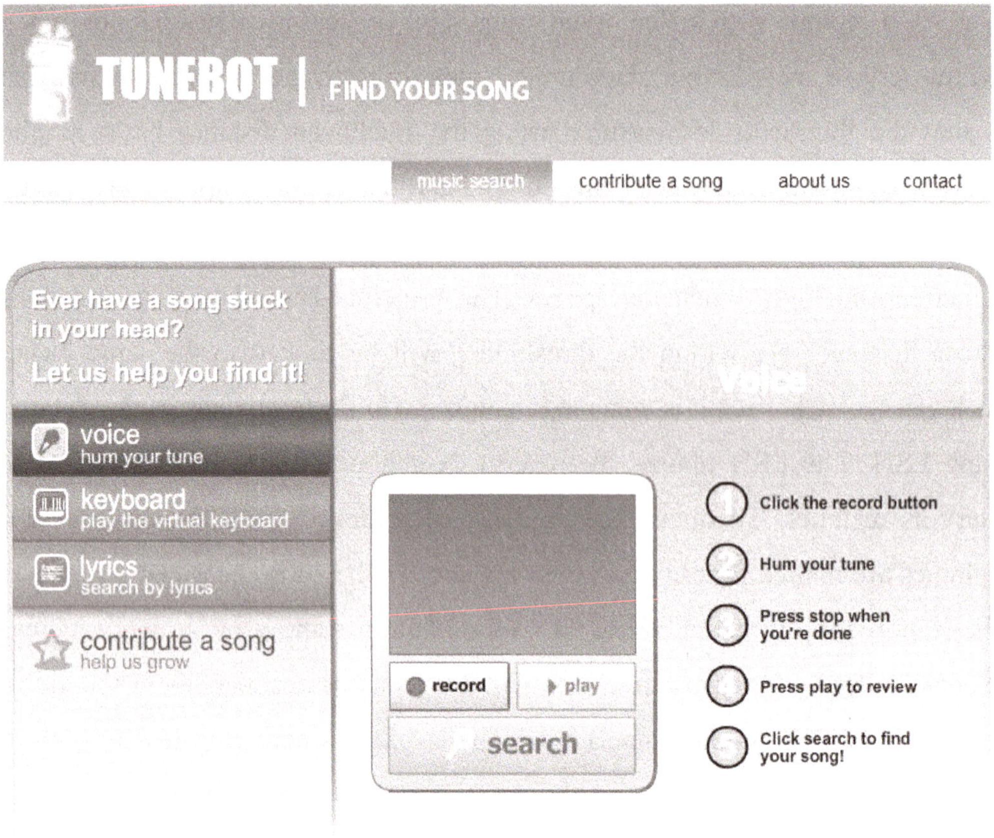

Figure 35: TuneBot user interface

TuneBot incorporates a transcription subsystem that transcribes a sung query into a pitch and duration interval representation. Pitch intervals are given as the semitone interval between adjacent note segments while duration intervals are given as the log of the ratio between the length of a note segment and the length of the subsequent note segment. Thus the authors claim the representation is both pitch and tempo invariant. TuneBot uses a genetic algorithm to tune the transcription subsystem so that the more instances a user corrects the system when it generates an incorrect result, the better the system performs. Matching in

TuneBot is achieved using dynamic programming to align queries with strings from the melody corpus (section 4.4). An evaluation of the system is reported in (Little et al. 2007), with a corpus of 1001 melodies of Beatles songs, folk songs and classical music used. After training, the system gives a Mean Reciprocal Rank (MRR) of 0.289 meaning that the correct match for queries was, on average, in the top four songs returned by the search engine.

5.4 Conclusions

This chapter presented a selection of the available literature on MIR systems. Three classifications of systems were presented; those that work on symbolic representations of music, those that work on digital signals and hybrid systems.

This work seems to demonstrate characteristics of two types of MIR systems. It is similar to the systems outlined in section 5.2 in the sense that the aim of the work is to annotate a digital recording. However the systems in section 5.2 work entirely in the signals domain. Their aim is to identify a digital recording as being an instance of another digital recording. These systems create hashes of recordings known as audio fingerprints in order to decrease computational complexity and minimise memory usage. In these systems two versions of the same piece of music will be annotated differently. In this work, the aim is to annotate different interpretations of the same piece of music identically. This is particularly important if the work is to facilitate the types of queries suggested in section 1.2. Several of the papers report on the difficulty of extracting performance data from digital signals and hence used either MIDI data, data captured from custom instruments or on-screen representations of instruments that a user must "play" using the mouse in the query by-example paradigm. It can therefore be concluded that there are additional challenges in developing MIR systems that work on audio from real instruments.

It seems reasonable to understand the aim of a typical QBH system to be to try to find a melody from a corpus which is similar to a hummed query. The systems outlined in section 5.3 would require adaptation to address P1-P10 from Table 10. To address P1-P10, it is necessary to identify the melodic query as being an *instance* of a melody from a corpus. The approach proposed in Chapter 6 maximises similarity between pieces of music played on different instruments, in different tempos and most importantly in different regional and individual styles and ground truth transcriptions of the musical pieces. In order to achieve this it is necessary to first *normalise* both the query and strings from the corpus, where normalisation involves removal of musical style elements. To do this requires a consideration of which parts of a melody are core, which parts are subject to interpretation and also the nature of the interpretation. This question is explored in section 2.9.1. Removal of musical features should increase accuracy. This is not the case in gross contour representations of melodies such as those described in section 5.3 used in many MIR systems, which as the literature suggests results in too many mismatches (Schlichte 1990; Adams et al. 2003; Lu et al. 2001). Gross contour representations of traditional melodies are evaluated in section 7.2. Instead the melody representation scheme should be fine grained enough to minimise the possibility of mismatches.

There should be no arbitrary limits in this system on the length of a query. Queries might conceivably consist of a melody fragment, an entire tune, or multiple tunes played segue in a set (Chapter 8). For longer phrases, it makes sense to extract the maximum amount of relevant information from a query to use in matching. Chapter 6 addresses the problem of how to normalise traditional music queries to maximise melodic similarity. It also addresses the problem of how to match melody fragments and entire melodies. Chapter 8 extends this to address the problem of how to annotate multiple segue melodies played in a set.

6 Machine Annotation of Traditional Tunes (MATT2)

In this chapter MATT2, a new system for automatically annotating recordings of traditional Irish dance music is presented. MATT2 addresses P1-P9, the main problems in performing MIR on traditional Irish dance music identified in Chapter 2 (Table 10, page 58). MATT2 represents Contribution 1 of this thesis. P10 is addressed using the Turn ANnotation in SEts using SimilaritY profiles (TANSEY) algorithm proposed in Chapter 8. TANSEY represents Contribution 4.

First, using Gainza's (2005) onset detection algorithm (section 3.1), a frequency domain pitch detection algorithm (section 3.2), and a pitch spelling algorithm based on Breathneach's (1985) observations about the transcription of traditional Irish dance music discussed in section 2.2, tunes are transcribed to strings of a reduced alphabet of ABC music notation (Contribution 2, section 2.7). The transcriptions are *normalised* to take account of various expressive transformations that can occur in the interpretation of traditional music, such as ornamentation (P7, section 2.9.1), the "long note", (P8, section 2.9.1), reversing (P3, section 2.9.1) and phrasing (P5, section 2.9.2). The purpose of normalisation is to extract the core melody from an augmented interpretation of the melody played by a musician. An algorithm known as Ornamentation Filtering is proposed to normalise queries played with ornamentation. Compensating for expressiveness in this way represents Contribution 3 of this thesis.

Once a transcription is made, the system compares it against a corpus of human made ground truth transcriptions of tunes. The corpus used is in ABC notation which has the advantage of being based on ASCII text and so tunes in ABC can be easily processed and analysed using algorithms for textual information retrieval. The transcriptions used are normalised in a five stage process, before comparison, to remove ornamentation, to compensate for reversing and to expand the tunes as they would be typically played by a musician interpreting the tune. Levenshtein's (1966) edit distance (section 4.4) is used to calculate a measure of melodic dissimilarity, with Navarro & Raffino's (2002) variation which allows for searching for substrings. Using the approach proposed in this chapter, a high success rate is reported for test audio consisting of long and short phrases of music, incipits and extracts from the middle of tunes, solo and ensemble playing, (with up to ten musicians on various traditional instruments), field recordings from concerts, informal pub sessions and badly degraded archive recordings. The work reported in this chapter was first presented at the Sixth International Workshop on Content-Based Multimedia Indexing as "A System for Automatically Annotating Traditional Irish Music Field Recordings" (Duggan et al. 2008a).

6.1 System design

A high level diagram of the subsystems which make up MATT2 are presented in Figure 36. The subsystems present in MATT2 will now be described.

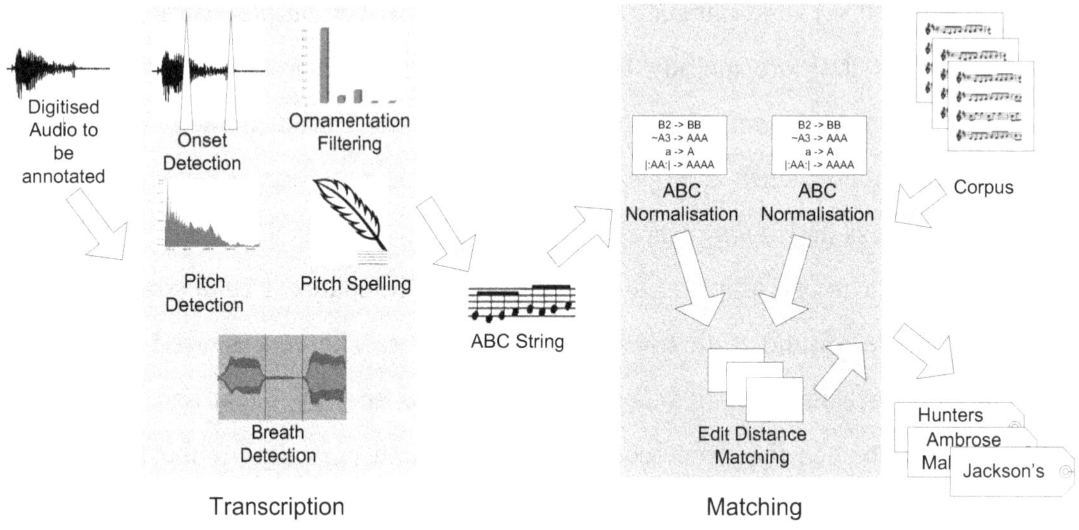

Figure 36: High level diagram of MATT2

MATT2 works on mono digital audio files in the WAV format recorded at 44.1KHz. There are two core components; a transcription algorithm and a matching algorithm. The transcription algorithm is made up of a number of subsystems for onset detection, pitch detection, pitch spelling, breath detection and Ornamentation Filtering. The output of the transcription algorithm can be considered to be the set N, where each element in N is a vector with various dimensions describing features of the audio being analysed. A string t is extracted from the notes, where t contains characters of the reduced alphabet of the ABC music notation language.

The matching algorithm compares the transcription t against transcriptions from Z, the corpus of known tunes allowing errors, and returns elements from Z in order of ascending dissimilarity. Elements in Z are preprocessed as described in section 6.8 before matching.

6.2 Onset detection

The audio file to be annotated is first segmented into candidate note onsets and offsets using an onset detection function adapted from (Gainza 2006; Gainza & Coyle 2007) (section 3.1). The onset detection function, ODCF (Onset Detection using Comb Filters) is based on time domain FIR comb filters. ODCF discovers harmonic characteristics of the input signal and is therefore tolerant to energy changes in an input signal not caused by note onsets and is also better at detecting onsets in legato playing typical of woodwind traditional instruments such as the concert flute, the tin-whistle and the uilleann pipes. The use of ODCF specifically addresses P1 from Table 10; that is support for queries played on the main instruments used in traditional music.

The input signal is first segmented into overlapping frames of 2048 samples (approximately 46 milliseconds). Each frame overlaps with the previous frame by 75%. Each frame is then passed through a bank of twelve FIR comb filters. A FIR comb filter works by summing the input signal with a delayed version of the same input signal. The delay of the filter is calculated as being the length in time of a single period of a waveform at the frequency. This has the effect of amplifying the frequency or a harmonic of the frequency in the input signal which matches the frequency being filtered. Thus, the energy of the input signal is doubled only if the peaks of the signal coincide with the peaks of the FIR comb filter (Smith 1997). Twelve filters with different delays are used. The delays are calculated as being the twelve semitones succeeding one octave below the *fundamental note* (Breathnach 1985) of the instruments in the audio file being analysed as per Equation 1 (Chapter 3, page 73). Figure 37 gives an extract from the author's implementation of Equation 1 in Java.

```
public class TimeDomainCombFilter {
  private float[] frame;
  private int frequency;
  private int sampleRate;
  private int delay;
  public void setFrequency(int frequency) {
    this.frequency = frequency;
    delay = (int) ((1.0f / (float) frequency) * (float)
sampleRate);
  }
  public float calculateOutputPower() {
    float power = 0;
    for (int i = 0; i < frame.length + delay; i++) {
      // Add 0's at the start
      if (i < delay) {
        power += Math.pow(frame[i], 2);
      } // Add 0's at the end
      else if (i >= frame.length) {
         power += Math.pow(frame[i - delay], 2);
      }
      else {
        power += Math.pow(frame[i] + frame[i - delay], 2);
      }
    }
    return power;
  }
  private float calculateInputPower() {
    float power = 0;
    for (int i = 0; i < frame.length; i++) {
      power += Math.pow(frame[i], 2);
    }
      return power;
  }
  public float calculateHarmonicity() {
    float inputPower, outputPower, power;
    inputPower = calculateInputPower();
    outputPower = calculateOutputPower();
    power = (float) outputPower / (4.0f * inputPower);
    return power;
  }
}
```

Figure 37: Extract from the author's implementation of a time domain comb filter (Equation 1) in Java

The usual fundamental note for traditional music is D (Breathnach 1985), however if the music is played on an instrument pitched as per Table 5, Table 6 or Table 7, then the fundamental note changes appropriately. In this way, P2 from Table 10 is addressed and the main modes and keys used to play traditional music are supported by the system. Table 13 shows the frequencies and corresponding delays for the fundamental notes used in traditional music (Chapter 2).

For each frame of audio examined, the outputs of the audio passed through each of the twelve filters are calculated. A value for the ODF is then calculated as being the sum of the difference between the outputs of each of the twelve filters in successive frames squared, as described in Equation 2 (Chapter 3, page 68).

In the case where the pitch of the input signal changes from one note to another, this will result in a peak in the ODF graph. A dynamic threshold is then calculated above which peaks in the ODF are recognised as being candidate note onsets (section 3.1).

Bb		**C**		**D**		**Eb**		**F**		**G**	
f	***D***	***f***	***D***	***f***	***D***	***f***	***D***	***f***	***D***	***f***	***D***
116	380	130	339	146	302	155	284	174	253	196	225
123	358	138	319	155	284	164	268	184	239	207	213
130	339	146	302	164	268	174	253	195	226	220	200
138	319	155	284	174	253	184	239	207	213	233	189
146	302	164	268	184	239	195	226	219	201	247	178
155	284	174	253	195	226	207	213	233	189	261	168
164	268	184	239	207	213	219	201	246	179	277	159
174	253	195	226	219	201	233	189	261	168	293	150
184	239	207	213	233	189	246	179	277	159	311	141
195	226	219	201	246	179	261	168	293	150	329	134
207	213	233	189	261	168	277	159	311	141	349	126
219	201	246	179	277	159	293	150	329	134	370	119

Table 13: Delays *D* in samples for frequencies *f* in Hz sampled at 44.1Khz, used in ODCF for differently pitched instruments. (See also Table 5, Table 6 and Table 7).

The peak detection algorithm identifies a peak in the ODF as being a value preceded by four ascending values and followed by four descending values, though MATT2 supports a configurable value for this. This value was discovered by experimenting with different values until the algorithm generated the fewest false positives. Onsets and offsets are considered by the system to be concurrent and so a candidate note is considered to be a segment bounded by two adjacent onsets.

Figure 38 shows the signal for the first bar of the tune "The Boyne Hunt" played on a concert flute (section 2.4.2) with the detected candidate note onsets marked. The second plot in this figure shows the ODF for the signal, with the dynamic threshold and the candidate onsets marked. In this plot, it is significant that the first note contains a dynamic energy change approximately half way through the note which the ODF has correctly ignored.

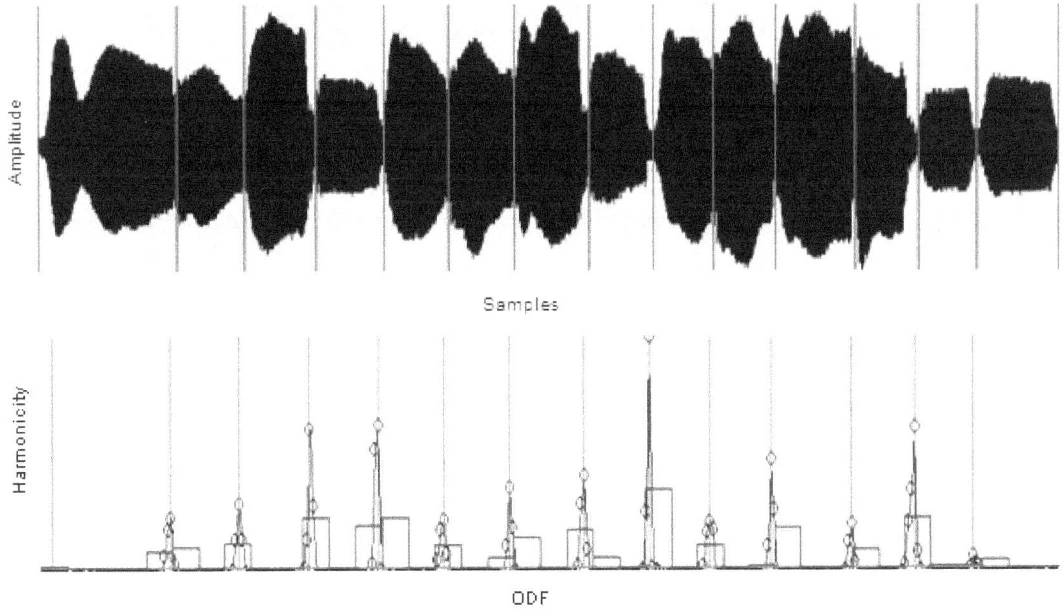

Figure 38: Signal and ODF plots of the first bar of the tune "The Boyne Hunt"

The onset detection function returns a set of candidate notes N indexed by j, where each element in $N_j \in N$ consists of the vector $\{os, of, dS, nD\}$ and $j \in \mathbb{N}$, $1 \leq j \leq J$. The dimension os_j is the onset point in samples, of_j is the offset point and dS_j is the length of the segment in samples, given by $of_j - os_j$. The dimension nD_j is the note duration in seconds and is calculated by dividing dS_j by the sample rate (44100Hz). The count of notes detected by the onset detection function is given by J.

6.3 Pitch detection

To estimate the perceived pitch of each note, the fundamental frequency (F0) of the note is derived. MATT2 makes use of a frequency domain pitch detector and so a Fast Fourier Transform (FFT, section 3.2) is first performed on each candidate note segment. As the FFT algorithm requires the frame size to be a power of two (Smith 1997), the pitch detector subsystem first calculates the highest number, which is a power of two nP_j, that is less than the length in samples dS_j of each segment N_j of audio bordered by onsets. For example, a note of length 0.28 seconds (Figure 41) and a sample rate of 44.1Khz, gives an audio segment of 12348 samples. This gives an nP_j of 8192. For a typical nP_j of 8192, the bin width of the FFT is 5.38Hz. This gives sufficient pitch discrimination to distinguish the notes playable on the instruments used to play traditional music and so interpolation is not necessary

An FFT is then performed on the segment of length nP_j. To determine the pitch, the system first evaluates the indices of frequency spectrum where peaks occur. A peak detection algorithm is again employed which identifies values bordered by two ascending/descending values. The algorithm extracts the bin indices of five peaks with the maximum amplitude from the spectrum as the set of candidate pitches cp_i. For each candidate pitch cp_i the algorithm calculates the harmonicity h_i by summing the amplitudes of the ten integer multiples of the candidate as per Equation 14. A border b is set each side of the integer multiple of the candidate index and the algorithm picks the maximum energy from the range. This gives the algorithm tolerance to inexact periodicity.

$$h_i = \sum_{m=0}^{10} max_{j=cp_i \times m-b}^{cp_i \times m+b}(fft(j))$$

Equation 14

The algorithm then picks the candidate with the highest harmonicity *cp*. The note frequency f_j is then calculated by multiplying *cp* by the FFT bin width. The algorithm adds f_j as a dimension to each element of *N* as $f_{j,}$. Figure 39 gives an extract from the implementation of this algorithm in Java.

```
int numCandidates = 5;
int numHarmonics = 10;
float maxEnergy = 0;
float maxCandidate = 0;

float binWidth = (float) sampleRate / (float) frameSize;
for (int i=0 ; i < numCandidates ; i ++)
{
    int candidate = peaks.elementAt(i).intValue();
    float energy = 0;
    int border = 2;
    for (int j = 0 ; j < numHarmonics ; j ++)
    {
        int harmonic = candidate + (j * candidate);
        float hLow = (int) ((float) harmonic - border);
        float hHigh = (int) ((float) harmonic + border);

        float harmonicity = -1;
        for (int k = (int) hLow; k <= (int) hHigh ; k ++)
        {
            if (k < fftMag.length)
            {
                if (fftMag[k] > harmonicity)
                {
                    harmonicity = fftMag[k];
                }
            }
        }
        energy += harmonicity;
    }

    if (energy > maxEnergy)
    {
        maxEnergy = energy;
        maxCandidate = candidate;
    }
}
frequency = maxCandidate * binWidth;
return frequency;
```

Figure 39: Extract from the author's frequency domain, harmonicity based pitch detector code in Java

6.4 Compensating for expressiveness in queries

At this stage *N*, the set of candidate notes is the set of note vectors consisting of $N_j = \{os, of, dS, nD, f\}$, where os_j is the onset point in samples, of_j is the offset point and dS_j is the length of the segment in samples, given by $of_j - os_j$, nD_j is the note duration in seconds and f_j is the detected pitch. The system next attempts to compensate for expressiveness in the playing that generated the transcription. Four expressive characteristics are accommodated: ornamentation (P7), the "long note" (P8), phrasing (P5) and reversing (P3) (section 2.9 and 2.9.1). Accommodation for ornamentation is discussed in section 6.4.1. Compensation for phrasing and reversing are discussed in sections 6.5, 6.8 and 6.7 respectively. Compensating for expressiveness represents Contribution 2 in this thesis.

6.4.1 Ornamentation Filtering

Firstly, the system attempts to identify *ornamentation notes* (section 2.9.1) in the transcription and filter them. An ornamentation note in traditional music takes duration from the subsequent note, so the aim of this algorithm is to identify the ornamentation notes, remove them from the transcription and give back duration to the subsequent note (Figure 17). This algorithm has no *a priori* knowledge of note durations and works equally well with tunes played at a variety of tempos (P9 from Chapter 1).

In order to achieve this, the system generates a histogram of note durations, nD_j from *N*, the set of transcribed notes. To count notes for inclusion in a histogram bin, the algorithm identifies bin widths on the fly. When a note is being considered, the algorithm first searches the histogram to see if there is a bin with a width, within +/- 33% of the duration of the note. 33% is the *fuzz* referred to in Figure 40.

The value 33% was chosen, because ornaments (notes of extremely short durations) get counted together, but triples (melodically significant) will get counted with quavers. The algorithm also updates the bin width each time a note is added to the bin, so that the bin widths contain the cumulative average note durations counted. The histogram bin with the highest count is considered to be the initial length of a quaver note *qL*. Pseudocode for this algorithm is given in Figure 40.

```
foreach (note in transcribed_notes)
begin
    found ← false
    foreach(bin in histogram)
    begin
        bin_start ← bin.width - fuzz
        bin_end ← bin.width + fuzz
      if (note.duration >= bin_start and
          note.duration <= bin_end)
      begin
          found ← true
          bin.count ++
        bin.width ← (bin.width  +
          note.duration) / 2
          break
        end
    if not found
    begin
      newNote.count ← 1
      newNote.width ← note.duration
      histogram.add(newNote)
    end
end
quaver_length ← max(histogram)
```

Figure 40: Pseudocode for the quaver duration calculation algorithm

Figure 41 shows the duration histogram for the incipit from the tune "The Kilmovee Jig". The system then calculates the integer, quaver multiple qQ_j of each note by dividing each duration nD_j by qL and rounding to an integer (Equation 15).

$$qQ_j = round\left(\frac{nD_j}{qL}\right)$$

Equation 15

From Figure 41, the bin counting notes of 0.28 +/- 33% seconds has the highest count and so this is considered to be the initial average length of a quaver in the piece of music analysed. Table 14 shows a subset of the durations measured by the onset detection function for the phrase of music used to generate Figure 41, with the rounded multiple of qL = 0.28. Tempo in jigs is counted as dotted crochets per minute (Table 3) and so a qL of 0.28 seconds represents a tempo of 71 BPM.

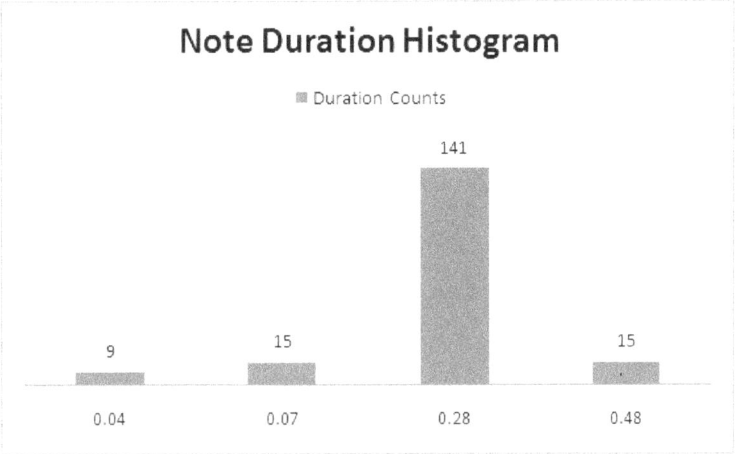

Figure 41: Histogram of candidate note durations in seconds, from a 25 second phrase from the tune "The Kilmovee Jig"

Notes whose multiples are zero are classified as ornamentation notes and removed from the transcription. These notes have their durations added to the subsequent notes. This has the effect of eliminating ornamentation notes such as those found in rolls, cuts taps and crans typical of traditional Irish music (section 2.9.1) and also of eliminating consecutive onsets (false positives caused by noisy onsets). The merging of ornamentation notes in this manner addresses P7 from Table 10. In Table 14, notes 3, 6, 7, 8, 23 and 29 will be removed and their durations added to the subsequent notes.

MATT2 then calculates the bin width, with the maximum bin count in a second histogram of the new note durations after ornamentation elimination as the quaver length may have changed as a result of merging ornamentation notes. The system uses this value to be the new length of a quaver qL'. The duration calculator then evaluates the nearest multiple qQ of the quaver length qL' for each candidate note as per Equation 15.

In order to compensate for "long notes" (P8) (section 2.9.1), the algorithm splits notes with durations $qQ_j > 1$ into multiple quaver length notes, so that all notes are quantised to be of quaver length. New notes have their frequencies recalculated using the pitch detection algorithm described in section 6.3. Table 15 (page 134) shows the results of this process on the transcription given in Table 14 (page 133). Notes added by "long note" compensation are highlighted in Table 15.

#	Onset Time	Duration	Multiple	Frequency	Energy
1	0.00	0.35	1	296.08	587.09
2	0.35	0.24	1	392.98	1806.87
3	0.59	0.07	0	430.66	1836.28
4	0.66	0.46	2	1181.63	2040.67
5	1.13	0.26	1	495.26	2736.67
6	1.38	0.05	0	559.86	1727.08
7	1.43	0.12	0	495.26	2269.23
8	1.54	0.03	0	430.66	1030.49
9	1.58	0.34	1	495.26	2820.16
10	1.92	0.24	1	392.98	2147.70
11	2.16	0.27	1	441.43	2486.53
12	2.43	0.29	1	495.26	2599.07
13	2.72	0.26	1	441.43	2347.55
14	2.97	0.27	1	392.98	2024.66
15	3.24	0.26	1	333.76	1129.72
16	3.49	0.27	1	296.08	1281.40
17	3.76	0.17	1	333.76	1161.26
18	3.94	0.35	1	392.98	2133.99
19	4.28	0.28	1	495.26	2523.68
20	4.56	0.23	1	586.78	1217.29
21	4.79	0.29	1	785.96	3093.80
22	5.09	0.22	1	667.53	1096.09
23	5.31	0.07	0	818.26	1254.11
24	5.38	0.46	2	664.84	1090.16
25	5.84	0.27	1	592.16	1257.22
26	6.11	0.26	1	489.88	1708.94
27	6.36	0.30	1	441.43	1996.61
28	6.66	0.26	1	392.98	1947.37
29	6.92	0.06	0	495.26	1668.10
30	6.98	0.49	2	785.96	1970.59

Table 14: Calculated note onset times, durations, quaver multiples, frequencies and energies for the first 30 notes from the tune "The Kilmovee Jig" played on a concert flute

In this way notes are quantised as being quavers, ornamentation notes are filtered and their durations added to the subsequent notes in the transcription.

#	Onset Time	Duration	Multiple	Frequency	Energy
1	0	0.35	1	296.08	587.09
2	0.35	0.24	1	392.98	1806.87
3	0.59	0.27	1	395.67	2103.44
4	0.86	0.27	1	392.98	1950.97
5	1.13	0.26	1	495.26	2736.67
6	1.38	0.16	1	495.26	2269.23
7	1.54	0.37	1	495.26	2820.16
8	1.92	0.24	1	392.98	2147.70
9	2.16	0.27	1	441.43	2486.53
10	2.43	0.29	1	495.26	2599.07
11	2.72	0.26	1	441.43	2347.55
12	2.97	0.27	1	392.98	2024.66
13	3.24	0.26	1	333.76	1129.72
14	3.49	0.27	1	296.08	1281.40
15	3.76	0.17	1	333.76	1161.26
16	3.94	0.35	1	392.98	2133.99
17	4.28	0.28	1	495.26	2523.68
18	4.56	0.23	1	586.78	1217.29
19	4.79	0.29	1	785.96	3093.80
20	5.09	0.22	1	667.53	1096.09
21	5.31	0.27	1	664.84	1112.75
22	5.57	0.27	1	667.53	1081.67
23	5.84	0.27	1	592.16	1257.22
24	6.11	0.26	1	489.88	1708.94
25	6.36	0.30	1	441.43	1996.61
26	6.66	0.26	1	392.98	1947.37
27	6.92	0.27	1	392.98	1940.54
28	7.19	0.27	1	392.98	2140.87

Table 15: Calculated note durations after Ornamentation Filtering and long note compensation of the data presented in Table 14

Ornamentation Filtering is carried out on a sliding window of the set of transcribed notes (with no overlaps). In this way Ornamentation Filtering accounts for tempo deviation (P9) which may occur in the audio being analysed. The window size used for the experiments described in Chapter 7 is six seconds. If the last window is of duration less than the window size, then the last window is combined with the previous window for analysis, so that no window is shorter than the window size.

	Whole Tunes (WT)				Excerpts (E)			
#	Original	Filtered	Inserted	New	Original	Filtered	Inserted	New
1	293	63	26	256	80	18	10	72
2	287	55	30	262	61	19	2	44
3	421	67	51	405	100	27	21	94
4	283	41	25	267	129	38	12	103
5	287	49	36	274	49	8	6	47
6	296	66	50	280	68	16	8	60
7	320	64	19	275	54	4	39	89
8	428	52	183	559	91	21	5	75
9	606	115	255	746	81	11	3	73
10	229	43	99	285	65	15	11	61
11	295	55	87	327	433	90	36	379
12	275	43	33	265	49	18	3	34
13	168	41	26	153	157	44	13	126
14	278	41	34	271	54	17	8	45
15	226	46	21	201	70	15	2	57
16	263	49	50	264	170	20	84	234
17	291	61	108	338	35	6	3	32
18	267	38	177	406	63	12	25	76
19	172	43	14	143	64	18	13	59
20	693	163	92	622	261	37	47	271

Table 16: Filtered and inserted note counts using Ornamentation Filtering. See also Appendix A

Table 16 (previous page) shows the number of notes filtered and inserted by Ornamentation Filtering for the first twenty pieces of test audio (WT & E) used in the experiment described in Chapter 7.

6.5 Breath detection

Flute and tin-whistles commonly used to play traditional music are woodwind instruments and hence a musician must periodically take breaths as a piece of music is being played (Larsen 2003; Hamilton 1990) (section 2.9.2). MATT2 incorporates an energy based breath detector subsystem to transcribe a breath in the signal. The breath detector first calculates amplitude for each candidate note segment and compares it with the average absolute amplitude of the entire signal. A breath is marked with a pitch spelling pS_j = "z" if the average amplitude of a candidate note is less than a 10% threshold of the average amplitude over the entire signal.

A "z" is the symbol used in ABC notation to denote a rest. Again, this threshold is configurable. Silence segments or breaths detected before the transcription of the first pitched note or at the end of the transcription are removed.

6.6 Pitch spelling

The pitch spelling subsystem assigns a symbol in ABC notation to each detected note frequency. Concert flutes, tin-whistles and uilleann pipes used to play traditional music have a range of two octaves, though this can be extended by cross fingering techniques (section 2.4.2) and consequently most traditional tunes have a range of two octaves. The pitch spelling algorithm employed again takes advantage of Breathnach's (1985) observation reported in section 2.2, that transcriptions should be made relative to the fundamental note of the instrument.

When an instrument is being transcribed, the frequencies in the spelling/frequency table (Table 17) are adjusted relative to the fundamental note of the instrument (Table 5, Table 6 and Table 7, Chapter 2). In this way, MATT2 addresses P2 from Table 10 and is transposition invariant to the keys used to play Irish traditional music. It also ensures that pitches are quantised to the nearest *playable* note rather than the nearest semitone as is the case with other transcription systems. Occasionally, tunes use notes below the fundamental note. On concert flutes, tin-whistles and uilleann pipes, these notes are transposed up one octave to make them playable, however on a fiddle, accordion or harp, these notes are played as per the score. The pitch spelling algorithm recognises pitches one octave below the fundamental note *fn* and three octaves above the fundamental note. To assign each note with a pitch spelling pS_j, each calculated note frequency is compared with the frequencies of the notes in the major key of the fundamental note *fn*. As the C natural note is used extensively in traditional tunes (particularly those transcribed in G), the C natural spelling is added to the frequencies of known notes and both the C and C# are spelled as C. This gives the pitch spelling algorithm a range of thirty three notes. The nearest match for the frequency f_j is the assigned the pitch spelling pS_j (Equation 16).

$$pS_j = \min\left(abs\left(f_j - k_m \mid 1 \geq m \geq 33, 1 \geq j \geq J\right)\right)$$

Equation 16

Frequencies and pitch spellings (the corresponding symbol from ABC notation) for the fundamental note D are given in Table 17 as an example.

Spelling	Frequency
D,	146.83
E,	164.81
F,	184.99
G,	195.99
A,	220.00
B,	246.94
C	261.62
C	277.18
D	293.66
E	329.62
F	369.99
G	391.99
A	439.99
B	493.88
c	523.24
c	554.36
d	587.32
e	659.24
f	739.98
g	783.98
a	879.99
b	987.75
c'	1046.49
c'	1108.71
d'	1174.64
e'	1318.49
f'	1479.96
g'	1567.96
a'	1759.97
b'	1975.50
c''	2092.97
c''	2217.43
d''	2349.28

Table 17: Pitch spellings for the D flute pitch model

P6 is the problem that tin-whistles are pitched an octave higher than other traditional instruments. To annotate tunes played on the tin-whistle, the system first counts the number of transcribed notes either side of half way between the combined pitch range of a flute *fc* and a tin-whistle *tc*. For a flute with a fundamental note of D4, this note would be G5 and is calculated as being seventeen semitones up from the fundamental note (Table 18). If *tc* > *fc*, then the pitch spelling algorithm is adjusted by one octave.

← **Flute Range *fc*** →																					
D	E	F	G	A	B	C	D	E	F	G	A	B	C	D	E	F	G	A	B	C	D
4	4	4	4	4	4	5	5	5	5	5	5	5	6	6	6	6	6	6	6	7	7
							← **Tin-Whistle Range *tc*** →														

Table 18: Pitch range of a flute and tin-whistle with overlap

As all notes are normalised to the same register for comparison, this has no effect on the melodic similarity, but it adapts the transcription algorithm to the pitch range of a tin-whistle.

Pitch spellings pS_j are added as a dimension to each element in the set N, so that the final set of transcribed notes consist of the set of vectors $\{os, of, dS, f, e, nD, qQ, pS\}$, where os_j is the onset point in samples, of_j is the offset point and dS_j is the length of the segment in samples, given by $of_j - os_j$. nD_j is the note duration in seconds, e_j is the energy of the note (calculated for breath detection), qQ_j is the quaver multiple (now always 1) and pS_j is the pitch spelling in ABC notation. The updated count of notes after Ornamentation Filtering and "long note" compensation is given by the variable J.

For many of the test recordings used to evaluate MATT2 recorded in imperfect conditions, this approach results in remarkably few transcription errors. A string t is then extracted from N, consisting of the ordered string of pitch spellings.

6.7 Corpus normalisation

The corpus used in the experiments described in Chapter 7 is Norbeck's reel and jig collection, which contains 1582 reels and jigs, with variations (Norbeck 2007). MATT2 supports ABC notation which, being a text format, requires minimal pre-processing before it can be compared using the edit distance algorithm. Before edit distance matching against the corpus is carried out, both the transcribed string and strings from the corpus are *normalised*. This step is necessary as ABC notation supports features such as repeated sections, which need to be expanded so that they can be correctly matched against transcribed phrases (Appendix B). It also removes ornamentation from the transcriptions. Normalisation involves five stages. Figure 42 shows examples of each stage in the ABC normalisation process. Appendix C and D give further examples of tunes before and after normalisation.

Firstly, all whitespace, ornamentation markers and text comments are removed. When ornamentation markers (~{ }) are filtered from ABC transcriptions, this has the effect of quantising the duration of the majority of notes in corpus strings to multiples of the duration of a quaver. The `(X` symbol in ABC is used to indicate a duplet, where `X` indicates the number of notes in the duplet. For example `(3` indicates a triplet. These markers are removed, but the notes in the duplet are left intact. This again addresses P7 from Chapter 1.

Original:
`d2BG dGBG|~G2Bd efge|d2BG dGBG|1 ABcd edBc:|2 ABcd edBd||`

After ornamentation filtering:
`d2BGdGBG|G2Bdefge|d2BGdGBG|1ABcdedBc:|2ABcdedBd||`

After note expansion:
`ddBGdGBG|GGBdefge|ddBGdGBG|1ABcdedBc:|2ABcdedBd||`

After section expansion:
`ddBGdGBGGGBdefgeddBGdGBGABcdedBc`
`ddBGdGBGGGBdefgeddBGdGBGABcdedBd`

After register normalisation:
`DDBGDGBGGGBDEFGEDDBGDGBGABCDEDBC`
`DDBGDGBGGGBDEFGEDDBGDGBGABCDEDBD`

Figure 42: Normalisation stages for the A part of the tune "Come West Along the Road". See also Figure 3, Figure 15 and Figure 44

Secondly, all notes of duration greater than that of a quaver are expanded to be multiple instances of a quaver. This removes the effect of long notes on distance calculations addressing P8 from Chapter 1.

Thirdly repeated sections are expanded and bar divisions are removed. ABC supports several notations for different types of repeated phrases (Mansfield 2007) (Appendix B). This means for example, that if the transcribed query was the A part of a tune played twice, this would be correctly matched against the expanded A part of a tune from the corpus.

Finally all notes are transformed to be in the same register. All octave (`',`) indicators are removed and all lower case characters in the ABC notation of tunes are transformed to upper case. This removes the skewing of melodic similarity measuring as a result of reversing (P3) in the interpretation of a tune.

6.8 Matching

One final transformation is carried out on strings from the corpus before they are compared with transcribed strings. Occasionally, strings from the corpus are shorter than transcribed strings. For example, the transcribed string might be from a double reel, while the string from the corpus could be from a single reel (a tune half the length). In order to gain the maximal usage from the transcription, corpus strings shorter then transcribed strings are duplicated until their length is greater than the length of the transcribed string. This approximates what a real musician would do in order to extend the duration of a tune (Vallely 1999; Mansfield 2007; Zheng & Duggan 2007).

The minimum edit distance (section 4.4) $eF(c)$ for each string c from the corpus Z then calculated using a cost of one for insertions, deletions and substitutions, for each pair consisting of the transcribed string s in substrings of c. In order to take a breath, a musician must leave out a note. Therefore, the edit distance cost function is adapted so that breath marks ("z") are allowed to match any character. This addresses P5 from Chapter 1. The substring variation of the classic edit distance algorithm, described in (Navarro & Raffinot 2002) and discussed in section 4.4 is used to search for the minimum edit distance for a search string in substrings of a target string. This way any phrase from a tune can be matched; not just complete tunes and not just incipits. MATT2 returns the top ten matching tunes in order of ascending distance from the automatically transcribed query string.

6.9 Interface

MATT2 is developed in Java. A screenshot of the system is presented in Figure 43.

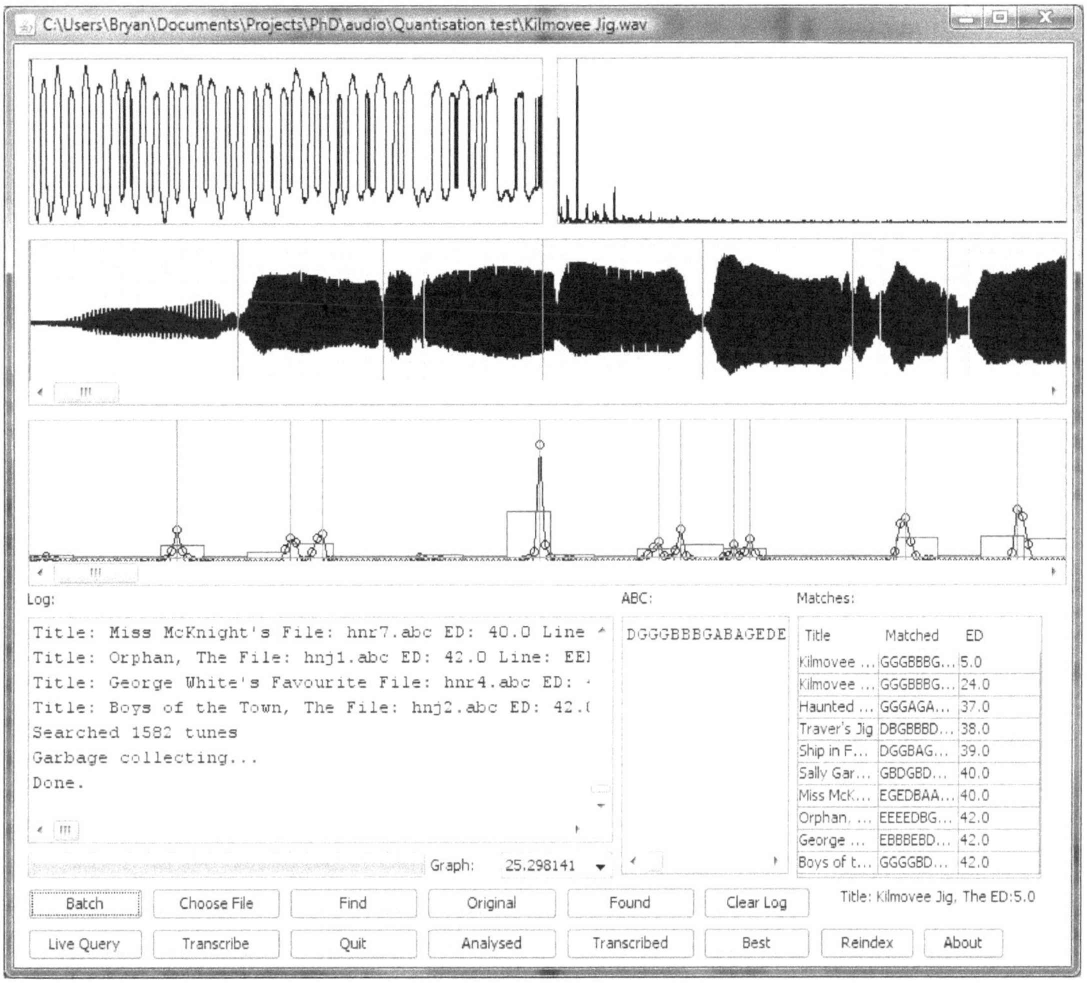

Figure 43: Screenshot of MATT2

The interface to MATT2 displays several useful plots of the outputs of each stage in the transcription and the matching algorithm such as the current frame being analysed, the onset detection function and the FFT of each detected note (the white graph). Additionally, the interface displays the transcription in ABC notation and the title of the current closest tune match. MATT2 can also play the original WAV file being analysed, the transcribed pitches, the transcription in ABC notation, the closest match and any of the matched tunes. When the matching algorithm terminates, MATT2 can play and display any of the top ten closest matching tunes, with their corresponding edit distances. It can also operate in batch mode where it will attempt to annotate all the WAV files in a folder. MATT2 also keeps several log files as it annotates through files in a folder. The source code for MATT2 is available under the GNU General Public License v2 from:

`http://code.google.com/p/matt2/`

6.10 Conclusions

In this chapter MATT2, a new system for annotating recordings of traditional Irish dance music with metadata was described. MATT2 combines a novel transcription system which makes use of ODCF to detect onsets and a pitch spelling algorithm based on Brendan Breathneach's observations about the transcription of traditional Irish music which provides transposition invariance for the keys and modes used to play traditional music thus addressing P1, P2 P4 and P6 given in Chapter 2. This complete, working system represents Contribution 1.

The automatic pitch spelling approach employed in MATT2, minimises pitch spelling errors by quantising to the nearest likely playable note and represents Contribution 2. A new algorithm for dealing with ornamentation and compensating for "the long note" in traditional music called Ornamentation Filtering was presented that addresses P7 and P8 given in Chapter 2. A matching technique was presented that aligns audio queries with complete tunes from a corpus and that takes account of phrasing and reversing effects in the interpretation of traditional Irish dance music thus addressing P3 and P5 from Chapter 2.

Compensating for expressiveness using the proposed Ornamentation Filtering algorithm, normalising ABC scores and adapting the edit distance cost function to account for breath marks represents Contribution 3.

In order to evaluate the effect of the expressiveness compensation algorithms described in this chapter, Chapter 7 presents a comprehensive evaluation of MATT2 and compares it with two standard approaches suggested by the MIR literature, reviewed in Chapter 4 and Chapter 5. The recordings used in the experiment described in Chapter 7 are of whole tunes and short excerpts of tunes. Chapter 8 presents Contribution 4, a new algorithm and an evaluation of the algorithm for annotating recordings of sets of tunes.

7 Evaluation

This chapter presents an experimental evaluation of MATT2. In order to evaluate the effect of the expressiveness compensation algorithms described in Chapter 6, MATT2 is compared with two alternative approaches common in the MIR literature that do not make any accommodation for expressive performance. These are an approach based on comparing melodic contours and an approach based on comparing pitch intervals. Studies of experimental evaluations sometimes critique the number of systems that are not evaluated on real-world problems (Prechelt 1996; Salzberg 1999) and so in order to evaluate MATT2, audio was acquired in real world conditions. Test audio contains fifty whole tunes and fifty short incipits and excerpts from tunes played by a variety of musicians on traditional instruments. This chapter also includes statistical significance tests that evaluate the significance of the results of the experiment. The work reported in this chapter was first presented at the 2009 International Computer Music Conference as "Compensating for Expressiveness in Queries to a Content Based Music Information System" (Duggan et al. 2009).

7.1 Experiment

For the experiment described in this section, audio was acquired from real-world sources including field-recordings of musicians, traditional music sessions and commercial recordings. More than thirty musicians made recordings which were used in testing. Appendix A lists the audio used in the experiment.

Field recordings were made in imperfect conditions such as a kitchen in a house, a school room, various concerts in public halls and various public sessions, and contain ambient noise such as chairs moving, doors opening, foot taps and crowd noises. The recordings were edited so that the audio being tested contained fifty whole tunes (WT) and fifty short excerpts (E) from tunes. Deliberately challenging audio was used, including degraded archive recordings, flute duets, flute and fiddle duets, fiddle solos, sessions with ensembles of up to ten musicians and ensemble playing in unusual keys with background noise. Table 19 classifies the test audio used by instrument.

Instrument	**WT**	**E**
Solo flute	21	29
Solo tin-whistle	4	6
Flute duets	3	0
Solo fiddle	5	0
Solo pipes	2	2
Flute & fiddle duet	4	1
Flute & guitar duet	1	3
Flute & pipes duet	0	1
Solo concertina	2	4
Solo accordion	1	1
Sessions (ensembles of up to 10 musicians)	7	3
Total	**50**	**50**

Table 19: Sources of MATT2 test audio by instrument

Table 20 classifies the test audio by fundamental note.

Fundamental note	**WT**	**E**
Bb	2	3
C	0	1
D	39	42
Eb	4	2
F	5	2
Total	**50**	**50**

Table 20: Sources of MATT2 test audio by fundamental note

Table 21 gives the durations in seconds of the audio used in the test. Audio used to develop the system was removed from the test audio.

	WT	E
Minimum	21.23	4.74
Maximum	84.00	65.43
Average	43.91	14.17

Table 21: Durations in seconds for MATT2 test audio

The ABC corpus mostly contains single instances of each tune. Some entries in the corpus are variations of the same tune, but no more than three variations of each tune is included and usually only a single variation is included if at all. In most cases the aim therefore is to retrieve the single match from the corpus and annotate the audio query recording appropriately and so precision and recall scores are not appropriate in this experiment (section 8.3). Three scenarios are evaluated:

MC-ED: Edit distance matching based on melodic contours. This approach is common in the literature and is similar to the approaches employed by (Downie 1999; Ghias et al. 1995; McNab et al. 1997; McNab et al. 1996; McPherson & Bainbridge 2001; Lu et al. 2001; Rho & Hwang 2004; Prechelt & Typke 2001). To perform this experiment, the corpus was first converted to MIDI format using the open source ABC2MIDI program from the ABC Music Project (Shlien 2008). ABC2MIDI creates a MIDI rendering of a transcription in ABC format. Significantly, ABC2MIDI creates MIDI versions of any ornaments included in the transcription. The sequence of MIDI note numbers (Table 22) was extracted from each file and an algorithm was developed to convert this sequence to a melodic contour of "U", "D" and "S" characters (section 4.1). Some examples of the output of the algorithm are given in Figure 44.

d2BG dGBG|~G2Bd efge|d2BG dGBG|1 ABcd edBc:|2 ABcd edBd||

|:g2bg egdg|(3efg dg edBd|1 g2bg egdB|ABcd edBd:|2 gabg efge|dega bage||

74,71,67,74,67,71,67,69,67,71,74,76,78,79,76,74,71,67,74,67,71,67,69,71,72,74,76,74,71,72,74,71,67,74,67,71,67,69,67,71,74,76,78,79,76,74,71,67,74,67,71,67,69,71,72,74,76,74,71,74,79,83,79,76,79,74,79,76,78,79,74,79,76,74,71,74,79,83,79,76,79,74,71,69,71,72,74,76,74,71,74,79,83,79,76,79,74,79,76,78,79,74,79,76,74,71,74,79,81,83,79,76,78,79,76,74,76,79,81,83,81,79,76

DDUDUDUDUUUUUDDDDUDUDUUUUUDDUUDDUDUDUDUUUUUDDDDUDUDUUUUUDDUUUDDUDUDUUDUDDDUUUDDUDDDUUUUDDUUUDDUDUDUUDUDDDUUUUDDUUDDUUUUDDD

Figure 44: Various representations of the tune "Come West Along the Road". (See also Figure 3, Figure 42 and Figure 15)

The transcription system was adapted so that instead of quantising to the nearest playable note as described in section 6.3, the detected pitches were spelled as the closest MIDI note numbers and the sequence of MIDI note numbers was extracted from the transcription. As can be seen in Table 22, MIDI notes are quantised to the nearest semitone.

Octave #	Note Numbers											
	C	C#	D	D#	E	F	F#	G	G#	A	A#	B
-1	0	1	2	3	4	5	6	7	8	9	10	11
0	12	13	14	15	16	17	18	19	20	21	22	23
1	24	25	26	27	28	29	30	31	32	33	34	35
2	36	37	38	39	40	41	42	43	44	45	46	47
3	48	49	50	51	52	53	54	55	56	57	58	59
4	60	61	62	63	64	65	66	67	68	69	70	71
5	72	73	74	75	76	77	78	79	80	81	82	83
6	84	85	86	87	88	89	90	91	92	93	94	95
7	96	97	98	99	100	101	102	103	104	105	106	107
8	108	109	110	111	112	113	114	115	116	117	118	119
9	120	121	122	123	124	125	126	127				

Table 22: MIDI note numbers (adapted from (Huber 1991))

From this sequence of MIDI note numbers, the melodic contour was generated. Matching was performed using Navarro & Raffinot's (2002) substring edit distance algorithm.

TI-ED: A transposition invariant edit distance matching between the corpus and transcribed queries was tested in the second scenario. For this experiment, the expressiveness compensation algorithms (Ornamentation Filtering, phrasing compensation, reversing and lengthening) described in Chapter 6 were not employed. This was carried out to evaluate the impact of these algorithms. To perform this experiment, distances were calculated using (Navarro & Raffinot 2002) substring edit distance algorithm between the MIDI note sequences for the query and MIDI note sequences derived from strings from the corpus as described above, with a transposition invariant edit distance cost function (Lemstrom & Ukkonen 2000). This experiment might be considered similar to the SEMEX system described in 5.1 (although technically SEMEX works entirely on symbols and does not have a transcription system). It is also similar to the many QBH systems that employ edit distances based on pitch intervals described in Chapter 5.

MATT2: The complete system as described in Chapter 6. The system annotated the test audio as described in Chapter 6. In this experiment, the expressiveness compensation algorithms of Ornamentation Filtering and ABC corpus normalisation were employed. Pitches were spelled as ABC characters as described in section 6.6 and transcriptions (and the corpus) were normalised to take account of reversing as described in section 6.7. The edit distance cost function was adapted to allow breath marks to match any character as described in section 6.8.

For each of the three scenarios, the results were validated by a human expert who verified the accuracy of the annotations by proof listening to confirm that the retrieved scores were correct. Each test audio file was annotated with the metadata from the corpus string with the minimum distance. In this way, the experiment only considered true positives *TP* and false positives *FP*. If there are *T* audio files to be annotated, then scores for *accuracy* and *error* are calculated as per Equation 17.

$$accuracy = \frac{TP}{T} \quad error = \frac{FP}{T}$$

Equation 17

7.2 Results

Table 23 presents the accuracy and error rates for the MC-ED, TI-ED and MATT2 for the fifty whole tunes (WT) and for the fifty excerpts (E).

	MC-ED		TI-ED		MATT2	
	WT	E	WT	E	WT	E
TP	10	1	28	19	47	46
FP	40	49	22	31	3	4
Total	50	50	50	50	50	50
accuracy	0.20	0.02	0.56	0.38	0.94	0.92
error	0.80	0.98	0.44	0.62	0.06	0.08
Total	1.00	1.00	1.00	1.00	1.00	1.00

Table 23: Results for MC-ED, TI-ED and MATT2 for WT and E

Table 24 gives the combined results for WT and E. When the results are combined, it can be seen that MC-ED gives 11% accuracy, TI-ED gives 47% accuracy and MATT2 gives 93% accuracy. MC-ED gives very poor accuracy and a high error rate for both WT and E. This can be attributed to the effect of ornamentation notes at higher and lower pitches on the generation of Parsons Code and to the minimal discriminative power of this format. TI-ED is able to successfully annotate about half the whole tunes and less than half of the excerpts. TI-ED is therefore better at discriminating melodies than MC-ED, even though the effect of ornamentation is still evident in the results. MATT2 however gives 93% accuracy for both WT and E leading to the conclusion that the expressiveness compensation algorithms employed have significantly increased annotation accuracy.

	MC-ED	TI-ED	MATT2
TP	11	47	93
FP	89	53	7
Total	100	100	100
accuracy	0.11	0.47	0.93
Error	0.89	0.53	0.07
Total	1.00	1.00	1.00

Table 24: Combined WT and E results for the 3 systems

7.3 Significance

The probability that these results could be achieved by random selection can be calculated with a binomial distribution. A Bernoulli process must possess the following properties (Walpole 2002):

1. An experiment consists of n queries to a system.
2. Each query results in an outcome that is classified as either a true positive or a false positive.
3. The probability of success denoted by p, is the same for all queries.
4. Repeated queries are independent.

In practice, there are some variations of the same tune in the corpus used in these experiments however for the purposes of this test; it is assumed that there is only one correct match in the corpus for each query audio file. Each query therefore can be considered as a Bernoulli trial with a possible outcome of either true positive or false positive. A true positive indicates that the query audio file was annotated with the correct melody from the corpus, with a false positive indicating that an incorrect melody was returned as the closest match. A Bernoulli trial can result in a true positive with a probability of p and a false positive with a probability of $q = 1 - p$. These experiments can therefore be considered as a Bernoulli process and consequently the probability of getting the results given in Table 24 using random selection can be calculated. The number of true positives in n Bernoulli trials is known as a binomial random variable and is denoted by X. The probability distribution of X (known as the binomial distribution) is denoted by $b(x;n, p)$. This can be calculated as per Equation 18, where $\binom{n}{x}$ is the binomial coefficient and p is the probability of a true positive in a single trial.

$$b(x; n, p) = \binom{n}{x} p^x q^{n-x}$$

Equation 18

The binomial coefficient $\binom{n}{x}$ is equal to the number of partitions of n outcomes into two groups, with x in one group and n-x in the second group. This can be calculated as per Equation 19.

$$\binom{n}{x} = \frac{n!}{x!\,(n-x)!}$$

Equation 19

If a query audio file is annotated by selecting a single melody at random from the corpus of 1582 melodies then the probability p of selecting the correct melody is calculated as $\frac{1}{1582}$. Table 25 gives the probabilities of getting x true positives, by random selection, calculated as per Equation 18.

x	N	p	$b(x; n, p)$
0	100	$\frac{1}{1582}$	0.93873
1	100	$\frac{1}{1582}$	0.05938
2	100	$\frac{1}{1582}$	0.00186
3	100	$\frac{1}{1582}$	0.00004
>0	100	$\frac{1}{1582}$	0.06127
>2	100	$\frac{1}{1582}$	0.00004
>3	100	$\frac{1}{1582}$	0.00000

Table 25: Probability of *x* true positives by random selection

The probability of getting no true positives is 0.93873 at five decimal places. It is therefore likely that with random selection, none of the tunes will be annotated correctly. The probability of annotating more than three tunes correctly by random selection approaches zero at five decimal places. It can therefore be concluded that each of the systems tested, MC-ED, TI-ED and MATT2 performs significantly better than random selection of tunes from the corpus.

The error rates of the three systems can be analysed using a McNemar's test which is used to determine statistical significance when comparing the performance of systems (Dietterich 1998). To apply McNemar's test, queries used to develop the system are removed from the set of queries used to evaluate the system. Given two systems A and B, for each example $x \in T$, where T is the set of test queries, a contingency table is constructed as per Table 26.

Number of examples misidentified by both A & B	Number of examples misidentified by A and identified correctly by B
Number of examples misidentified by B and identified correctly by A	Number of examples identified correctly by both A and B

Table 26: McNemar's contingency table

The notation given in Table 27 is used to represent the cells in Table 26 where $n = n_{00} + n_{01} + n_{10} + n_{11}$ is the total number of examples in the test set T.

n_{00}	n_{01}
n_{10}	n_{11}

Table 27: Representation of McNemar's contingency table

A null hypothesis is a hypothesis set up to be nullified, refuted, or rejected in order to support an alternative hypothesis. Under the null hypothesis, the systems being compared should have the same error rate, which means that $n_{01} = n_{10}$. McNemar's test is based on a X^2 (chi squared) test for goodness of fit which compares the distribution of counts expected under the null hypothesis to the observed counts. X^2 is calculated as per Equation 20 (Dietterich 1998).

$$X^2 = \frac{(|n_{01} - n_{10}| - 1)^2}{n_{01} + n_{10}}$$

Equation 20

This statistic is distributed (approximately) as X^2 with one degree of freedom.

If the null hypothesis is correct then the probability that $X^2_{1,0.95} > 3.841459$ is less than 0.5. The null hypothesis can therefore be rejected in favour of the hypothesis that the two systems have different performance. McNemar's test has a lower probability of incorrectly detecting a difference when no difference exists but it also possesses good discriminative power (the ability to detect a difference where one does exist) (Dietterich 1998).

To establish the statistical significance of the results given in section 7.2, contingency tables are presented in Table 28, Table 29 and Table 30. Table 28 presents a contingency which that compares MC-ED and TI-ED. Table 29 presents a contingency table which compares MC-ED and MATT2, while Table 30 presents a contingency table which compares TI-ED and MATT2. The data used to generate these tables are given in Appendix F.

53	36
0	11

Table 28: Contingency table for MC-ED and TI-ED

7	82
0	11

Table 29: Contingency table for MC-ED and MATT2

7	46
0	47

Table 30: Contingency table for TI-ED and MATT2

The X^2 value for MC-ED and TI-ED (Table 28) is calculated as per Equation 20 as 34.03. It can therefore be concluded that as $X^2 > 3.841459$, TI-ED improves on the annotation accuracy of MC-ED. The X^2 value for MC-ED and MATT2 (Table 29), calculated as per Equation 20 is 80.01. The X^2 value for TI-ED and MATT2 (Table 30) calculated as per Equation 20 is 44.02. That both of these values are above 3.841459 indicates that there is a statistical significant improvement in the performance of MATT2 compared with both MC-ED and TI-ED.

While Dietterich (1998) suggests a significance level of 0.05, in all cases the X^2 scores calculated are above the significance level of 0.001 for a X^2 test with one degree of freedom which is 10.83. If the null hypothesis is correct that the systems performance is equal, then the probability that $X^2 > 10.83$ is less than 0.001. It can therefore be concluded that the improvement in annotation accuracy offered by MATT2 over MC-ED and TI-ED is statistically significant at a confidence level of 0.001.

7.4 Conclusions

Chapter 7 presented an experimental evaluation that used MATT2 from Chapter 6 to annotate one hundred real-world field recordings of traditional music consisting of whole tunes and extracts from sessions, classes and concerts. Results were reported using standard measures from the field of information retrieval (IR) of accuracy and error and the system was compared to two alternatives suggested by the literature.

From the results of the experiment, it can be concluded that MATT2 substantially improves on pitch contour representations of music applied to MIR for traditional music. Pitch contour representations give very poor accuracy when queries and the corpus contain ornamentation. In comparing MATT2 with a SEMEX like approach, it is evident that the proposed system also substantially improves accuracy over a system that has better discriminative power than Parsons Code, but has no specific accommodation for expressiveness. Further, to the authors knowledge, MATT2 represents a unique attempt to adapt MIR to the specific characteristics of traditional Irish dance music.

The experiments presented in this chapter give MATT2 an accuracy of 93% for the one hundred real world queries against a 1582 piece corpus. By comparison, Cornell's Query-By-Humming (Ghias et al. 1995) reports accuracy of 90% for queries of between ten and twelve notes against a corpus of 183 pieces. Tuneserver (Prechelt & Typke 2001) is reported as having 44% accuracy for 100 whistled queries against its corpus of 10,370 pieces. The QBH system described by Lu *et al.* (2001) has an accuracy of 59% for queries against a database of 1000 pieces, while Ryynanen & Klapuri (2008) report an accuracy of 89% for 2797 sung queries against a 6030 piece corpus. MATT2 therefore compares very favourably with other similar systems.

In successfully testing MATT2 with audio acquired from real world sources it can be further concluded that the approaches outlined in Chapter 6 are robust to variations in musician, style and instrument and it is hoped that the work presented can be further developed for use on the many thousands of hours of archived recordings of traditional music that currently exist and that are being collected representing an important contribution to the traditional music community.

8 Annotating Sets of Tunes Played Segue

The work described in Chapter 6 solves the problem of annotating single tunes, however in traditional music tunes are rarely played singly. More commonly tunes are played in groups of at least two tunes known as a set of tunes. The aim of this chapter is to present a new algorithm for annotating sets of traditional Irish dance tunes.

A set typically consists of two, three or four tunes played in succession without an interval (Vallely 1999; Duggan et al. 2008b). Typically each tune in the set is played twice or three times before musicians advance to the subsequent tune in the set. A *turn*[5] in a tune represents the point when the B or subsequent part of the melody is introduced. For the purposes of this work, the meaning is expanded so that a turn in a set is taken to mean the time when a repetition of a tune begins or a second or subsequent tune is introduced. As tunes in sets are always in the same time signature and often in the same key, the challenge therefore is in segmenting sets into tunes and repetitions. Carson (1997) writes:

> *"Such is the bent of Irish traditional music that tunes repeat: they are played at least twice, or maybe three, four or more times; then the players generally change to another tune. Getting "the change" is a skill; it has to be watched for, and listened for even if the number of repeats has been determined in advance (some players can't count). If the repeats have not been predetermined, the players will use body language to communicate the change – eyes, shoulders, elbows, knees, feet and hands may be deployed.*

---

[5] A *turn* in traditional music is distinguished here from a turn in classical music, which is a four note ornament with a similar note sequence to a roll in traditional music (Virginia Tech 2009)

Hence the manic widening of the flute-player's eyes at the end of the first tune the third time round, or the shaking of her head which means you play the first tune again. If not agreed in advance, it will be assumed that the second tune will always be that which is normally associated with the first; that is they will form a set, as in 'The Boys of Ballisodare' and 'The Five Mile Chase', or 'The Sally Gardens' and 'The Sligo Maid'. But sometimes there may be two or three possibilities for the second tune in the set, or you are playing with unfamiliar musicians who have a different notion of the set. Or maybe someone is inspired to form a new set there and then..."

The approach presented in this chapter addresses this problem by making use of melodic similarity *profiles* calculated using Navarro & Raffinot's (2002) variant of the *edit distance* string matching algorithm described in section 4.4 which searches for strings in substrings of a target string. The TANSEY (Turn ANnotation from SEts using SimilaritY profiles) algorithm described in this chapter can retrieve the start and end of each repetition of a tune, can count the repetitions and can identify the title and associated metadata associated with each tune in a set. This chapter also includes experimental results using precision and recall scores for the algorithm which establish its effectiveness. Work in this chapter was originally presented at the Ninth International Conference on Music Information Retrieval (ISMIR) as "Machine Annotation of Sets of Traditional Irish Dance Tunes" (Duggan, et al. 2008b).

8.1 Sets of traditional Irish dance tunes

Traditional Irish dance tunes are typically played as sets. Certain common sets were originally put together to accompany set dances (Vallely 1999), while other sets have become popular as a result of recordings made by emigrant Irish musicians in America during the early part of the twentieth century. Figure 45 shows a waveform plot from a turn from one tune to the subsequent tune played in a set.

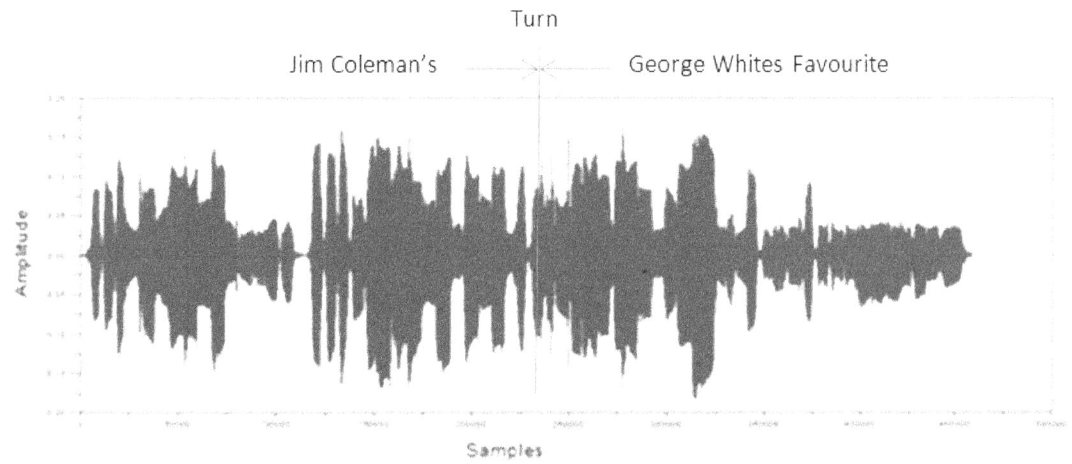

Figure 45: Waveform of the last phrase from the tune "Jim Coleman's" and the first phrase from the tune "George Whites Favourite" played in a set

The tunes were played on a concert flute and as can be seen in the plot, there is no obvious indication of the end of the first tune and the start of the second tune. Maddage *et al.* and other audio segmentation approaches generally look for repetitive patters in a music recording (Maddage et al. 2004). This is not the case in the approach presented in this chapter, where each tune in the set can be played once or many times. The origin of many sets of tunes is unknown and musicians often compile new sets "on the fly" in traditional music sessions.

8.2 TANSEY (Turn ANnotation from SEts using SimilaritY profiles) Algorithm

In this section TANSEY is described. TANSEY is an enhancement to MATT2 described in the previous chapter. TANSEY makes use of the transcription algorithm and expressiveness compensation algorithms from the previous chapter.

The purpose of TANSEY is to annotate tunes played in sets consequently TANSEY will now be described.

The shortest tune in the corpus Z used by TANSEY is a single jig. A single jig sj is a tune in 6/8 time with an A and B part played singly (forty eight quaver notes in duration). The length of sj is given by $|sj|$. The shortest possible set therefore would contain two single jigs (ninety six notes) played with no repetitions. To annotate a set of tunes, the input audio is first analysed, transcribed, ornamentation filtered and normalised as described in sections 6.2, 6.3, 6.4, 6.5, 6.6, and 6.8, to produce t, a string in the reduced alphabet of the ABC music notation language. The vector N consisting of $Nj = \{os, of, dS, f\}$, where os_j is the onset point in samples, of_j is the offset point and dS_j is the length of the segment in samples, given by $of_j - os_j$ and f_j is the detected pitch (section 6.2) is retained for later use as this vector contains the onset times of all the notes in t. TANSEY first uses a heuristic to determine if the string of transcribed notes t is longer than the length of the shortest set $|sj| \times 2$. When this is the case, the TANSEY algorithm is used instead of the minimum edit distance algorithm described in sections 4.4 and 6.8. Pseudocode for the TANSEY algorithm is presented in Figure 46.

The TANSEY algorithm first extracts a substring ss from t the transcription. If the length ss is given by $|ss|$, then $|ss| = |sj|$ at position $p=1$ in t. TANSEY then searches the corpus Z using the edit distance algorithm described in sections 4.4 and 6.8 to find the closest match for ss. When a match is found TANSEY knows the name of the first tune and has c', a transcription of the tune played with no repetitions from the corpus Z. TANSEY then generates a similarity profile *edp* for c', the matching tune, in t the transcription. The profile *edp* is given as the last row of the edit distance matrix and can be understood as the positions where substrings in t match c' with the minimum edit distance .

```
p ← 0
rem ← length(t) - p
while (rem >= sj)
begin
  ss ← substring(t, p, p + sj)
  foreach (c in Z)
  begin
      ed_c ← min(ed(ss, c))
      if (ed_c < min_ed)
      begin
        min_ed ← ed_c
        c' ← c
      end
  end
  edp ← ed(c', t)
  edp ← normalise(edp)
  edp ← filter(edp, 10)
  th ← 0.3
  v ← troughs(edp, th)
  foreach (tr in v)
  begin
    convertToTime(tr)
  end
  r ← length(v)
  p ← v[r]
  print c', r
  rem ← length(t) - p
end
```

Figure 46: Pseudocode for the TANSEY set annotation algorithm

Figure 47 shows the similarity profiles for the set of tunes "Jim Coleman's", "George Whites Favourite" and "the Virginia" played in a set. The algorithm has identified the first tune as "Jim Coleman's" and has subsequently generated a similarity profile (plot B in Figure 47) for the first tune in the transcription. The two troughs in this graph indicate the end of the two repetitions of the tune in the transcription. These can be considered as turns in the set.

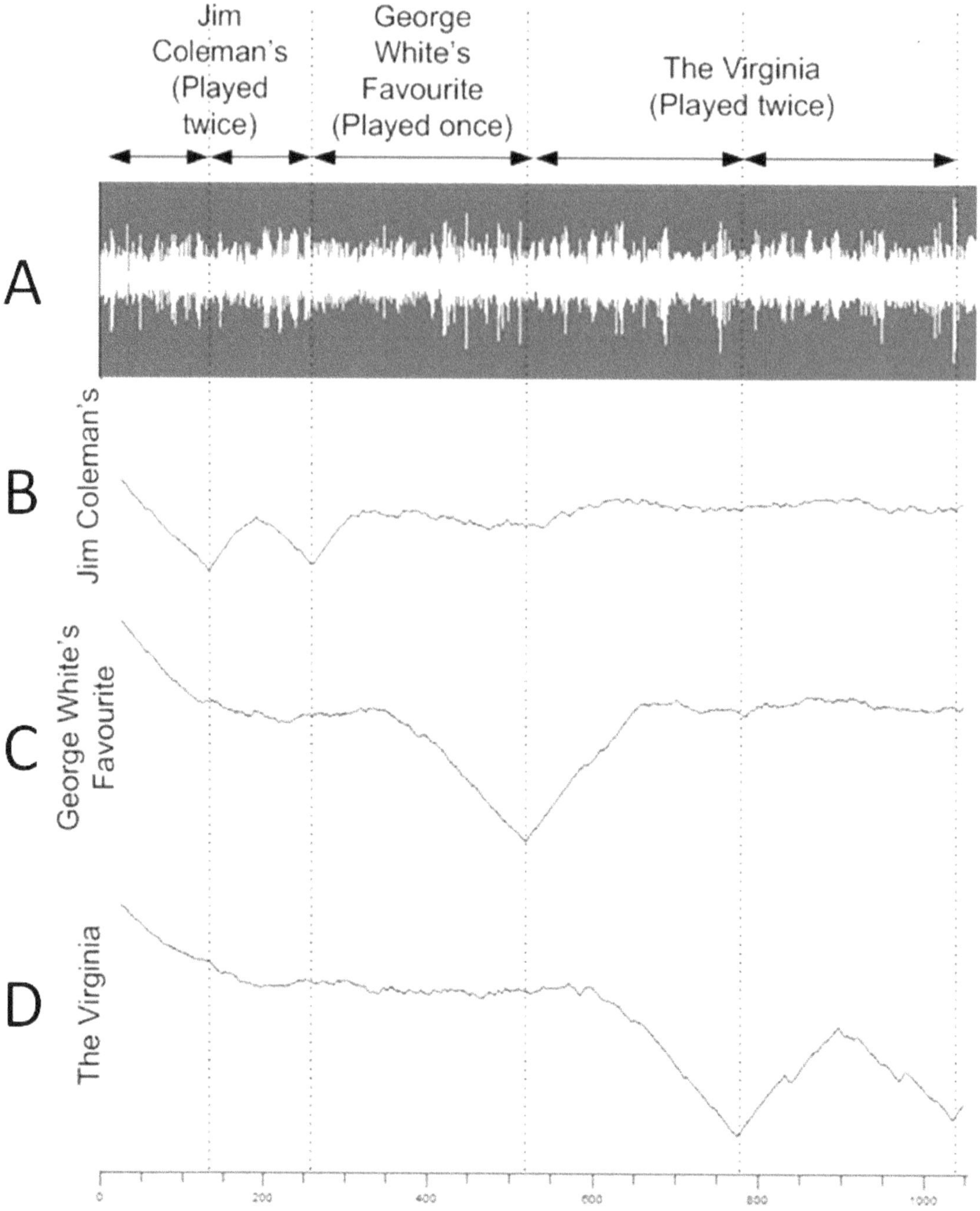

Figure 47: Similarity profiles for three tunes played in a set

The TANSEY algorithm passes the profile through a low pass filter which filters frequencies less than 10Hz. This has the effect of smoothing the profile. An example of a smoothed similarity profile is given in Figure 48. This graph illustrates plot B in Figure 47 after low pass filtering has been applied.

The algorithm then detects troughs in the graph less than a threshold initially set to $t=0.3$. The algorithm varies this threshold dynamically by trying different values until the number of troughs in the graph is between one and five. It is rare in traditional music for a tune to be played more than five times in a set.

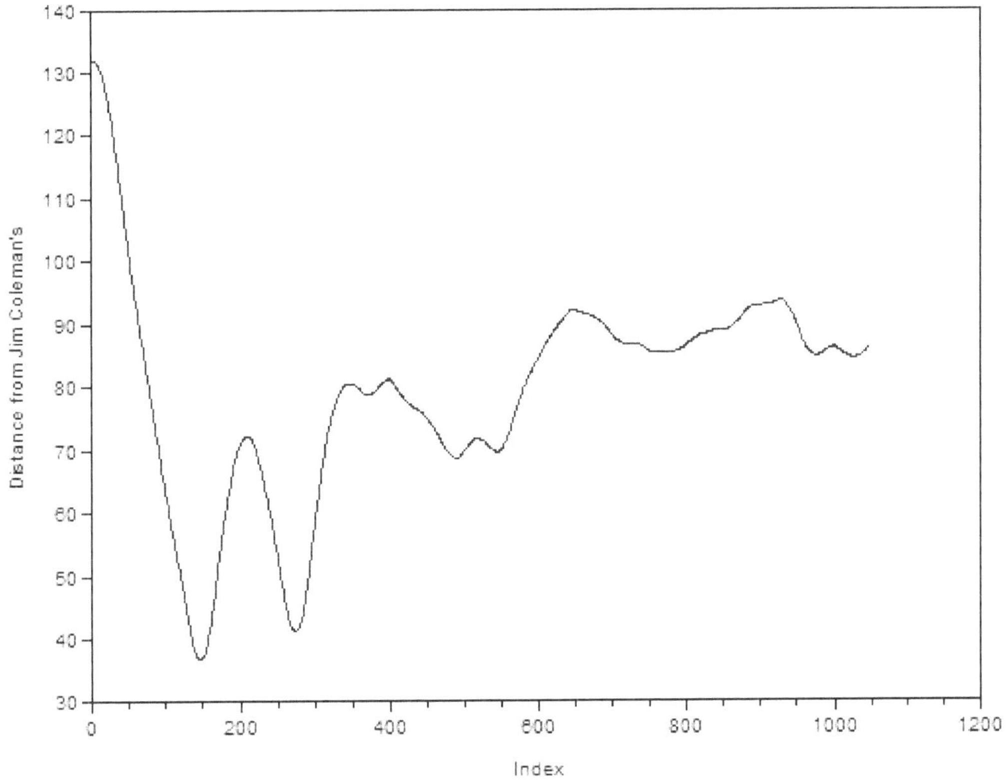

Figure 48: Filtered version of plot B from Figure 47.

The trough detection algorithm in TANSEY returns a vector of troughs v, such that $|v|$ is the number of troughs (elements in the troughs vector) and the elements in v are the positions of the bottom of the troughs. A heuristic is applied which eliminates troughs less than $|sj|$ apart, which removes consecutive troughs which might be marked as false positives. A trough in TANSEY need only have a *descending* wall as a trough can occur at the end of a tune and hence may not contain an ascending wall. An example of this is the plot D in Figure 47. Each element in v is used to retrieve the note onset time os_j from N. This value is output from the algorithm as the turn time.

The algorithm repeats this process with a new p given as the last entry in the troughs vector to extract the second and subsequent tunes in the set until it is no longer possible to extract a substring ss, where $|ss| = |sj|$ starting at p because we have reached the end of t. The second tune in the set, "George Whites Favourite" was played once and there is a corresponding single trough in the graph of the edit distance function (plot C in Figure 47) for the tune from the corpus c' in the transcription t. The third tune "the Virginia" was repeated twice and so there are two troughs in plot D in Figure 47.

8.3 Experiment

To evaluate MATT2, standard measures from information retrieval (IR) of *precision* and *recall* are presented (Manning 1999). These measures are based on the concept of relevancy of results. Given a retrieval strategy S, precision and recall evaluate the similarity between the set of results retrieved by S and the set of results provided by experts, thus providing an estimation of the usefulness of S. Precision gives a measure of the accuracy of a system. From an IR perspective, if a system returns ten documents and only two of the documents are relevant, then the system has a precision of 0.2. Recall counts how many relevant documents are returned. In Figure 49 *tn* is true negatives, *fp* is false positives, *tp* is true positives and *fn* is false negatives.

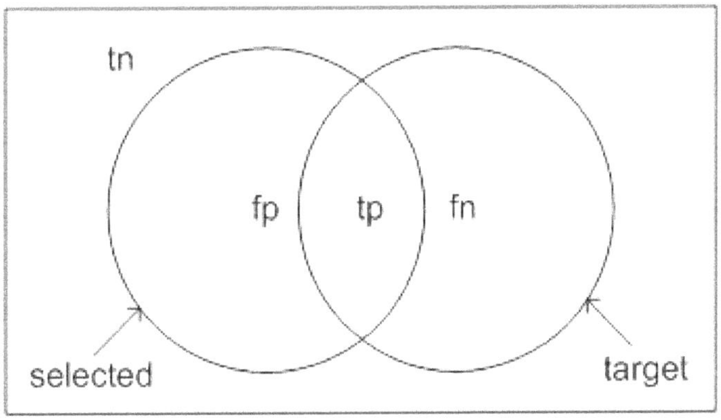

Figure 49: A diagram motivating the measures of precision and recall (Manning 1999)

In order to test the robustness of MATT2 with TANSEY, thirty audio files of musicians playing sets of tunes on traditional instruments were used. The sets consisted of single and double jigs and reels played multiple times in sets (segue). Table 31 classifies the test audio used by instrument.

Instrument	Count
Solo flute	15
Solo tin-whistle	6
Flute duet	1
Flute & fiddle duet	2
Session (ensembles of at least 5 musicians)	1
Solo concertina	3
Solo fiddle	1
Solo uilleann pipes	1

Table 31: Sources of TANSEY test audio by instrument

Table 32 classifies the test audio by fundamental note. The test audio contains mostly flute and tin-whistle music, but fiddle, uilleann pipes and concertina music was also included, where available. Appendix A details the audio used in the experiment.

Fundamental note	Count
Bb	3
D	26
F	2

Table 32: Sources of TANSEY test audio by fundamental note

Table 33 gives the durations in seconds of the audio used in the test. The total duration of the test audio annotated was 1 hour 27 minutes and 18 seconds. In total, the test audio contained 64 separate tunes with 141 turns.

Minimum	70.53
Maximum	322.08
Average	174.61
Total	5238.25

Table 33: Durations in seconds for TANSEY test audio

The end of a set is the time when the last tune in the set concludes and so this is also considered as a turn for annotation purposes. As each test audio file begins with the start of a set at a time of 0 seconds, the starts of sets are not considered. In carrying out this experiment, the aim was to establish if MATT2 could correctly identify the names of the tunes and if TANSEY could figure out the timings of turns. To establish a ground truth for the experiment, a human domain expert manually annotated the turns in the sets of tunes. A true positive *TP* is a turn annotated by the system which agrees with a human annotated turn within a threshold timeframe *tf*. The threshold used in this experiment was +/- 2 seconds.

A false positive (FP) is a turn identified by the system which does not correspond with a human annotated turn within a threshold *tf* of +/- 2 seconds. A false negative is a turn identified by the human expert, but missed by the algorithm. Precision and recall are calculated as per Equation 21 and Equation 22.

$$recall = \frac{TP}{TP + FN}$$

Equation 21

Precision is the fraction of the retrieved documents which is relevant (Equation 22).

$$precision = \frac{TP}{TP + FP}$$

Equation 22

8.4 Results

MATT2 successfully identified 63 out of the 64 tunes in the experiment, and recognised each input audio file as a set and so used the TANSEY set annotation algorithm (Table 34). Interestingly, the one tune missed was a result of the TANSEY algorithm missing a turn and hence not being able to extract a substring to use to identify the subsequent tune.

	Actual	**Percentage**
Correctly identified:	63	98.44%
Incorrectly identified:	1	1.56%
Total:	64	100.00%

Table 34: Correctly and incorrectly identified tunes

Table 35 shows a sample of the data collected in this experiment for the audio file used to generate Figure 47 and Figure 48. The full table is given in Appendix G.

The Tune column in Table 35 gives the name of the tune introduced at the time given by the Human column. The Human and Machine columns in Table 35 list the onset times in seconds for turns in the set.

Set	Tune	Human	Machine	|Human – Machine|
15	Jim Coleman's	0.00	0.00	
		20.80	21.90	1.10
	George White's Favourite	41.50	43.15	1.65
	The Virginia	83.00	84.24	1.24
		124.00	125.41	1.41
		166.30	166.78	0.48
			Average:	1.18

Table 35: Human & machine annotated turns

From this table it can be seen that for this piece of audio, TANSEY was on average within 1.18 seconds of the human annotations. The overall annotation accuracy is obtained by calculating precision and recall. Table 36 shows the annotation accuracy with a threshold t of 2.0 seconds. It can be seen from precision and recall that the algorithm provides a high degree of accuracy at detecting turns. Because the algorithm can successfully identify turns, it can also correctly extract a suitable prefix from the subsequent tune in the set and so can identify the subsequent tune. The precision score given means that 86.36% of the turns returned by the TANSEY algorithm were within two seconds of the human annotations. The recall score given means that TANSEY recalled 80.28% of the human annotated turns from the test audio. *FN*'s were caused by the algorithm failing to correctly identify the transitions between tunes in a set.

TP	*FN*	*FP*	*precision(%)*	*recall(%)*
114	28	18	86.36%	80.28%

Table 36: Annotation accuracy

When this happens the algorithm cannot extract a representative prefix from the next tune and so all subsequent turns are usually misidentified. In some cases, *FP*'s were within a few seconds of the two second threshold set. Table 37 and Figure 50 give precision and recall scores for different values of *t*.

t	*TP*	*FN*	*FP*	*precision(%)*	*recall(%)*
1	92	50	40	69.70%	64.79%
2	114	28	18	86.36%	80.28%
3	122	20	10	92.42%	85.92%
4	125	17	7	94.70%	88.03%
5	126	16	6	95.45%	88.73%
6	128	14	4	96.97%	90.14%
7	128	14	4	96.97%	90.14%
8	128	14	4	96.97%	90.14%
9	128	14	4	96.97%	90.14%
10	129	13	3	97.73%	90.85%

Table 37: Precision and recall scores for TANSEY with different values of *t*

These values are plotted in Figure 50.

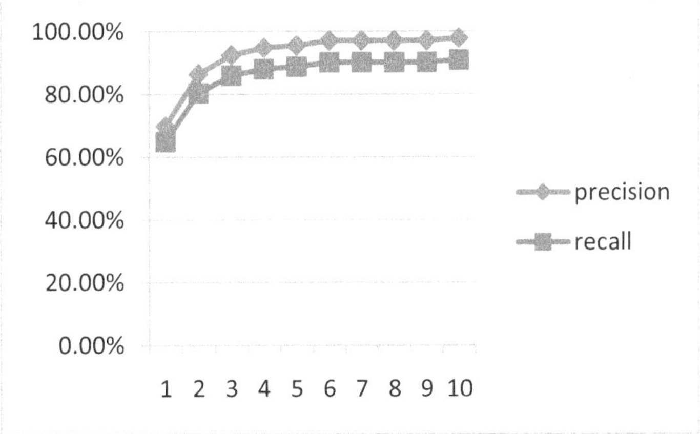

Figure 50: Graph of precision and recall scores for TANSEY with different values of *t*

8.5 Conclusions

Irish traditional dance tunes are almost never played singly. Instead, tunes are usually repeated several times individually and grouped into sets of multiple tunes played segue (without an interval). Any annotation system for traditional music must take this fact into consideration and be able to annotate a recording of a set of tunes played in this fashion. Due to tempo deviation in the performance of traditional dance tunes (section 2.2), it is difficult to determine the timings of turns in sets by using calculated timing information. Also it is possible in a set, for a single tune to be played once or many times and so looking for repetitive patterns in the overall recording is also not an option.

This chapter presented a novel algorithm which addresses this problem in the domain of Irish traditional dance music. A set can contain an arbitrary number of tunes played segue without an interval and tunes in sets are repeated an arbitrary number of times. Tunes in a set are always in the same time signature and often in the same key and so there is a significant challenge in recognising where one tune ends and the next tune starts. TANSEY solves this problem by first extracting a melodic subsequence from the start of a recording and then using that subsequence to identify the first tune. TANSEY takes advantage of the transcription and expressiveness compensation algorithms which address P1-P9 from Chapter 2, presented in Chapter 6. A similarity profile is then used to find instances of that tune in the transcription of the overall recording. The end of last instance of the tune in the similarity profile is used to identify the turn, whereby a second and subsequent subsequence can be extracted. TANSEY represents a unique solution to P9 from Chapter 2 and Contribution 4 of this PhD thesis.

An experiment was carried out using TANSEY to annotate thirty recordings of sets of tunes played on a variety of traditional instruments. Results were presented using standard measures of precision and recall from the field of information retrieval. The results of this experiment prove that the approach of using similarity profiles is effective at segmenting sets, counting repetitions and at annotating individual tunes played in a set. To the authors knowledge this is the first time this specific problem has been addressed in an MIR system and it is suggested that the proposed approach can be adapted to segmenting repeated tunes from other genres played segue.

9 Conclusions & Future Work

As described in Chapter 1, Irish traditional music is an aural tradition and for many hundreds of years, repertoire was acquired through a process of listening and learning. Due to geographic isolation of rural communities and the creativity of musicians who played and composed the music, the canon has grown to include over seven thousand compositions. The work of collectors and archivists from the pre-digital age such as Petrie, Bunting, Joyce, O'Neill, Small, Breathneach, O' Riada and Tansey, and those from the digital age such as Walshaw, Norbeck, Beimborn, Chambers and Keith has ensured that this heritage is available for future generations. It is hoped that the work presented in this thesis will make a contribution towards this goal. This chapter summarises the main contributions made and presents a number of important ways in which this work may be extended.

9.1 Conclusions

Chapter 2 distilled ten problems which make the task of Content Based Music Information Retrieval (CBMIR) challenging when applied to the domain of traditional Irish dance music. This work proposes a solution for each of these problems.

P1: Support for traditional instruments: The QBH MIR (Query-by-Humming Music Information Retrieval) systems described in Chapter 5 require a vocal articulation at the onset of new notes. Consequently, these systems typically do not give positive results when queries are presented in the form of melodies played on traditional instruments such as the concert flute or tin-whistle. These instruments have slow onsets which are difficult to detect using the onset detection techniques discussed in Chapter 3. This work presents a transcription system which makes use of Onset Detection using Comb Filters (ODCF) (Gainza et al. 2005). This algorithm was specifically developed and tested on recordings of woodwind traditional instruments. Similarly, the frequency domain harmonic energy-based pitch detection algorithm employed works well at extracting pitch features from harmonic traditional instruments. Results presented in sections 7.2 and 8.4 establish the effectiveness of the transcription system developed, in transcribing audio from a variety of traditional instruments.

P2: Commonly used keys and modes: Table 5, Table 6 and Table 7 from Chapter 2 present the fundamental notes for traditional instruments. A pitch spelling approach was presented in Chapter 6 which follows from Breathnach's (1985) observations that transcriptions should be made relative to the fundamental note of the instrument as if the fundamental note was D. This approach ignores the pitch of the instrument and quantises pitches to the nearest playable note rather than the nearest semitone. Using this pitch spelling approach, transcriptions can be compared against transcriptions from corpora in ABC format. This approach also minimises pitch spelling transcription errors that might occur if pitches were quantised to the nearest semitone and avoids the double weighting of substitutions, insertions and deletions that occurs when edit distances are calculated on pitch intervals.

P3: Reversing: Reversing as an expressiveness technique was described in Chapter 2. Reversing means that segments of melodies will be transposed by an octave, with a corresponding increase in distance between queries and corpus strings. MATT2 normalises melodies by transposing all melodies to be in the same register thus compensating for this.

P4: C, C# similarity: Transcriptions of traditional tunes in ABC format represent C and C# identically as the key of a tune is encoded into the header of the tune. Also, due to the physical characteristics of the instruments used to play traditional music and fingerings used to produce C and C#, the pitches of these notes are difficult to distinguish, even for human listeners and particularly when these notes are played at speed. The pitch spelling algorithm proposed in Chapter 6 therefore spells C and C# identically, so that the pitch can be matched against a transcription in ABC format.

P5: Phrasing: When taking a breath, a musician is required to leave out one or more notes. As described in sections 6.5 and 6.8, MATT2 detects when a musician takes a breath and allows a transcribed breath to correspondingly match with any character from a corpus string.

P6: Transposition in tin-whistles: The literature suggests that the tin-whistle is the most popular of the instruments used to play traditional music, being played by most musicians as a first or second instrument. The tin-whistle is a transposing instrument as pitches are played one octave higher than written. The pitch spelling algorithm proposed in section 6.6 first automatically detects if the query was played on a tin-whistle and if so, the frequencies used by the pitch spelling algorithm are increased by twelve semitones, so that tunes are transcribed correctly.

P7: Ornamentation: The playing of ornamentation is a defining characteristic of traditional music. Ornamentation is feature which can distinguish both individual and regional styles of playing. Ornamentation can be played or not played and differences exist in the fingerings used to play ornamentation on different instruments and by different musicians. It is both difficult to transcribe accurately and will have an impact on melodic distances that do not compensate for the playing of ornamentation. Section 6.4.1 proposes a filtering method called Ornamentation Filtering which extracts the core melody from a performance played with ornamentation by merging ornamentation notes with subsequent notes. Section 6.7 describes how corpus strings in ABC notation are normalised so that the core melody is extracted. These techniques combined mean that appropriate distances can be calculated between melodies that otherwise would be considered to be different.

P8: The long note: Related to P7 is the problem of how to compensate for the playing of "the long note" as described by Small (Breathnach 1996). Ornamentation Filtering splits long notes into multiple quaver length notes in transcriptions (section 6.4.1) and expands notes from the corpus whose durations are greater than a quaver to be multiple quaver length notes (section 6.7).

P9: Tempo deviation: Section 2.2 gives Breathnach's (1963) recommended tempo for that playing of traditional tunes, but as explained, tempos vary widely from musician to musician and from performance to performance. Additionally tempo deviation is common in traditional music even within the performance of the same piece of music, particularly in ensemble playing where, if one musician increases the tempo the other musicians will usually follow. Consequently, the Ornamentation Filtering algorithm presented in section 6.4.1 makes no *a priori* assumption about the tempo used to play the query being processed and adapts to the tempo being played. It also operates on a sliding window across the audio being analysed and so takes account of tempo deviations that occur within the performance. Results presented in sections 7, 7.2, 8.3 and 8.4 with test audio recorded by many real musicians playing without a metronome establish that the work presented in this thesis works equally well with music played at various tempos.

P10: The playing of melodies in sets, segue: The playing of tunes in sets as is typical in traditional music presents particular segmentation problems. As tunes in sets are always in the same time signature, often in the same key and can be repeated several times or not at all, there is a significant challenge in counting the repetitions of each tune and determining where each new tune begins, so that the subsequent tune can be annotated. Chapter 8 proposed a novel algorithm called TANSEY (Turn ANnotation from SEts using SimilaritY profiles) which makes use of similarity profiles to address this challenge. Precision and recall scores for MATT2 with the TANSEY algorithm indicate a high degree of accuracy in segmenting sets of traditional tunes.

The work presented in Chapter 6 addresses P1-P9, the main challenges to MIR in traditional dance music. This work was validated in experiments on real world field recordings and compared with two alternatives suggested by the MIR literature in Chapter 7. From the experimental results reported in Chapter 7 it can be concluded that making specific accommodations for expressive elements present in recordings made by traditional musician's results in significant improvement in annotation accuracy over systems that do not compensate for expressiveness. Chapter 8 address P10 from Chapter 2. From the experimental results reported in sections 8.3 and 8.4, it can be concluded that the TANSEY algorithm proposed in this chapter gives good accuracy in annotating sets of traditional music.

These solutions to these problems form the basis for four specific contributions to the body of knowledge:

Contribution 1: The development of a content based music information retrieval system (MATT2) which supports the input of queries played on traditional instruments. This is addressed in solutions to P1, P2, P4 and P6 discussed in Chapter 2 and is presented in Chapter 6.

Contribution 2: The development of a new automatic transcription approach for traditional music that supports transposition invariance for the keys and modes used to play traditional music, while minimising pitch spelling errors and avoiding the double weighting of substitutions, insertions and deletions that occurs when edit distances are calculated on pitch intervals.. This is addressed in the solution to P2 presented in Chapter 6.

Contribution 3: The development of a framework of algorithms to accommodate expressiveness in audio queries to a content based music information retrieval system is addressed in solutions to P5, P7 and P8 discussed in Chapter 2 and presented in Chapter 6.

Contribution 4: The development of a novel algorithm based on similarity profiles to annotate sets of traditional Irish dance tunes. This is addressed in the solution to P10 presented in Chapter 8.

9.2 Future work

Recent work in MIR has focused on mining the web for information on artists and performances (Widmer et al. 2005; Schedl 2008). The most obvious method of disseminating the work presented in this thesis to the wider traditional music community would be to develop a version of MATT2 which could be hosted in a web browser. This is feasible as MATT2 is entirely written in Java and can be easily divided into a client component which would run as a Java applet and a server component. The client component would be responsible for recording and transcribing audio, while the server component could perform matching. This work should also extend the corpus of tunes to include those transcribed by the traditional music community and hosted by websites such as thesession.org. Interestingly, thesession.org often contains detailed discographies and discussions on each of the tunes transcribed, which could be made available through MATT2 (see Appendix E).

It is common in traditional music sessions where groups of musicians meet informally to play together for tunes to be played that none of the musicians know the names off. Consequently, musicians wishing to add the tune to their repertoire cannot easily do so. The algorithms developed could be made available on a mobile device such as a smartphone, so that CBMIR can be performed *insitu*. It would also be interesting to study the impact of the usage of such technology on the transmission of music in an aural idiom. It is hoped that disseminating this work over the web and on mobile devices will make a significant contribution decreasing the number of *gan ainm*'s being played.

In the cases where MATT2 did not identify the correct tune, it can be concluded that the transcription subsystem was not able to accurately transcribe the tune. This is also the cause of set segmentation errors reported in section 8.4. While it is often possible to identify a single tune from an approximate transcription, the TANSEY algorithm depends on there being measurable troughs in the similarity profiles, which do not occur if the transcriptions have too many errors. It is therefore proposed that improving transcription accuracy will lead to more accurate matching and this will be the focus of future work. In particular, the usage of a less sensitive onset detection function, which would be more appropriate for ensemble playing, is suggested. Currently, setting the correct fundamental note for transcription is done manually, but it should be straightforward to derive this automatically from a chromagram of the audio being analysed.

Interesting work is reported by (Repp 1992; R.B. Dannenberg et al. 1997; León & Iñesta 2004; Widmer & Goebl 2004; Widmer et al. 2005), who use various techniques to try and model the cognition of musical style. Repp's (1992) statistical analysis of performances of the same piece of piano music by twenty four pianists showed notable differences in both note level features and also phrasing between the performances. To acquire a corpus for testing, the performances were manually transcribed and thus, due to the difficulty of this task, Repp's analyses were limited to one particular piece. Later work mainly uses machine learning to induce structure level expressive patterns from music performances, often from augmented music instruments. Currently this work extracts many of the features that characterise individual and regional style such as ornamentation and phrasing, and with further development it will be possible to classify audio being annotated. One possible approach would be to use graph theory to develop models to represent the stylistic similarities between musicians and see if this maps onto real world relationships that might have led to this similarity.

One interesting feature not yet exploited is the metadata typically present in an ABC transcription. Effectively the time signature and key of an input audio file can be determined by melodic similarity with a known tune. This can be exploited in several interesting ways. Firstly, if the first tune in a set were to be identified as a reel, the search for subsequent tunes can be limited to reels, thus speeding up annotation. Conversely, if a number of reels were to be identified in a set and a single tune in a different time signature was to be identified this could be recognised as a potential error. Finally, the approaches and systems presented in this thesis have applicability in other musical genres which remains to be explored.

"They have been worn into shape by many ears...and have been contemplated often. But every time is new because the time is new, and there is no time like now...

Then he passes round the rosin and the other fiddle-players take a ritual rub of it. They start to play. They hit the time just right and everybody else joins in."

- (Carson 1997)

Appendix A – Test Audio Listing

Test audio used in the experiments described in Chapters 7 and Chapter 8 can be downloaded from:

`http://www.comp.dit.ie/bduggan/music/`

1 – 50 are the whole tunes (WT) test audio

51 – 100 are the excerpts (E) test audio

101 – 130 are the sets (S) test audio

#	Title	Source
1	Ambrose Moloney's	Solo Flute
2	Boy in the Boat, The	Solo Flute
3	Christmas Eve	Solo Flute
4	Cooley's	Solo Flute
5	Dan Breen's	Solo Flute
6	Devanny's Goat	Solo Tin-whistle
7	Fisherman's Island	Solo Fiddle
8	Jackson's	Solo Flute
9	Last Night's Fun	Solo Flute
10	Frost is all over, The	Session
11	McFadden's Favourite	Session
12	Micho Russell's	Solo Flute
13	Rolling in the Ryegrass	Solo Pipes
14	Sean Reid's	Solo Flute
15	Ship in Full Sail, The	Solo Flute
16	Sonny Martin's	Flute & Fiddle Duet
17	Speed the Plow	Flute & Guitar
18	Sweeney's Dream	Session
19	Five Mile Chase, The	Solo Fiddle
20	Ashplant, The	Session
21	Banshee, The	Flute & Fiddle Duet

22	Boys of the Town, The	Solo Flute
23	Bucks of Oranmore, The	Solo Flute
24	Burnt Old Man, The	Solo Fiddle
25	College Groves, The	Solo Fiddle
26	Corner House, The	Solo Concertina
27	Dublin Lasses, The	Session
28	Dublin Reel, The	Session
29	Earl's Chair, The	Solo Pipes
30	Golden Keyboard, The	Solo Flute
31	Green Mountain, The	Solo Flute
32	Humours of Lissadell, The	Flute & Fiddle Duet
33	Kilmovee Jig, The	Solo Flute
34	Kilmovee Jig, The	Solo Tin-whistle
35	Banks of the Liffey, The	Flute Duet
36	Morning Star, The	Solo Flute
37	Otter's Holt, The	Solo Flute
38	Ravelled Hank of Yarn, The	Solo Tin-whistle
39	Reel of Rio, The	Flute Duet
40	Roscommon Reel, The	Session
41	Salamanca Reel, The	Solo Fiddle
42	Salamanca Reel, The	Solo Tin-whistle
43	Shaskeen Reel, The	Solo Flute
44	Skylark, The	Solo Flute
45	Swallow's Tail, The	Solo Flute
46	Tarbolton, The	Solo Accordion
47	Touch Me If You Dare	Flute & Fiddle Duet
48	Traver's Jig	Solo Concertina
49	Trim the Velvet	Solo Flute
50	Young Tom Ennis	Flute Duet
51	Ambrose Moloney's	Solo Flute
52	Butlers of Glen Avenue, The	Solo Tin-whistle
53	Christy Barry's	Solo Tin-whistle
54	Colonel Frazer	Flute & Guitar
55	Cooley's	Solo Flute

56	Dan Breen's	Solo Flute
57	Dinky Dorian's	Session
58	Dowd's #9	Solo Flute
59	Drowsy Maggie	Solo Flute
60	Gorman's	Solo Flute
61	Green Fields of Rossbeigh, The	Solo Flute
62	Happy to Meet and Sorry to Part	Solo Concertina
63	Happy to Meet and Sorry to Part	Solo Flute
64	Jackson's Bottle of Brandy	Solo Concertina
65	Jackson's	Solo Flute
66	Jackson's	Solo Flute
67	Mrs McLeod's	Solo Tin-whistle
68	O'Connell's Trip to Parliament	Solo Flute
69	Paddy in London	Solo Concertina
70	Rakish Paddy	Solo Flute
71	Rolling in the Ryegrass	Solo Flute
72	Rolling in the Ryegrass	Solo Pipes
73	Scartaglen Reel, The	Session
74	Strop the Razor	Solo Flute
75	Five Mile Chase, The	Solo Flute
76	Banks of the Ilen	Session
77	Belles of Tipperary, The	Flute and Pipes
78	Bucks of Oranmore, The	Solo Flute
79	Corner House, The	Solo Concertina
80	Earl's Chair, The	Solo Pipes
81	Galway Rambler, The	Solo Flute
82	Golden Keyboard, The	Solo Flute
83	Gooseberry Bush, The	Solo Flute
84	Green Groves of Erin, The	Flute & Guitar
85	Green Groves of Erin, The	Solo Flute
86	Green Mountain, The	Solo Flute
87	Green Mountain, The	Solo Flute
88	Humours of Ballyloughlin, The	Solo Tin-whistle
89	Humours of Lissadell, The	Flute & Fiddle Duet

90	Humours of Loughrea, The	Solo Flute
91	Jolly Clamdiggers, The	Flute & Guitar
92	Killavel Jig, The	Solo Flute
93	Lilting Fisherman, The	Solo Tin-whistle
94	Skylark, The	Solo Flute
95	Sporting Pitchfork, The	Solo Tin-whistle
96	Tarbolton, The	Solo Accordion
97	Virginia, The	Solo Flute
98	Touch Me If You Dare	Solo Flute
99	Trim the Velvet	Solo Flute
100	Upstairs in a Tent	Solo Flute
101	Concert reel, The; Salute to Baltimore, The	Flute & Fiddle Duet
102	Touch Me if you Dare	Flute & Fiddle Duet
103	McKenna's 1 & 2	Flute Duet
104	Billy Brocka's; Green Mountain, The	Session
105	Happy to Meet sorry to Part; Jackson's Bottle of Brandy	Solo Concertina
106	Cornerhouse The, Boys of Portaferry, The	Solo Concertina
107	Travers Jig, Paddy in London	Solo Concertina
108	Dublin Lassies, The 5 Mile Chase	Solo Fiddle
109	Connie O ' Connells 1, 2, 3	Solo Flute
110	Cooley's set	Solo Flute
111	Down the broom, the Gatehouse maid	Solo Flute
112	Galway Rambler London Lassies	Solo Flute
113	Geese in the bog, Connaughtman's rambles	Solo Flute
114	Green mountain, John Stenson's #2	Solo Flute
115	Humours of Ballyloughlan	Solo Flute
116	Jim Coleman's, George Whites Favourite, the Virginia	Solo Flute
117	Strop the Razor, The Kilaval, Boys of the Town	Solo Flute
118	The Copper Plates (Old & new)	Solo Flute
119	The Cup of Tea, Upstairs in a tent	Solo Flute
120	The Gooseberry Bush, The Limestone Rock, the Humours of Loughrea	Solo Flute
121	The Humours of Ballyconnell	Solo Flute
122	The Skylark, Roaring Mary	Solo Flute
123	Tonres & the Kilaval	Solo Flute

124	The Wandering Minstrel	Solo Pipes
125	Christy Barry's, The Butlers of Glenavenue	Solo Tin-whistle
126	Devaney's Goat, Tommy Peoples	Solo Tin-whistle
127	Micho Russell's, The Maids of Moncisco, the Green Groves of Erin	Solo Tin-whistle
128	Scully Casey's, The Kilmovee Jig	Solo Tin-whistle
129	The Lilies in the Field, Tommy Peoples	Solo Tin-whistle
130	The Lilting Banshee, The Mouse in the Cupboard, The Tenpennybit	Solo Tin-whistle

Appendix B – ABC Notation

Appendix B presents a summary of the main features of ABC notation. It is adapted from Mansfield's (2007) tutorial available from:

`http://www.lesession.co.uk/abc/abc_notation.htm`

ABC notation is an ASCII musical notation format, devised by Chris Walshaw in 1992. ABC is widely used for the notating and distribution of traditional Irish music and is the native music notation language supported by website thesession.org amongst others. A tune notated in ABC can be played directly from the notation, or alternatively converted into MIDI, printed as sheet music or played by the computer.

Notes

Middle C is notated as:

`C`

The D immediately above middle C is notated as:

`D`

The E above which is notated as:

`E`

And so on up the scale. Starting at middle C, the notes in that octave are shown as

`CDEFGAB`

The next note up is a C again – but to show it is in the higher octave than C is shown in lowercase as:

`c`

So a full one-octave C major scale from middle C is:

`CDEFGABc`

Going from middle C to the B one octave and seven notes above that is therefore:

`CDEFGABcdefgab`

The next octave up is shown by an apostrophe immediately after the note name:

`c'`

The scale now runs two octaves from middle C:

`CDEFGABcdefgabc'`

Using the apostrophe to denote the upper octave the scale can be extended further:

`CDEFGABcdefgabc'd'e'f'g'a'b'`

The octave below middle C is shown by a comma immediately following the note name:

`B,`

This gives a range of 4 octaves, but the range can be extended further by adding more commas or apostrophes.

Notes of different lengths (the `L:` field)

ABC allows the setting of a default note length for each tune. This is set as a fraction in the tune header in the `L:` field. The following table shows the most common default note lengths for traditional music, with the equivalent terms from standard music notation:

Default note length	'English' terminology	'American' terminology
1/2	Minim	Half note
1/4	Crotchet	Quarter note
1/8	Quaver	Eighth note
1/16	Semi-quaver	Sixteenth note

For example, a tune where the default note length is a quaver, or eighth note, would have:

`L:1/8`

in its header.

The C major scale:

`CDEFGABcdefgabc'`

If this had a default note length of `L: 1/8` field is:

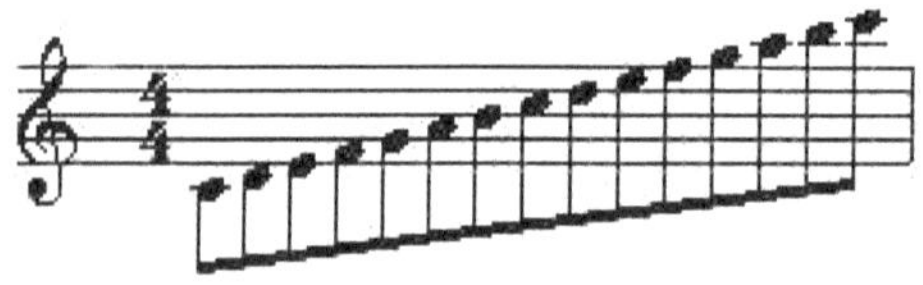

If the default length was `1/4`, `L:1/4`, the scale is now a scale of crotchets:

If the current note is half the length of the default note length, it is shown with a forward slash immediately after it:

`C/`

This can also be written as:

`C/2`

Other fractions (`/3, /5, /7, /16` etc.) are also legal.

If the current note is twice the default note length, it is shown as:

`C2`

If the current note is four times the default note length, it is shown as:

`C4`

Other multiples (`3, 5, 7, 8` etc.) are also legal.

The length of any particular note is always calculated according to the default note length of the tune.

The hornpipe rhythm is useful to illustrate an additional method to represent notes of differing length.

A hornpipe could be notated with a default note length of 1/16:

```
L:1/16
D3EF3G
```

An alternative is to set the default note length to 1/8 and use the > symbol:

```
L:1/8
D>EF>G
```

The greater than (and less than) sign can be used wherever groups of dotted notes are found.

The < symbol has the same effect in the other direction, that is shortening the first note and lengthening the second, as found in strathspeys.

Standard note lengths for different tune types are given:

Jig	1/8
Reel	1/8
Schottische	1/8
Waltz	1/4
Polka	1/8
Bourree	1/8

An L: field can be placed in the middle of a tune to denote a change of default note length.

Rests

Rests are indicated by the (lower case) letter `z`. The length of rest is set in a similar way to the length of note:

```
z4
```

Key (the K: field)

The key is specified by the K: field:

```
K:G
```

The G major scale can be written as:

`K:G`

`GABcdefg`

The G minor scale as

`K:Gm`

`GABcdefg`

In the key field sharps are noted by character # and flats by the letter `b`:

B flat	`K:Bb`
C sharp	`K:C#`

Modal keys (the Lydian, Ionian, Mixolydian, Dorian, Aeolian, Phrygian and Locrian modes) can be specified by either name in full or by the first 3 letters of the mode.

Sharps, flats and naturals

To sharpen a note it should be preceded with the circumflex or caret ^

`^c`

To flatten a note it should be preceded with an underscore _

`_B`

To naturalise a note it should be preceded with an equals sign =

`=c`

So a scale of G major could be notated as:

`GABcde^fg`

The scale of G minor as:

`GA_Bcd_efg`

However as standard Western musical notation has a key, the player automatically knows to (for example) play all Fs as F# in the key of G

Time signatures (the M: field) and the rhythm R: field

Time signatures, or meters, are shown as fractions in the M: field:

Jig	`M:6/8`
Reel	`M:4/4`
Waltz	`M:3/4`

Common time is shown as C, and cut time as C| (the letter C followed by the pipe symbol).

ABC also includes a rhythm field, `R:` which is free text and used for cataloguing and sorting collections of ABC tunes.

Bar lines and spaces

Bar lines are denoted by the pipe symbol | as:

```
ABAF DFAF|G2BG dGBG|~A3F DFAF|GBAF EFDF|
```

A double bar is shown by `||`

Repeats

The start of a repeated section is shown by:

```
|:
```

The end of a repeated section by:

```
:|
```

Where the end of one repeated section, and the beginning of the next, the symbols

```
::
```

Are used.

Numbered and alternate repeats are indicated by `[1` and `[2` (etc.). Where the start of a section coincides with a bar line the `[` symbol may be omitted:

```
DE FF |[1 GA Bc :|[2 GA BG ||
```

Can also be written as:

```
DE FF |1 GA Bc :|2 GA BG ||
```

Ornaments and grace notes

The general symbol for an ornament is the tilde ~.

The symbol is placed before the note to be ornamented:

```
~G2
```

Note that the tilde is a general mark to indicate the presence of an ornament, and does not specify a particular ornamentation - it is usually interpreted as a roll or a cran.

Triplets, quadruplets, and the various other tuplets

The basic notation for duplets, triplets and quadruplets is an opening round bracket, the number, and the notes within the tuplet:

Duplet	`(2GA`
Triplet	`(3GAB`
Quadruplet	`(4GABA`

And so on, up to

(9GABcdcBAG

The values of the particular tuplets are:

`(2`	2 notes in the time of 3
`(3`	3 notes in the time of 2
`(4`	4 notes in the time of 3
`(5`	5 notes in the time of *n*
`(6`	6 notes in the time of 2
`(7`	7 notes in the time of *n*
`(8`	8 notes in the time of 3
`(9`	9 notes in the time of *n*

Appendix C – Example Tunes in ABC Format (Norbeck 2007)

```
X:16
T:Tenpenny Bit, The
T:Three Little Drummers, The
R:jig
Z:id:hn-jig-16
M:6/8
K:Ador
eAA eAA|BAB GBd|eAA eAA|def gfg|eAA eAA|BAB GBd|~e3
gdB|BAG A3:|
|:eaa aga|bab age|eaa aga|bgf ~g3|eaa aga|bab ged|~e3
gdB|BAG A3:|

X:19
T:Old Maid, The
T:Hag at the Spinning Wheel, The
T:Maid at the Spinning Wheel, The
T:Old Maid at the Spinning Wheel, The
R:jig
D:Paddy Moloney & Sean Potts: Tin Whistles.
Z:id:hn-jig-19
M:6/8
K:G
~G3 B2G|BcA B2D|~G3 cAG|F2G AFD|~G3 B2G|BcA B2g|fed
cAF|1 GAG G2D:|2 GAG G2c||
|:BAG AFD|~D3 AFD|~D3 AFD|EFG ABc|BAG AFD|~D3 AFD|ded
cAF|1 GAG G2c:|2 GAG G2D||
|:GBd gba|gdB ecA|dBG cAG|EFG AFD|GBd gba|gdB ecA|fed
cAF|1 GAG G2D:|2 GAG G2c||
|:BAG Agd|Bgd Agd|Bgd cBA|EFG ABc|BAG AFD|~D3 AFD|ded
cAF|1 GAG G2c:|2 GAG G2D||

X:30
T:Morrison's Jig
T:Stick Across the Hob, The
R:jig
```

```
Z:id:hn-jig-30
M:6/8
K:Edor
~E3 ~B3|~E3 AFD|~E3 BAB|dcB AFD|~E3 BAB|~E3 AFD|~G3
FGA|dAG FED:|
Bee fee|aee fed|Bee fee|a2g fed|Bee fee|aee fed|gfe
d2A|BAG FED|
Bee fee|aee fed|Bee fee|faf def|~g3 gfe|def g2d|edc
d2A|BAG FED||
"Variation"
EBE BEB|EBE AFD|EDE BAB|dcB AFD|EBE BEB|EBE AFD|~G3
FGA|dAG FED:|
Bee fee|aee fed|Bee fee|a2g fed|Bee fee|aee fed|gfe
d2A|BAG FED|
Bee fee|aee fed|Bee fee|faf def|~g3 gfe|def g2d|edc
d2A|BAG FED||


X:2
T:Trim the Velvet
R:reel
S:Mary Bergin
H:Similar to "Kiss the Maid behind the Barrel", #549
D:Mary Bergin: Feadoga Stain 2.
Z:id:hn-reel-2
M:C|
K:G
~G3B AGFD|GBdB BAFA|~G3B AGFA|defd cAFA|
~G3B ~A3c|BcdB BAFA|~G3B AGFA|defd cAFA||
dgeg dg~g2|dedB cAFA|dgeg dg~g2|defd cAFA|
d3e dBGB|dGBd cAFA|dgeg dg~g2|defd cAFA||
~g3a bgaf|g2ab c'baf|g2af g2af|defd cAFA|
~g3a bgaf|g2ab c'ba2|bg~g2 af~f2|defd cAFA||
BGdG BG~G2|(3BAG dB cAFA|BGdG BG~G2|defd cAFA|
BGdG BG~G2 |DGBd cAFA|~B3G c2ce|defd cAFA||

X:6
T:Mullingar Lee, The
T:Nine Pint Coggie, The
R:reel
S:Kevin Burke
D:Milestone at the Garden
```

```
D:Hugh Gillespie 1937
Z:id:hn-reel-6
M:C|
K:Gmix
BG~G2 GFDE|F2AF CFAc|BG~G2 DEFE|1 FAdc BGGA:|2 FAdc
BG~G2||
|:~g3d Bcde|~f3c ABcd|1 ~g3d BddB|dgga bga^f:|2 ed~d2
DEFE|FAdc BGGA||

X:7
T:For the Sakes of Old Decency
T:Farewell to Old Decency
R:reel
D:Chieftains Live.
D:Michael Tubridy: The Eagle's Whistle.
Z:id:hn-reel-7
M:C|
K:G
d2BG AGEG|DGBG A2AB|d2BG AGEG|1 DGAG EGAB:|2 DGAG
EG~G2||
|:~G3B d2Bd|eaag eg~g2|~G3B d2Bd|1 dega bged:|2 dega
bage||

X:8
T:Over the Moor to Maggie
R:reel
D:Oisin: Over the Moor to Maggie.
D:Music at Matt Molloy's.
Z:id:hn-reel-8
M:C|
K:G
~G3A BGBd|efge dBAG|EAAG ABAG|EAAG A2DE|
~G3A BGBd|efge dBAG|EG~G2 BGAG|1 EGGF G2DE:|2 EGGF
G2ga||
|:~b3g ~a3f|gage d2Bd|eaag abag|eaag a2ga|
bg~g2 af~f2|gage d2Bd|eg~g2 bgag|1 eggf g2ga:|2 eggf
g2Bd||
|:~e3c d2dB|c2cA B2AG|EAAG ABAG|EAAG ABcd|
~e3c dedB|cA~A2 B2AG|EG~G2 BGAG|1 EGGF G2Bd:|2 EGGF
G2DE||
```

```
X:11
T:Star of Munster, The
R:reel
H:Also in Edor, #626. Also as jig#282
D:Chieftains Live.
Z:id:hn-reel-11
M:C|
K:Ador
c2Ac BAGB|AGEF GEDG|EAAG ABcd|e2af gfed|
c2Ac BAGB|AGEF GEDG|EAAG ABcd|ecdB cA~A2:|
|:eaag ageg|a2bg agef|~g3a gdBd|gaba gedg|
eaag ageg|a2bg agef|g2~g2 a2ga|1 bgaf gedg:|2 ~b3a
gedB||
"Variations:"
|:c2cA B2BG|AGEA GEDG|EAAB cBcd|e2ge dBGB|
(3cde cA (3Bcd BG|EAAF GEDG|EAAG ABcd|(3efg dB ~A3z:|
|:eaab ae~e2|aebe aeef|g2fa gede|geae gedB|
Aaab ae~e2|aebe agef|~g3e a2ga|1 ~b3a gedg:|2 bgaf
gedB||
```

Appendix D – Example Tunes after Normalisation

Tenpenny Bit, The

EAAEAABABGBDEAAEAADEFGFGEAAEAABABGBDEEEGDBBAGAAAEAAEAAB
ABGBDEAAEAADEFGFGEAAEAABABGBDEEEGDBBAGAAAEAAAGABABAGEEA
AAGABGFGGGEAAAGABABGEDEEEGDBBAGAAAEAAAGABABAGEEAAAGABGF
GGGEAAAGABABGEDEEEGDBBAGAAA

Old Maid, The

GGGBBGBCABBDGGGCAGFFGAFDGGGBBGBCABBGFEDCAFGAGGGDGGGBBGB
CABBDGGGCAGFFGAFDGGGBBGBCABBGFEDCAFGAGGGCBAGAFDDDDAFDDD
DAFDEFGABCBAGAFDDDDAFDDEDCAFGAGGGCBAGAFDDDDAFDDDDAFDEFG
ABCBAGAFDDDDAFDDEDCAFGAGGGDGBDGBAGDBECADBGCAGEFGAFDGBDG
BAGDBECAFEDCAFGAGGGDGBDGBAGDBECADBGCAGEFGAFDGBDGBAGDBEC
AFEDCAFGAGGGCBAGAGDBGDAGDBGDCBAEFGABCBAGAFDDDDAFDDEDCAF
GAGGGCBAGAGDBGDAGDBGDCBAEFGABCBAGAFDDDDAFDDEDCAFGAGGGD

Morrison's Jig

EEEBBBEEEAFDEEEBABDCBAFDEEEBABEEEAFDGGGFGADAGFEDEEEBBBE
EEAFDEEEBABDCBAFDEEEBABEEEAFDGGGFGADAGFEDBEEFEEAEEFEDBE
EFEEAAGFEDBEEFEEAEEFEDGFEDDABAGFEDBEEFEEAEEFEDBEEFEEFAF
DEFGGGGFEDEFGGDEDCDDABAGFED

Morrison's Jig (Variation)

EBEBEBEBEAFDEDEBABDCBAFDEBEBEBEBEAFDGGGFGADAGFEDEBEBEBE
BEAFDEDEBABDCBAFDEBEBEBEBEAFDGGGFGADAGFEDBEEFEEAEEFEDBE
EFEEAAGFEDBEEFEEAEEFEDGFEDDABAGFEDBEEFEEAEEFEDBEEFEEFAF
DEFGGGGFEDEFGGDEDCDDABAGFED

Trim the Velvet

GGGBAGFDGBDBBAFAGGGBAGFADEFDCAFAGGGBAAACBCDBBAFAGGGBAGF
ADEFDCAFADGEGDGGGDEDBCAFADGEGDGGGDEFDCAFADDDEDBGBDGBDCA
FADGEGDGGGDEFDCAFAGGGABGAFGGABCBAFGGAFGGAFDEFDCAFAGGGAB
GAFGGABCBAABGGGAFFFDEFDCAFABGDGBGGGBAGDBCAFABGDGBGGGDEF
DCAFABGDGBGGGDGBDCAFABBBGCCCEDEFDCAFA

Mullingar Lee, The

BGGGGFDEFFAFCFACBGGGDEFEFADCBGGABGGGGFDEFFAFCFACBGGGDEF
EFADCBGGGGGGDBCDEFFFCABCDGGGDBDDBDGGABGAFGGGDBCDEFFFCAB
CDEDDDDEFEFADCBGGA

For the Sakes of Old Decency

DDBGAGEGDGBGAAABDDBGAGEGDGAGEGABDDBGAGEGDGBGAAABDDBGAGE
GDGAGEGGGGGGBDDBDEAAGEGGGGGGBDDBDDEGABGEDGGGBDDBDEAAGEG
GGGGGBDDBDDEGABAGE

Over the Moor to Maggie

GGGABGBDEFGEDBAGEAAGABAGEAAGAADEGGGABGBDEFGEDBAGEGGGBGA
GEGGFGGDEGGGABGBDEFGEDBAGEAAGABAGEAAGAADEGGGABGBDEFGEDB
AGEGGGBGAGEGGFGGGABBBGAAAFGAGEDDBDEAAGABAGEAAGAAGABGGGA
FFFGAGEDDBDEGGGBGAGEGGFGGGABBBGAAAFGAGEDDBDEAAGABAGEAAG
AAGABGGGAFFFGAGEDDBDEGGGBGAGEGGFGGBDEEECDDDBCCCABBAGEAA
GABAGEAAGABCDEEECDEDBCAAABBAGEGGGBGAGEGGFGGBDEEECDDDBCC
CABBAGEAAGABAGEAAGABCDEEECDEDBCAAABBAGEGGGBGAGEGGFGGDE

Star of Munster, The

CBABAGAGEGEDEAAABDEAFGEDCBABAGAGEGEDEAAABDEDBAAACBABAGA
GEGEDEAAABDEAFGEDCBABAGAGEGEDEAAABDEDBAAAEAAAGEAAAAGEGG
GGEDGAGGEDEAAAGEAAAAGEGGGAGABBAGEDEAAAGEAAAAGEGGGGEDGAG
GEDEAAAGEAAAAGEGGGAGABBAGED

Star of Munster, The (Variation)

CCCABBBGAGEAGEDGEAABCBCDEEGEDBGBCDECABCDBGEAAFGEDGEAAGA
BCDEFGDBAAAZCCCABBBGAGEAGEDGEAABCBCDEEGEDBGBCDECABCDBGE
AAFGEDGEAAGABCDEFGDBAAAZEAABAEEEAEBEAEEFGGFAGEDEGEAEGED
BAAABAEEEAEBEAGEFGGGEAAGABBBAGEDGEAABAEEEAEBEAEEFGGFAGE
DEGEAEGEDBAAABAEEEAEBEAGEFGGGEAAGABGAFGEDB

Appendix E – Extract from a discussion on the tune "Down the Broom" from thesession.org (Accessed 22 August, 2008)

Reel: "Down The Broom"

Here's a set with this reel that was played by a band known as THE IRISH TRADITION They played CONGRESS REEL / DOWN THE BROOM / STAR OF MUNSTER. It's on their CD "The Corner House" (Green Linnet recording #1016; 1978). It's also one of the tracks on Green Linnet's double-CD "25 Years Of Celtic Music" (Green Linnet, 2000).

Posted on January 31st 2002 by Munsondr

By the by, that's a really good album.

Posted on February 4th 2002 by Josh Kane

At a summer school for ITM that I attended last year, the teacher (from Sligo I believe) said that this tune ALWAYS was played in set with the Gatehouse Maid.

Posted on April 13th 2003 by lars
Classic Set!

Lars, det har du ratt i! And as an illustration of this -- this tune came up yersterday at a session "somewhere in the USA" and, when the change was signaled, I immediately went roaring into "The Gatehouse Maid" and temporarily ground the set
to a halt as my American friends had started another tune. Automatic reflex on my part. I wonder if this is the first time I have ever heard "Down The Broom" not followed by "Gatehouse Maid". A classic set and not heard all that often here. Halsa Uppsala fran mig. Jag bodde dar i nastan tre ar.

Posted on April 13th 2003 by LongNote
Down the Broom

I finally learned this session standard today. It shares almost the same second part with "The Bag of Spuds," so it was easy to pick up. Mayo flute player Paul

Smyth's solo album is the source. That's a cracking track, joined by a piper. I might misremember it but the version on the recording is something like this:

K: Ador
G|EAAG A2Bd|eg~g2 egdc|BGGF GAGE|D2BD GABG|
EAAG A2Bd|eg~g2 egdg|eg~g2 dgba|gedB BAA:|
g|a2ea ageg|agbg agef|gedc BGBd|~g3a bgeg|
a2ea ageg|agbg ageg|dg~g2 dgba|gedB BAA:|

I happened to record Clare flute player Christy Barry play the tune, and found he has a very similar version to this.

I heard it played coupled with "The Gatehouse Maid" just once, but this tune is still referred to as the tune before "The Gatehouse Maid" quite often.

Posted on October 26th 2004 by slainte
Down the Broom

Here is the link to the northern versions of the tune:
http://thesession.org/tunes/display.php/3871

Posted on December 12th 2004 by slainte

Link to the old setting of the tune:
http://www.thesession.org/tunes/display.php/837

Posted on April 7th 2005 by slainte
Regarding the Tune Down the Broom

Does anyone know which version of "Down the Broom" is on the CD, Traditional Irish Fiddle Music, by the Kilfenora Ceili Band? I am uncertain as to whether the Down the Broom reel that is linked to the Recording on the session is the same version they play.

Posted on August 25th 2006 by enirehtac
Re: Regarding the Tune Down the Broom

I think I've got this recording on a compilation and also one by Paddy Killoran (which is a knockout - absolutely love his playing). This seems to be close (copied from another archive - credit as below):
X:1

T:DOWN BROOM (THE)
R:Reel
S:Paddy Canny and Peter O'Loughlin, Clare (fiddles)
N:As played (P O'L much the louder)
Z:Bernie Stocks
H:Played with "The Gatehouse Maid"
M:4/4
K:G
EA(3.A.A.A A2Bd | eg~g2 egdc | BG~G2 ~G3E | {G}EDB,D GABG |
EA(3.A.A.A A2Bd |
eg~g2 egdg | eg~g2 dgbg | {a}gedB {d}BAA2 :| a2ea {b}ageg | agbg agef | g2dg Bgdg |
{a}geaf gedg | a2ea {b}ageg | agbg ageg | dg~g2 dgba | gedB {d}BAA2 :|

Posted on August 25th 2006 by RichardB

You can actually listen to Killoran play this tune:
http://tedmcgraw.com/mp3/KilloranBroom.mp3
From N. American Archive of Traditional Irish Music:
http://tedmcgraw.com/recimages/Irish_clips.htm

Posted on August 25th 2006 by slainte
"The Cottage in the Glen / Grove" / "The Crosses of Annagh"

Damn, I was trusting slainte to make these connections...

The Cottage in the Glen ~ reel
Key signature: E Dorian
Submitted on February 21st 2002 by barney morgan.
http://www.thesession.org/tunes/display/558

The Crosses Of Annagh ~ reel
Key signature: A Dorian
Submitted on November 30th 2002 by gian marco.
http://www.thesession.org/tunes/display.php/1170

Appendix F – Results of MC-ED, TI-ED and MATT2 (sections 7, 7.2 and 7.3)

1 = True Positive, 0 = False Positive

				MC-ED, TI-ED				MC-ED, MATT2				TI-ED, MATT2			
Audio	**T 1**	**T 2**	**T 3**	n_{00}	n_{01}	n_{10}	n_{11}	n_{00}	n_{01}	n_{10}	n_{11}	n_{00}	n_{01}	n_{10}	n_{11}
1	1	1	1	0	0	0	1	0	0	0	1	0	0	0	1
2	0	1	1	0	1	0	0	0	1	0	0	0	0	0	1
3	1	1	1	0	0	0	1	0	0	0	1	0	0	0	1
4	1	1	1	0	0	0	1	0	0	0	1	0	0	0	1
5	0	0	1	1	0	0	0	0	1	0	0	0	1	0	0
6	1	1	1	0	0	0	1	0	0	0	1	0	0	0	1
7	0	1	1	0	1	0	0	0	1	0	0	0	0	0	1
8	0	0	1	1	0	0	0	0	1	0	0	0	1	0	0
9	0	0	0	1	0	0	0	1	0	0	0	1	0	0	0
10	0	0	1	1	0	0	0	0	1	0	0	0	1	0	0
11	0	0	1	1	0	0	0	0	1	0	0	0	1	0	0
12	0	1	1	0	1	0	0	0	1	0	0	0	0	0	1
13	0	0	1	1	0	0	0	0	1	0	0	0	1	0	0
14	0	1	1	0	1	0	0	0	1	0	0	0	0	0	1
15	0	0	1	1	0	0	0	0	1	0	0	0	1	0	0
16	0	0	1	1	0	0	0	0	1	0	0	0	1	0	0
17	0	0	0	1	0	0	0	1	0	0	0	1	0	0	0
18	0	0	0	1	0	0	0	1	0	0	0	1	0	0	0
19	0	1	1	0	1	0	0	0	1	0	0	0	0	0	1
20	0	0	1	1	0	0	0	0	1	0	0	0	1	0	0
21	0	1	1	0	1	0	0	0	1	0	0	0	0	0	1
22	0	0	1	1	0	0	0	0	1	0	0	0	1	0	0
23	0	1	1	0	1	0	0	0	1	0	0	0	0	0	1
24	0	1	1	0	1	0	0	0	1	0	0	0	0	0	1
25	0	1	1	0	1	0	0	0	1	0	0	0	0	0	1
26	1	1	1	0	0	0	1	0	0	0	1	0	0	0	1
27	0	0	1	1	0	0	0	0	1	0	0	0	1	0	0

28	0	0	1	1	0	0	0	0	1	0	0	0	1	0	0
29	0	1	1	0	1	0	0	0	1	0	0	0	0	0	1
30	0	0	1	1	0	0	0	0	1	0	0	0	1	0	0
31	0	0	1	1	0	0	0	0	1	0	0	0	1	0	0
32	0	1	1	0	1	0	0	0	1	0	0	0	0	0	1
33	1	1	1	0	0	0	1	0	0	0	1	0	0	0	1
34	1	1	1	0	0	0	1	0	0	0	1	0	0	0	1
35	1	1	1	0	0	0	1	0	0	0	1	0	0	0	1
36	0	0	1	1	0	0	0	0	1	0	0	0	1	0	0
37	0	1	1	0	1	0	0	0	1	0	0	0	0	0	1
38	0	1	1	0	1	0	0	0	1	0	0	0	0	0	1
39	0	0	1	1	0	0	0	0	1	0	0	0	1	0	0
40	0	0	1	1	0	0	0	0	1	0	0	0	1	0	0
41	0	1	1	0	1	0	0	0	1	0	0	0	0	0	1
42	1	1	1	0	0	0	1	0	0	0	1	0	0	0	1
43	0	0	1	1	0	0	0	0	1	0	0	0	1	0	0
44	0	1	1	0	1	0	0	0	1	0	0	0	0	0	1
45	1	1	1	0	0	0	1	0	0	0	1	0	0	0	1
46	0	0	1	1	0	0	0	0	1	0	0	0	1	0	0
47	0	1	1	0	1	0	0	0	1	0	0	0	0	0	1
48	0	1	1	0	1	0	0	0	1	0	0	0	0	0	1
49	0	0	1	1	0	0	0	0	1	0	0	0	1	0	0
50	0	1	1	0	1	0	0	0	1	0	0	0	0	0	1
51	0	0	0	1	0	0	0	1	0	0	0	1	0	0	0
52	0	1	1	0	1	0	0	0	1	0	0	0	0	0	1
53	0	1	1	0	1	0	0	0	1	0	0	0	0	0	1
54	0	0	0	1	0	0	0	1	0	0	0	1	0	0	0
55	0	0	1	1	0	0	0	0	1	0	0	0	1	0	0
56	0	0	1	1	0	0	0	0	1	0	0	0	1	0	0
57	0	0	0	1	0	0	0	1	0	0	0	1	0	0	0
58	0	0	1	1	0	0	0	0	1	0	0	0	1	0	0
59	0	0	1	1	0	0	0	0	1	0	0	0	1	0	0
60	0	0	1	1	0	0	0	0	1	0	0	0	1	0	0
61	0	0	1	1	0	0	0	0	1	0	0	0	1	0	0
62	0	1	1	0	1	0	0	0	1	0	0	0	0	0	1
63	0	0	1	1	0	0	0	0	1	0	0	0	1	0	0
64	0	0	1	1	0	0	0	0	1	0	0	0	1	0	0

65	0	0	1	1	0	0	0	0	1	0	0	0	1	0	0
66	0	0	1	1	0	0	0	0	1	0	0	0	1	0	0
67	0	0	1	1	0	0	0	0	1	0	0	0	1	0	0
68	0	1	1	0	1	0	0	0	1	0	0	0	0	0	1
69	0	1	1	0	1	0	0	0	1	0	0	0	0	0	1
70	0	1	1	0	1	0	0	0	1	0	0	0	0	0	1
71	0	1	1	0	1	0	0	0	1	0	0	0	0	0	1
72	0	0	1	1	0	0	0	0	1	0	0	0	1	0	0
73	0	0	1	1	0	0	0	0	1	0	0	0	1	0	0
74	0	1	1	0	1	0	0	0	1	0	0	0	0	0	1
75	0	1	1	0	1	0	0	0	1	0	0	0	0	0	1
76	0	0	1	1	0	0	0	0	1	0	0	0	1	0	0
77	0	1	1	0	1	0	0	0	1	0	0	0	0	0	1
78	0	0	1	1	0	0	0	0	1	0	0	0	1	0	0
79	0	1	1	0	1	0	0	0	1	0	0	0	0	0	1
80	0	1	1	0	1	0	0	0	1	0	0	0	0	0	1
81	0	0	1	1	0	0	0	0	1	0	0	0	1	0	0
82	0	0	1	1	0	0	0	0	1	0	0	0	1	0	0
83	0	1	1	0	1	0	0	0	1	0	0	0	0	0	1
84	0	0	1	1	0	0	0	0	1	0	0	0	1	0	0
85	0	0	0	1	0	0	0	1	0	0	0	1	0	0	0
86	0	1	1	0	1	0	0	0	1	0	0	0	0	0	1
87	0	1	1	0	1	0	0	0	1	0	0	0	0	0	1
88	0	1	1	0	1	0	0	0	1	0	0	0	0	0	1
89	0	0	1	1	0	0	0	0	1	0	0	0	1	0	0
90	0	0	1	1	0	0	0	0	1	0	0	0	1	0	0
91	0	0	1	1	0	0	0	0	1	0	0	0	1	0	0
92	0	0	1	1	0	0	0	0	1	0	0	0	1	0	0
93	0	0	1	1	0	0	0	0	1	0	0	0	1	0	0
94	1	1	1	0	0	0	1	0	0	0	1	0	0	0	1
95	0	0	1	1	0	0	0	0	1	0	0	0	1	0	0
96	0	1	1	0	1	0	0	0	1	0	0	0	0	0	1
97	0	1	1	0	1	0	0	0	1	0	0	0	0	0	1
98	0	0	1	1	0	0	0	0	1	0	0	0	1	0	0
99	0	0	1	1	0	0	0	0	1	0	0	0	1	0	0
100	0	0	1	1	0	0	0	0	1	0	0	0	1	0	0
Total	11	47	93	53	36	0	11	7	82	0	11	7	46	0	47

(1)															
Total (0)	89	53	7												

Appendix G – Results of TANSEY Evaluation described in sections 8.3 and 8.4

Set	Tune	Human	Machine	|Human - Machine|	TP	FP	FN
1	Billy Brocker's	0.00	0.00		0	0	0
		19.20			0	0	1
		38.13	37.96	0.17	1	0	0
		56.95	57.43	0.48	1	0	0
	Green Mountain, The	76.00			0	0	1
		113.20			0	0	1
		150.63			0	0	1
		188.02			0	0	1
2	Christy Barry's	0.00	0.00		0	0	0
		34.40			0	0	1
	Butlers of Glenavenue, The	69.80	72.71	2.91	0	1	1
		105.10	110.32	5.22	0	1	1
		141.53	141.30	0.23	1	0	0
3	Connie O'Connell's	0.00	0.00		0	0	0
		46.40	46.68	0.28	1	0	0
	Cullen Jig, The	92.63	92.69	0.06	1	0	0
		123.23	123.52	0.29	1	0	0
	Cordal Jig, The	153.73	154.34	0.61	1	0	0
		184.73	184.65	0.08	1	0	0
		217.93	217.80	0.13	1	0	0
4	Cooley's	0.00	0.00		0	0	0
		41.10	41.51	0.41	1	0	0
	Dick Gossip's	82.30	82.76	0.46	1	0	0
		122.50	123.70	1.20	1	0	0
	Bird in the Bush, The	164.84	165.06	0.22	1	0	0
		206.44	207.30	0.86	1	0	0

		248.54	250.06	1.52	1	0	0
5	Devaney's Goat	0.00	0.00		0	0	0
		44.48	45.26	0.78	1	0	0
	Tommy Peoples	89.48	87.14	2.34	0	1	1
		111.86	114.35	2.49	0	1	1
		134.13	134.78	0.65	1	0	0
6	Down the broom	0.00	0.00		0	0	0
		43.70			0	0	1
	Gatehouse Maid, The	86.30	87.67	1.37	1	0	0
		107.60	109.18	1.58	1	0	0
		128.90	129.80	0.90	1	0	0
		152.50	153.22	0.72	1	0	0
7	Dublin Lasses, The	0.00	0.00		0	0	0
		28.10	28.49	0.39	1	0	0
	Five Mile Chase, The	47.28	47.42	0.14	1	0	0
		66.38	66.70	0.32	1	0	0
		86.55	87.14	0.59	1	0	0
8	Galway Rambler, The	0.00	0.00		0	0	0
		20.50	20.75	0.25	1	0	0
		39.70	40.12	0.42	1	0	0
		59.00	59.34	0.34	1	0	0
	London Lasses, The	78.40	78.91	0.51	1	0	0
		117.50	118.21	0.71	1	0	0
		158.20	161.04	2.84	0	1	1
9	Geese in the bog	0.00	0.00		0	0	0
9		33.20	32.94	0.26	1	0	0
	Connaughtman's Rambles, The	64.00	64.78	0.78	1	0	0
		95.10	96.77	1.67	1	0	0
	Black Rogue, The	125.80	128.16	2.36	0	1	1
		156.30	157.59	1.29	1	0	0
		187.00	189.44	2.44	0	1	1
		219.00	215.42	3.58	0	1	1
10	Green Mountain, The	0.00	0.00		0	0	0
		39.10	48.46	9.36	0	1	1

		77.30		77.30	0	0	1
	John Stensons # 2	115.10	115.62	0.52	1	0	0
		152.80	153.36	0.56	1	0	0
		189.70	189.81	0.11	1	0	0
		227.50	227.65	0.15	1	0	0
11	Happy to Meet Sorry to Part	0.00	0.00		0	0	0
		41.80	42.54	0.74	1	0	0
	Jacksons Bottle of Brandy	82.30	83.58	1.28	1	0	0
		122.30	124.24	1.94	1	0	0
		163.45	163.28	0.17	1	0	0
12	Humours of Bally Loughlan	0.00	0.00		0	0	0
		63.58	64.00	0.42	1	0	0
		126.65	127.47	0.82	1	0	0
		191.24	191.09	0.15	1	0	0
13	McKenna's #1	0.00	0.00		0	0	0
		41.50	41.31	0.19	1	0	0
		81.10	82.41	1.31	1	0	0
	McKenna's # 2	121.00	122.28	1.28	1	0	0
		140.73	141.64	0.91	1	0	0
		160.50	161.36	0.86	1	0	0
		182.90	183.88	0.98	1	0	0
14	Micho Russles	0.00	0.00		0	0	0
		46.00	46.32	0.32	1	0	0
	Maid of Mount Kisco, The	91.50	91.80	0.30	1	0	0
		144.39	145.86	1.47	1	0	0
	Green Groves of Erin, The	196.09	197.64	1.55	1	0	0
		237.99		237.99	0	0	1
		279.10	281.32	2.22	0	1	1
		321.19	321.91	0.72	1	0	0
15	Jim Coleman's	0.00	0.00		0	0	0
		20.80	21.90	1.10	1	0	0

	George White's Favourite	41.50	43.15	1.65	1	0	0
	The Virginia	83.00	84.24	1.24	1	0	0
		124.00	125.41	1.41	1	0	0
		166.30	166.78	0.48	1	0	0
16	Scully Casey's	0.00	0.00		0	0	0
		31.30	31.25	0.05	1	0	0
	Kilmovee Jig, The	62.01	60.97	1.04	1	0	0
		94.10	94.53	0.43	1	0	0
		126.60	126.45	0.15	1	0	0
17	Strop the Razor	0.00	0.00		0	0	0
		47.70	47.88	0.18	1	0	0
	Killavel Jig, The	94.10	94.64	0.54	1	0	0
		124.30		124.30	0	0	1
	Boys of the Town, The	154.70	155.46	0.76	1	0	0
		185.71	189.42	3.71	0	1	1
		215.70	220.23	4.53	0	1	1
		247.11	247.93	0.82	1	0	0
18	Concert Reel, The	0.00	0.00		0	0	0
		39.65	39.61	0.04	1	0	0
		77.67	77.82	0.15	1	0	0
	Baltimore Salute, The	115.67	115.75	0.08	1	0	0
		153.67	153.72	0.05	1	0	0
		193.84	193.67	0.17	1	0	0
19	Copperplate, The	0.00	0.00		0	0	0
		40.10	40.16	0.06	1	0	0
	Old Copperplate, The	80.00	80.04	0.04	1	0	0
		120.00	120.02	0.02	1	0	0
		161.20	161.53	0.33	1	0	0
20	Corner House, The	0.00	0.00		0	0	0
		54.30	55.51	1.21	1	0	0
	Boys of Portaferry, The	108.54	110.62	2.08	0	1	1
		135.13	136.21	1.08	1	0	0
		161.63	162.83	1.20	1	0	0
21	Cup of Tea, The	0.00	0.00		0	0	0

		62.10	62.31	0.21	1	0	0
	Upstairs in a Tent	122.00	122.06	0.06	1	0	0
		161.70	162.14	0.44	1	0	0
		204.50	203.68	0.82	1	0	0
22	Gooseberry Bush, The	0.00	0.00		0	0	0
		61.20	61.56	0.36	1	0	0
	Limestone Rock	121.30	121.68	0.38	1	0	0
		141.78	141.50	0.28	1	0	0
		162.08	161.27	0.81	1	0	0
23	Humours of Loughrea, The	181.88	181.80	0.08	1	0	0
		201.88	201.26	0.62	1	0	0
		221.78	221.33	0.45	1	0	0
		242.91	242.43	0.48	1	0	0
24	Humours of Ballyloughlin, The	0.00	0.00		0	0	0
		65.27	65.47	0.20	1	0	0
		130.81	131.22	0.41	1	0	0
25	Lillies in the Field, The	0.00	0.00		0	0	0
		20.30	21.28	0.98	1	0	0
		40.50	41.18	0.68	1	0	0
	Tommy Peoples	61.16	62.12	0.96	1	0	0
		81.16	81.96	0.80	1	0	0
		101.26	102.05	0.79	1	0	0
		122.50	123.01	0.51	1	0	0
26	Lilting Banshee, The	0.00	0.00		0	0	0
		30.80	54.94	24.14	0	1	1
		62.00	86.13	24.13	0	1	1
	Mice in the Cupboard	92.90	107.23	14.33	0	1	1
		123.40	124.96	1.56	1	0	0
	Tenpenny Bit, The	154.30	155.02	0.72	1	0	0
		185.30	186.40	1.10	1	0	0
		217.00	217.47	0.47	1	0	0
27	Skylark, The	0.00	0.00		0	0	0
		43.80	43.07	0.73	1	0	0

	Roaring Mary	86.40	85.91	0.49	1	0	0
		129.20	129.44	0.24	1	0	0
		173.27	173.95	0.68	1	0	0
28	Wandering Minstrel, The	0.00	0.00		0	0	0
		52.14	52.04	0.10	1	0	0
		104.29	104.13	0.16	1	0	0
29	Touch Me If You Dare	0.00	0.00		0	0	0
		34.10	34.05	0.05	1	0	0
		70.53	70.41	0.12	1	0	0
30	Traver's Jig	0.00	0.00		0	0	0
		43.70	46.92	3.22	0	1	1
		84.30	89.55	5.25	0	1	1
		124.21	123.91	0.30	1	0	0
	Total:	**142**			**114**	**18**	**28**

Appendix H – Example transcriptions in ABC notation discussed in section 2.9.4

```
X:1
T:Ambrose Maloneys
R:Reel
H:No ornamentation
M:C|
L:1/8
K:G
B3G ABGE|DGBG A3d|
BGGG A2ef|gedg eAAA|
B3G ABGE| DGBG A3d|
BGGG A2ef |ged=c BGGG:|
dgbg a2fa|gedB GABd|
eaag agef|g2bgage2|
dgbg a2fa|gedB GABd|
eaag e2fa|ged=cBggg:|

X:2
T:Ambrose Maloneys
R:Reel
D:Catherine McEvoy: Recorded The Cobblestone 01/02/2006
M:C|
L:1/8
K:D
Bd{c}BG A{c}BGE|DG{c}BG ~A3d|
B~G3 Azeg|{c'}gedg e~A3|
(3Bcd BD ABGE| DzBG ~A3d|
B~G3 ABea |{c'}ged=c B~G3|

Bz{c}BG A{c}BGE|D~G3 AzaD|
B~G3 ABea|{c'}gedg e~A3|
(3Bcd {c}BD ABGE| dz{c}BG ~A3D|
B~G3 Azeg |{c'}ged=c B~g3|

dzb a{c'}ag{g}ea|{c'}g{g}edB ~g3d|
{f}a4{c'}a {b}g{b}ed|gzbgabge|
dgbz {c'}agea|{c'}gedB ~g3z|
```

```
~a3g (3efg fa|{b}ged=cB~g3|

dgba {c'}a ge z | {c'}gedb gabd|
ea{c'}a^g {c'}a=ged |~g3b abge|
dzbg{c'}agea|{c'}gedB~g3z|
~a3g ezfa |{c'}ged=c B~G3|

Bz{c}BG A{c}BGE|DG{c}BG ~A3d|
B~G3 ABea|{c}gedg e~A3|
(3Bcd BD ABGE| Dz{c}BG ~A3d|
B~G3 Azea |{c'}ged=c B~G3|

BdBD ABGE|Dz{c}BG AGAD|
B~G3 Azea|{c'}gedg e~A3|
(3Bcd BD ABGE| Dz{c}BG ~A3D|
B~G3 Azeg |{c'}ged=c B~g3|

dzb a{c'}agea|gedB ~g3d|
~a3b  aged|gzbga{c'}bge|
d~g3 {c'}agez|{c'}gedB GABD|
gzag egfa |{b}ged=cB~g3|

{a}b3 a {b}agea | {c'}gedB ~g3 z|
~a3b aged |gz{c'}bg a{c'}bge|
d~g3 {c'}agea|{b}gedB ~g3z|
~a3g ez fa|{b}ged=cB~g3|

Bz{c'}BG A{c}BGE|D~G3 ~A3d|
B~G3 ABea|{c'}gedg e~a3|
Bz{c}BG A{c}BGE| DzBG ~A3D|
B G{A}g{e}g azeg |{c'}ged=c B~G3|

Bz{c}BG ABGE|DGBG ~A3D|
B~G3 ABea|{c'}gedg e~a3|
Bz{c}BG AGGE| D2BG ~A3z|
B ~G3 ABea |{c'}ged=c B~GGB|

dgb z{c'}agea|{c'}gedB GABD|
ea{b}ag  aged|~g3z abge|
d~g3 ~a3b | {c'}gedB GzBD|
~a3ge zfg | gedGB~G3|
```

```
dgba {c'}agea|{c'}gedB GzBD|
ea{b}ag  aged|gb{c'}bg abge|
Dzbg ~a3e|{c'}gedB ~g3z|
~a3g ez fa|{c'}gedG BDAD|
{c}G4|


X:3
T:Ambrose Maloneys
R:Reel
D:Eamon Cotter: Traditional Irish Music From County
Clare
M:C|
L:1/8
K:D
"A1 1:12:00"
~B3G A{c}BGE|DGBG ~A3d|
B~G3 Azef|{a}g{ef}edg e~A3|
BdBG A{c}BGE| DGBG ~A3d|
B~G3 Azef |~g2d=c B~G3|
"A2 1:20:58"
BdBG A{c}BGE|DGBG ~A3d|
B~G3 Azef|g{b}gda e~A3|
BdBG A{c}BGE|DzBD ~A3d|
B~G3 Azef |~g2d=c B~g3|
"B1 1:30:00"
dgbg ~a2f{ag}a|gedB GDBD|
ea{b}a^g a{gf}=gef|gzbg{b}a{gf}gez|
dgbg ~a2f{ag}a|gedB GA(3Bcd|
ea{b}a{gf}g ezfa|{gf}ged=cB~g3|
"B2 1:38:50"
bdga ~a2fa|{gf}gedB GDBz|
ea{b}a^g a{gf}=gef|gzbg{b}a{gf}gez|
dgbg ~a2f{ag}a|gedB GA(3Bcd|
ea{b}a{gf}g ezfa|{gf}ged=cB~G3|
"A3 1:47:00"
~B3G A{c}BGE|DGBG ~A3d|
B~G3 Azef|{a}geda e~A3|
BdBG A{c}BGE| DzBD ~A3d|
B~G3 Azef |~g2d=c B~G3|
"A4 1:56:10"
BdBG A{c}BGE|DGBD ~A3d|
```

```
B~G3 Azef|g{a}gda e~A3|
BdBG AzG{EG}E| DGBD ~A3d|
B~G3 Aze=c |{a}g{ef}ed=c B~G3|
"B3 2:05:10"
dgbg ~a2f{ag}a|gedB GDBz|
ea{b}a^g a{gf}=gef|~g2bg{b}a{gf}gez|
dgbg azfa|{fa}gedB GA(3Bcd|
ea{b}a{gf}g eafd|{a}ged=cB~g3|
"B4 2:13:00"
dgbg azfa|{ge}gedB {Ga}GDBz|
ea{b}a^g a{gf}=gef|gzbg{b}a{gf}geg|
dgbg ~a2fa|{fa}gedB GA(3Bcd|
ea{b}a{gf}g ezfa|{a}ged=cB~G3|
```

References

The Humdrum Toolkit: Software for Music Research. Available at: http://www.musiccog.ohio-state.edu/Humdrum/ [Accessed July 16, 2008].

The Session. Available at: http://www.thesession.org/ [Accessed January 31, 2008].

Adams, N., Bartsch, M. & Wakefield, G., 2003. Coding of sung queries for music information retrieval. *Applications of Signal Processing to Audio and Acoustics, 2003 IEEE Workshop on.*, 139-142.

Allamanche, E. et al., 2001. Content-based identification of audio material using MPEG-7 low level description. *Proceedings of the International Symposium of Music Information Retrieval.*

Andoni, A. & Indyk, P., 2006. Near-optimal hashing algorithms for approximate nearest neighbor in high dimensions. *Proceedings of the Symposium on Foundations of Computer Science.*

Apple, 2008. Apple - iPhone. Available at: http://www.apple.com/iphone/ [Accessed August 10, 2008].

Baeza-Yates, R. & Perleberg, C., 1996. Fast and practical approximate pattern matching. *Information Processing Letters*, 59(1), 21-27.

Barlow, H. & Morgenstern, S., 1948. *A Dictionary of Musical Themes*, Reprint Services Corp.

Bello, J. et al., 2005. A Tutorial on Onset Detection in Music Signals. *IEEE TRANSACTIONS ON SPEECH AND AUDIO PROCESSING*, 13(5), 1035.

Bello, J. et al., 2004. On the use of phase and energy for musical onset detection in the complex domain. *Signal Processing Letters, IEEE*, 11(6), 553-556.

Bello, J. & Sandler, M., 2003. Phase-based note onset detection for music signals. *Acoustics, Speech, and Signal Processing, 2003. Proceedings.(ICASSP'03). 2003 IEEE International Conference on*, 5.

Birmingham, W. et al., 2001. Musart: Music Retrieval Via Aural Queries. *2nd Annual International Symposium on Music Information Retrieval, Indiana University Bloomington, Indiana, USA October 15-17, 2001*, 1001, 48109-2110.

Blum, T. et al., 1999. Method and article of manufacture for content-based analysis, storage, retrieval, and segmentation of audio information.

Boden, M., 1996. *Dimensions of creativity*, Cambridge, Massachusetts: MIT Press.

Breathnach, B., 1963. Ceol Rince na hÉireann Cuid I [Dance Music of Ireland] Vol I.

Breathnach, B., 1976. Ceol Rince na hÉireann Cuid II [Dance Music of Ireland] Vol II.

Breathnach, B., 1985. Ceol Rince na hÉireann Cuid III [Dance Music of Ireland] Vol III.

Breathnach, B., 1996. Ceol Rince na hÉireann Cuid IV [Dance Music of Ireland] Vol IV.

Breathnach, B., 1999. Ceol Rince na hÉireann Cuid V [Dance Music of Ireland] Vol V.

Breathnach, B., 1977. *Folk music and dances of Ireland*, Mercier Press Cork [Ireland.

Brown, J., 1993. Determination of the meter of musical scores by autocorrelation. *Journal of the Acoustical Society of America*, 94(4), 1953-1957.

Brown, J., 1992. Musical fundamental frequency tracking using a pattern recognition method. *JASA 1992*, 3, 1394-1402.

Bunting, E., 1840. *The Ancient Music of Ireland: Arranged for Piano*,

Burges, C., Platt, J. & Jana, S., 2002. Extracting noise-robust features from audio data. *Acoustics, Speech, and Signal Processing, 2002. Proceedings.(ICASSP'02). IEEE International Conference on*, 1.

Canainn, T., 1978. *Traditional Music in Ireland*, London: Routledge and Keegan-Paul Ltd.

Cano, P. et al., 2005. A Review of Audio Fingerprinting. *The Journal of VLSI Signal Processing*, 41(3), 271-284.

Carson, C., 1997. *Last Night's Fun: A Book about Irish Traditional Music*, North Point Press.

Chafe, C. & Jaffe, D., 1986. Source separation and note identification in polyphonic music. *Acoustics, Speech, and Signal Processing, IEEE International Conference on ICASSP'86.*, 11.

Chambers, J., 2007. O' Neills Books. Available at: http://trillian.mit.edu/~jc/music/book/oneills/.

Chávez, E. et al., 2001. Searching in metric spaces. *ACM Computing Surveys (CSUR)*, 33(3), 273-321.

Cheveigne, A., 1991. A Mixed Speech F0 Estimation Algorithm. *Second European Conference on Speech Communication and Technology.*

Chordia, P., Godfrey, M. & Rae, A., 2008. Extending Content-Based Recommendation: the Case of Indian Classical Music. *Ninth International Conference on Music Information Retrieval, Drexel University in Philadelphia, Pennsylvania USA.*

Clark, N.J., 2003. *Story of the Irish Harp Its History and Influence* 1st ed., North Creek Press.

Collins, N., 2005. Using a Pitch Detector for Onset Detection. *Proc. of ISMIR2005.*

Dannenberg, R., Thom, B. & Watson, D., 1997. A Machine Learning Approach to Musical Style Recognition. In *1997 International Computer Music Conference.* International Computer Music Association, pp. pp. 344-347.

Dietterich, T., 1998. Approximate statistical tests for comparing supervised classification learning algorithms. *Neural Computation*, 10(7), 1895-1923.

Dixon, S., 2004. On the analysis of musical expression in audio signals. *Proceedings of SPIE.*

Dixon, S., 2006. Onset Detection Revisited. *Proceedings of the 9th International Conference on Digital Audio Effects (DAFx06), Montreal, Canada.*

Dolson, M., 1986. The phase vocoder: A tutorial. *Computer Music Journal*, 10(4), 14-27.

Doraisamy, S., Adnan, H. & Norowi, N., 2006. Towards a MIR System for Malaysian Music. *7th International Conference on Music Information Retrieval, Victoria, Canada, 8 - 12 October 2006.*

Downie, J., 1999. Evaluating a Simple Approach to Music Information Retrieval: Conceiving Melodic N-Grams as Text.

Downie, J., 2003. Music information retrieval. *Annual Review of Information Science and Technology*, 37(1), 295-340.

Dubnowski, J., Schafer, R. & Rabiner, L., 1976. Real-time digital hardware pitch detector. *Acoustics, Speech, and Signal Processing [see also IEEE Transactions on Signal Processing], IEEE Transactions on*, 24(1), 2-8.

Duggan, B., 2007a. A Portable Tune Teaching Tool for Traditional Musicians. *DIT Annual Showcase of Learning & Teaching Activities.*

Duggan, B., 2007b. Enabling Access to Irish Traditional Music Archives on a PDA. *Eight Annual Irish Educational Technology Users Conference, DIT Bolton St, Ireland.*

Duggan, B., 2006. Learning Traditional Irish Music using a PDA. *IADIS Mobile Learning Conference, Trinity College Dublin.*

Duggan, B., Cui, Z. & Cunningham, P., 2006. MATT - A System for Modelling Creativity in Traditional Irish Flute Playing. In *Third ECAI Workshop on Computational Creativity.* Riva Del Garda, Italy.

Duggan, B. et al., 2009. Compensating for Expressiveness in Queries to a Content Based Music Information Retrieval System. *2009 International Computer Music Conference.*

Duggan, B., O'Shea, B. & Cunningham, P., 2008. A System for Automatically Annotating Traditional Irish Music Field Recordings. *Sixth International Workshop on Content-Based Multimedia Indexing, Queen Mary University of London, UK.*

Duxbury, C. et al., 2003. A combined phase and amplitude based approach to onset detection for audio segmentation. In pp. 275-280.

Duxbury, C., Davies, M. & Sandler, M., 2001. Separation of transient information in musical audio using multiresolution analysis techniques. *Proceedings of the COST G-6 Conference on Digital Audio Effects (DAFX-01), Limerick, Ireland.*

Duxbury, C., Sandler, M. & Davies, M., 2002. A hybrid approach to musical note onset detection. *Proc. Digital Audio Effects Conf.(DAFX, '02).*

Eagan, C., 1998. *Irish Book of Days*, Universe.

Eppstein, D. et al., 1992a. Sparse dynamic programming I: linear cost functions. *Journal of the ACM (JACM)*, 39(3), 519-545.

Eppstein, D. et al., 1992b. Sparse dynamic programming II: convex and concave cost functions. *Journal of the ACM (JACM)*, 39(3), 546-567.

Foote, J., 2000. Automatic audio segmentation using a measure of audio novelty.

Forney Jr, G., 1973. The viterbi algorithm. *Proceedings of the IEEE*, 61(3), 268-278.

Gainza, M., 2006. *Music Transcription within Irish Traditional Music*, PhD Thesis, Dublin Institute of Technology, Faculty of Engineering.

Gainza, M. & Coyle, E., 2007. Automating Ornamentation Transcription. *Acoustics, Speech and Signal Processing, 2007. ICASSP 2007. IEEE International Conference on*, 1.

Gainza, M., Coyle, E. & Lawler, B., 2005. Onset Detection Using Comb Filters. In *IEEE Workshop on Applications of Signal Processing to Audio and Acoustics*. New Paltz, NY.

Gardner, H., 1993. *Creating Minds: An Anatomy of Creativity Seen Through the Lives of Freud, Einstein, Picasso, Stravinsky, Eliot, Graham, and Gandhi*, Basic Books.

Ghias, A. et al., 1995. Query by humming: musical information retrieval in an audio database. *Proceedings of the third ACM international conference on Multimedia*, 231-236.

Götz, I., 1981. On Defining Creativity. *Journal of Aesthetics and Art Critism*, (39), 297-301.

Grachten, M., Arcos, J. & Lopez de Mantaras, R., 2005. Melody Retrieval using the Implication/Realization Model. *MIREX http://www. music-ir. org/evaluation/mirex-results/article/s/similarity/grachten. pdf.*

Hamilton, C., 1990. *The Irish Flute Players Handbook*, Cork: Breac Publications.

Hayes, M. & Cahill, D., 1997. *The Lonesome Touch (CD Recording)*,

Hitchcock, F., 1941. The distribution of a product from several sources to numerous localities. *J. Math. Phys. Mass. Inst. Tech*, 20, 224-230.

Hofstadter, D., 1979. *Gödel, Escher, Bach: An Eternal Golden Braid*, Basic Books.

Hoos, H., 2001. GUIDO/MIR—an Experimental Musical Information Retrieval System based on GUIDO Music Notation. *Symposium on Music Information Retrieval: ISMIR*, 41-50.

Howard, J., 1997. Plaine and Easie Code: a code for music bibliography. *Beyond MIDI: the handbook of musical codes table of contents*, 362-372.

Humdrum, 2008. *The Humdrum Toolkit: Software for Music Research*,

Hurley, B., 2005. An Interview with Eamon Cotter. Available at: http://www.firescribble.net/flute/cotter.html.

Jensen, K., Xu, J. & Zachariasen, M., 2005. Rhythm-based segmentation of popular chinese music. *Proceedings of 6th International Conference on Music Information Retrieval (ISMIR'05)*, 374-380.

Joyce, W., 1909. *Old Irish Folk Music and Song*,

Kassler, M., 1966. Toward musical information retrieval. *Perspectives of New Music*, 4(2), 59-67.

Keane, J.B., 1959. *Sive*,

Keane, J.B., 1986. *The Bodhrán Makers*,

Kearns, T. & Taylor, B., 2003. *A Touchstone for the Tradition - The Willie Clancy Summer School*,

Keegan, N., 1992. *The Words of Traditional Flute Style*, MPhil Thesis, University College Cork, Music Department.

Kenneally, C., 2008. So you think humans are unique? *New Scientist*.

Klapuri, A., 1998. Automatic Transcription of Music. *MSc Thesis, Tampere University of Technology*.

Klapuri, A., 1999. Sound onset detection by applying psychoacoustic knowledge. *Acoustics, Speech, and Signal Processing, 1999. ICASSP'99. Proceedings., 1999 IEEE International Conference on*, 6.

Klapuri, A., 2003. Multiple fundamental frequency estimation based on harmonicity and spectral smoothness. *Speech and Audio Processing, IEEE Transactions on*, 11(6), 804-816.

Kohonen, T., 2001. *Self-Organizing Maps*, Springer Verlag.

Kornstadt, A., 1998. Themefinder: A web-based melodic search tool. *Computing in Musicology*, 11, 231-236.

Krassen, M., 1975. *O' Neil's Music of Ireland*, Waltons.

Kunieda, N., Shimamura, T. & Suzuki, J., 1996. Robust method of measurement of fundamental frequency by ACLOS: autocorrelation of log spectrum. *Acoustics, Speech, and Signal Processing, 1996. ICASSP-96. Conference Proceedings., 1996 IEEE International Conference on*, 1.

Lacoste, A. & Eck, D., 2005. Onset Detection with Artificial Neural Networks for MIREX 2005. *Extended abstract of the 1 stAnnual Music Information Retrieval Evaluation eXchange (MIREX 2005), held in conjunction with ISMIR.*

Larsen, G., 2003. *The Essential Guide to Irish Flute and Tin Whistle*, Mel Bay Publications, Inc.

Lemstrom, K. et al., 2003. The C-BRAHMS Project. *Proceedings of the 4th Internationoal Conference on Music Information Retrieval (ISMIR 2003)*, 237-238.

Lemstrom, K. & Perttu, S., 2000. SEMEX-An Efficient Music Retrieval Prototype. *First International Symposium on Music Information Retrieval (ISMIR).*

Lemstrom, K. & Ukkonen, E., 2000. Including interval encoding into edit distance based music comparison and retrieval. *Proceedings of the AISB'2000 Symposium on Creative & Cultural Aspects and Applications of AI & Cognitive Science', Birmingham*, 53-60.

León, P. & Iñesta, J., 2004. Musical style classification from symbolic data: A two-styles case study. *Lecture Notes in Computer Science*, 2771, pp. 166-177.

Lerdahl, F. & Jackendoff, R., 1983. *A Generative Theory of Tonal Music*, MIT Press.

Levenshtein, V., 1966. Binary Codes Capable of Correcting Deletions, Insertions and Reversals. *Soviet Physics Doklady*, 10, 707.

Little, D., Raffensperger, D. & Pardo, B., 2007. A Query By Humming System That Learns From Experience. *Proceedings of the 8th International Conference on Music Information Retrieval, Vienna, Austria.*

Lu, L., You, H. & Zhang, H., 2001. A new approach to query by humming in music retrieval. *Proceedings of the IEEE International Conference on Multimedia and Expo.*

Lynch, B., 2008. 2008 Willie Clancy Summer School. Available at: http://www.setdancingnews.net/wcss/wcsst.htm [Accessed August 16, 2008].

Maddage, N. et al., 2004. Content-based music structure analysis with applications to music semantics understanding. *Proceedings of the 12th annual ACM international conference on Multimedia*, 112-119.

Makinen, V., Navarro, G. & Ukkonen, E., 2003. Algorithms for transposition invariant string matching. *Proc. STACS*, 191-202.

Manning, C., 1999. *Foundations of statistical natural language processing*, MIT Press.

Mansfield, S., 2007. How to Interpret ABC Notation. Available at: http://www.lesession.co.uk/abc/abc_notation.htm.

Masri, P., 1996. Computer Modeling of Sound for Transformation and Synthesis of Musical Signals. *Unpublished doctoral dissertation, University of Bristol, UK.*

M-AUDIO, 2008. M-AUDIO - MicroTrack II - Professional 2-Channel Mobile Digital Recorder. Available at: http://www.m-audio.com/products/en_us/MicroTrackII-main.html [Accessed August 16, 2008].

McCullough, L., 1987. *The Complete Irish Tinwhistle Tutor*, Music Sales Corp.

McEvoy, C., 1998. *Traditional Flute Music in the Sligo-Roscommon Style*, CD Recording.

McNab, R. et al., 1997. The New Zealand Digital Library MELody inDEX. *D-Lib Magazine*, 3(5), 4-15.

McNab, R. et al., 1996. Towards the digital music library: tune retrieval from acoustic input. *Proceedings of the first ACM international conference on Digital libraries*, 11-18.

McPherson, J. & Bainbridge, D., 2001. Usage of the MELDEX Digital Music Library. *Proceedings of the Second Annual International Symposium on Music Information Retrieval (Bloomington, IN, USA*, 15-17.

Meyer, L., 1989. *Style and Music. Theory, History and Ideology*, Philadelphia: University of Pensylvania Press.

Mihgak, M. & Venkatesan, R., 2001. A Perceptual Audio Hashing Algorithm: ATool for Robust Audio Identification and Information Hiding. *Information Hiding: 4th International Workshop, IH 2001, Pittsburgh, PA, USA, April 25-27, 2001: Proceedings.*

Miwa, T., Tadokoro, Y. & Saito, T., 2000. The Problems of Transcription using Comb Filters for Musical Instrument Sounds and Their Solutions. *IEIC Technical Report (Institute of Electronics, Information and Communication Engineers)*, 100(328), 25-32.

Mongeau, M. & Sankoff, D., 1990. Comparison of musical sequences. *Computers and the Humanities*, 24(3), 161-175.

Moorer, J., 1975. On the segmentation and analysis of continuous musical sound by digital computer.

MusicBrainz, 2008. Welcome to MusicBrainz! - MusicBrainz. Available at: http://musicbrainz.org/ [Accessed August 10, 2008].

Narmour, E., 1992. *The Analysis and Cognition of Melodic Complexity: The Implication-Realization Model*, University Of Chicago Press.

Navarro, G. & Raffinot, M., 2002. *Flexible Pattern Matching in Strings: Practical On-Line Search Algorithms for Texts and Biological Sequences*, Cambridge University Press.

Nesbit, A., Hollenberg, L. & Senyard, A., 2004. Towards Automatic Transcription of Australian Aboriginal Music. *5th International Conference on Musical Information Retrieval, Barcelona, Spain October 10-14, 2004.*

Norbeck, H., 2007. ABC Tunes. Available at: http://www.norbeck.nu/abc/index.html, [Accessed May 13, 2009].

ÓhAllmhuráin, G., 1998. Pocket History of Irish Traditional Music.

O'Murchu, M., 1997. *O Bhéal go Béal*,

O'Neill, F., 1907. *The Dance Music of Ireland – 1001 Gems*, Chicago, USA.

O'Neill, F., 1903. *The Music of Ireland*,

O'Shea, H., 2006. Getting to the Heart of the Music: Idealizing Musical Community and Irish Traditional Music Sessions. *Journal of the Society for Musicology in Ireland*, 2(7), 1.

Papaodysseus, C. et al., 2001. A new approach to the automatic recognition of musical recordings. *J. Audio Eng. Soc*, 49(1/2), 23-35.

Parsons, D., 1975. *The directory of tunes and musical themes*, New York: Spencer Brown.

Peiszer, E., 2007. *Automatic Audio Segmentation: Segment Boundary and Structure Detection in Popular Music.* Vienna University of Technology.

Peiszer, E., Lidy, T. & Rauber, A., 2008. Automatic audio segmentation: Segment boundary and structure detection in popular music. *Proceedings of the 2nd International Workshop on Learning the Semantics of Audio Signals (LSAS), Paris, France.*

Petrie, G., 1855. *The Petrie Collection of the Ancient Music of Ireland*,

Prechelt, L., 1996. A quantitative study of experimental evaluations of neural network learning algorithms: Current research practice. *Neural Networks*, 9(3), 457-462.

Prechelt, L. & Typke, R., 2001. An interface for melody input. *ACM Transactions on Computer-Human Interaction (TOCHI)*, 8(2), 133-149.

Rabiner, L. et al., 1976. A comparative performance study of several pitch detection algorithms. *Acoustics, Speech, and Signal Processing [see also IEEE Transactions on Signal Processing], IEEE Transactions on*, 24(5), 399-418.

Rabiner, L., 1989. A tutorial on hidden Markov models and selected applications inspeech recognition. *Proceedings of the IEEE*, 77(2), 257-286.

Relatable, 2008. Relatable | Tech. Available at: http://www.relatable.com/tech/trm.html [Accessed August 10, 2008].

Repp, B., 1992. Diversity and Commonality in Music Performance: an Analysis of Timing Microstructure in Schumann's 'Traumerei'. *Journal of the Acoustical Society of America*, (104).

Rho, S. & Hwang, E., 2004. FMF (Fast Melody Finder): AWeb-Based Music Retrieval System. *Computer Music Modeling and Retrieval: International Symposium, CMMR 2003, Montpellier, France, May 26-27, 2003: Revised Papers*.

Robinson, M., 1999. The Fiddle Music of Donegal. *Fiddler Magazine*.

Rubner, Y., Tomasi, C. & Guibas, L., 2000. The Earth Mover's Distance as a Metric for Image Retrieval. *International Journal of Computer Vision*, 40(2), 99-121.

Ryynanen, M. & Klapuri, A., 2008. Query by humming of midi and audio using locality sensitive hashing. *Acoustics, Speech and Signal Processing, 2008. ICASSP 2008. IEEE International Conference on*, 2249-2252.

Ryynanen, M. & Klapuri, A., 2006. Transcription of the Singing Melody in Polyphonic Music. *ISMIR 2006*, 1.

Salzberg, S., 1999. On comparing classifiers: A critique of current research and methods. *Data Mining and Knowledge Discovery*, 1(1).

Schedl, M., 2008. *Automatically Extracting, Analyzing, and Visualizing Information on Music Artists from the World Wide Web*. PhD Thesis. Johannes Kepler Universitat Linz.

Scheirer, E., 1998. Tempo and beat analysis of acoustic musical signals. *The Journal of the Acoustical Society of America*, 103, 588.

Schlichte, J., 1990. Der automatische Vergleich von 83 243 Musikincipits aus der RISM-Datenbank: Ergebnisse-Nutzen-Perspektiven. *Fontes artis musicae*, 37, 35-46.

Schloss, W., 1985. On the Automatic Transcription of Percussive Music: From Acoustic Signal to High-level Analysis.

Settel, Z. & Lippe, C., 1994. Real-time musical applications using the FFT-based resynthesis. *Proc International Computer Music Conference, Aarhus.*

Shazam, 2008. Shazam - The amazing music discovery engine. Join our Community. Available at: http://www.shazam.com/music/portal [Accessed August 10, 2008].

Shields, H., 1998. *Tunes of the Munster Pipers: Irish Traditional Music from the James Goodman Manuscripts*, Irish Traditional Music Archive.

Shlien, S., 2008. The ABC Music project - abcMIDI. Available at: http://abc.sourceforge.net/abcMIDI/ [Accessed August 14, 2008].

Smith, S., 1997. *The scientist and engineer's guide to digital signal processing*, California Technical Publishing San Diego, CA, USA.

Storey, B., 2002. Computing Fourier Series and Power Spectrum with MATLAB.

Subramanya, S. et al., 1997. Transform-Based Indexing of Audio Data for Multimedia Databases. *IEEE Int'l Conference on Multimedia Systems.*

Tadokoro, Y., Morita, T. & Yamaguchi, M., 2003. Pitch detection of musical sounds noticing minimum output of parallel connected comb filters. *TENCON 2003. Conference on Convergent Technologies for Asia-Pacific Region*, 1.

Tansey, S., 2006. *Personal Communication*, The Cobblestone Pub, Dublin.

Tansey, S., 1999. *The Bardic Apostles of Innisfree*, Tanbar Publications.

thesession.org, 2007. The session.org Forums. Available at: http://www.thesession.org.

Typke, R., 2007. Music Retrieval Based on Melodic Similarity. *Doctoral thesis, Utrecht University.*

Typke, R. et al., 2003. Using transportation distances for measuring melodic similarity. *Proceedings of the 4th International Conference on Music Information Retrieval (ISMIR 2003)*, 107-114.

Typke, R., Veltkamp, R. & Wiering, F., 2004. Searching notated polyphonic music using transportation distances. *Proceedings of the 12th annual ACM international conference on Multimedia*, 128-135.

Typke, R., Wiering, F. & Veltkamp, R., 2005. A Survey of Music Information Retrieval Systems. *Proceedings of the International Conference on Music Information Retrieval*, 153-160.

Ukkonen, E., Lemström, K. & Mäkinen, V., 2003. Geometric Algorithms for Transposition Invariant Content-Based Music Retrieval. *ISMIR 2003*, 2, 3.

Vallely, F., 1999. *The Companion to Irish Traditional Music*, New York University Press.

Vallely, F., 1986. *Timbre: The Wooden Flute Tutor*, Dublin, Ireland: Walton Manufacturing Company Ltd.

Virginia Tech, 2009. Virginia Tech Multimedia Music Dictionary. Available at: http://www.music.vt.edu/musicdictionary/ [Accessed January 19, 2009].

Viterbi, A., 1967. Error bounds for convolutional codes and an asymptotically optimum decoding algorithm. *Information Theory, IEEE Transactions on*, 13(2), 260-269.

Vos, J. & Rasch, R., 1981. The perceptual onset of musical tones. *Percept Psychophys*, 29(4), 323-35.

Wallis, G. & Wilson, S., 2001. *The Rough Guide to Irish Music*, London: Rough Guides.

Walpole, R., 2002. *Probability & Statistics for Engineers & Scientists*, Prentice Hall.

Walshaw, C., 2007. The ABC home page. Available at: http://www.walshaw.plus.com/abc/.

Widmer, G. et al., 2005. From Sound to `Sense' via Feature Extraction and Machine Learning: Deriving High-Level Descriptors for Characterising Music. *Sound to Sense:Sense to Sound: A State-of-the-Art*.

Widmer, G. & Goebl, W., 2004. Computational Models of Expressive Music Performance: The State of the Art. *Journal of New Music Research*, 33(3), 203–216.

Wiggins, G., Lemstrom, K. & Meredith, D., 2002. SIA (M) ESE: An algorithm for transposition invariant, polyphonic content-based music retrieval. *Proceedings of the 3rd International Conference on Music Information Retrieval (ISMIR 2002)*, 283-284.

Wise, J., Caprio, J. & Parks, T., 1976. Maximum likelihood pitch estimation. *Acoustics, Speech, and Signal Processing [see also IEEE Transactions on Signal Processing], IEEE Transactions on*, 24(5), 418-423.

Wright, M., Tzanetakis, G. & Schloss, A., 2008. Analyzing Afro-Cuban Rhythm Using Rotation-Aware Clave Template Matching With Dynamic Programming. *Ninth International Conference on Music Information Retrieval, Drexel University in Philadelphia, Pennsylvania USA.*

Zheng, N. & Duggan, B., 2007. A Combinational Creativity Approach to Composing Traditional Irish Reels. *18th Irish Conference on Artificial Intelligence and Cognitive Science, Dublin Institute of Technology, Ireland.*

CPSIA information can be obtained
at www.ICGtesting.com
Printed in the USA
LVHW061457250321
682471LV00015B/622

9 781449 521899